Community and Growth

By the same author

Becoming Human
Befriending the Stranger
The Broken Body
Drawn into the Mystery of Jesus through the Gospel of John
Made for Happiness
Man and Women He Made Them

Community and Growth

JEAN VANIER

Revised edition

DARTON · LONGMAN + TODD

First published in Great Britain in 1979 by
Darton, Longman and Todd Ltd
1 Spencer Court
140–142 Wandsworth High Street
London SW18 4JJ

Originally published as
La Communauté: Lieu du Pardon et de la Fête
by Les Editions Flurus, Paris and
Les Editions Bellarmin, Montreal

Translation © 1979 Jean Vanier
2nd revised edition © 1989 Jean Vanier

This edition 2007
Reprinted 2010, 2011

ISBN–10 0–232–52697–4
ISBN–13 978–0–232–52697–4

A catalogue record for this book
is available from the British Library.

Printed and bound in Great Britain by
Good News Digital Books

To Father Thomas Philippe
with whom I made my first steps in community

Contents

Preface   xiii

Acknowledgements   xvi

Introduction   1

1 One Heart, One Soul, One Spirit   13
  Community as belonging   13
  Community as openness   18
  Community as caring   20
  Community and co-operation   24
  Community, a place of healing and growth   25
  Sympathies and antipathies   31
  Community as forgiveness   35
  Have patience   38
  Mutual trust   41
  The right to be oneself   42
  Called by God just as we are   44
  Share your weakness   47
  Community is a living body   49
  Using our gifts   50
  From 'the community for myself' to 'myself for the
    community'   55

2 Walking Toward the Covenant   61
  A birth of hope   61
  The call to families   64
  Other paths   66
  The first call   68
  Leave your father, your mother, your culture   72

The beginning of the journey 76
Recognising the bonds 78
Choice for rooting 79
The final 'Yes' 82

3 Mission 84
Coming together for a purpose 84
Universal mission to give life 85
General and specific mission 88
Clarifying the goals 90
The yearning for God and the cry of the poor 93
Jesus is the poor 95
The cry for love 97
Inner pain 98
The waters flowing over humanity 101

4 Growth 104
A community grows like a child 104
From heroism to dailiness 108
The vision is clarified 109
From monarchy to democracy 113
Openness to the neighbourhood and the world 115
Times of trial: a step towards growth 118
Tensions 120
Sending people away 126
The outsider's eye, or external authority 128
Growth in individuals and growth in community 131
Losing illusions 134
The second call 139
Prayer, service and community life 141
From doing to listening 142
Signs of sickness and health in community 143
Openness to others 144
The focal point of fidelity 149
Generating life 152
Expansion and taking root 155
Born from a wound 155
The role of Providence 157
The dangers of becoming rich 158

The risk of growth   160
I was a stranger and you welcomed me   161
Be zealous and repent!   162

5 Nourishment: Give Us Our Daily Bread   165
Growth needs nourishment   165
Food for each day   169
Times of wonder and of awe   171
Affirmation from outside   173
The Word as bread   174
Rest and relaxation: 'the Sabbath Day'   177
Food for thought   181
Growth as nourishment   182
The friend   183
Sharing   185
The eyes of the poor   185
Personal prayer   189
Becoming bread   194
Communal prayer and Eucharist   195
The bread of pain   199
The bread of unity anticipated   203

6 Authority as a Gift   205
Authority   205
A mission from God   209
Being a servant   212
The danger of pride   216
Sharing responsibility   218
Community structures   221
Learning to listen and to exercise authority   224
Don't hide!   227
Personalised authority   229
Attitudes to authority   231
The sign of forgiveness   236
Letting the community evolve.   238

7 Other Gifts in Community   240
The spiritual guide   240
The specific role of the priest or ordained minister   247

Community and work accompaniment 249
Psychological accompaniment 250
Each person has a gift to share 251
The gift of listening 253
The gift of discernment 254
Fidelity over time 254
The gift of wonderment 255
The gift of the 'grandmother' 255
The gift of men and women 256
The anti-gift 260
The gift of animation 260
The gift of availability 261
The gift of the poor 262

8 Welcome 265
Giving space 265
Who welcomes? 270
Welcome: true and false 272
Welcoming Providence 273
Welcoming the vulnerable 274
Marginal people at the heart of the community 280
Welcome and service 282
The need for community 283

9 Meetings 284
Coming together to share 284
Coming together in the Spirit 288
Leading a meeting 290

10 Living with Every Day 297
Daily rhythm 300
Spirituality of movement and spirituality of the circle 302
The laws of matter 303
Love and poverty 304
The conflict between living littleness and political
  commitment 307
Political dimension of the community 308

11 Celebration 313
At the heart of community: celebration 313

Meals   322
Preparing the celebration   325
Invited to the wedding feast   328

Conclusion   329

Preface

This new edition of *Community and Growth* is essentially the book on Community which I wrote over ten years ago, but enlarged and revised.

Over these ten years I have learned a great deal about community life, both through mistakes I have made in l'Arche and through the evolution of our communities. Some of these have gone through an immense amount of pain and have nearly collapsed; two had to be closed for various reasons and the people with a handicap who were there welcomed into other l'Arche communities. All our communities have lived times of crisis and growth. We have seen some assistants put down roots, flower and give life; others have left, some angry, some with their hearts transformed in love and taking elsewhere the gifts and the vision they had received. And, of course, I have learnt a great deal from other new communities, particularly the communities of Faith and Light[1] with which I have been involved since their beginning in 1971.

In some ways, when I began l'Arche in 1964, I was a bit idealistic. I felt people could begin a community as I had begun, without too much outside help. I encouraged people to start and they did. Quite quickly serious difficulties cropped up. I had begun l'Arche with Father Thomas Philippe; but other founders were often alone and needed more support than I could give or was available from others. Over these last ten years I have seen how much leaders and communities need support, accompaniment and challenge if they are to fulfil their task and remain open and faithful to their call. I have seen also how much assistants need this same support, accompaniment and challenge to make the transition from a life of independence in society to community life. I have also seen

how much assistants need a spiritual guide. When there is a priest
committed to a community, assistants seem able to put down roots
more firmly. All these aspects I have enlarged upon in this new
edition.

I have also expanded a great deal on the question of mission in
community. What I wrote about this in the first two chapters of
the first edition have been taken out, enlarged and made the basis
for the third chapter of this new edition. Over the last ten years
L'Arche, and also Faith and Light[1] have developed ecumenical
communities in the United Kingdom, Scandinavia, Germany,
North America, Switzerland and Australia. They have taught me a
great deal about the pain and hope contained in such communities.

And so it is that in many parts of this book I have made additions
and corrections. My thought, born from daily experience of community life, has thus become clearer and more precise.

This new edition is a work of community; many from the l'Arche
communities sent me, at my invitation, their reflections and
suggestions. My thanks go to each one who brought light to this
book.

After a further ten years I imagine I will have many other
reflections and corrections to add. Every day I am discovering
new things. Maybe it will be someone else who will make those
corrections. The important thing for me and for each one of us is
to grow in the wisdom of community and never to hide behind
clichés, rules and regulations. This growth means a continual and
deeper listening to God, to people, and to communities as they
grow and live through crises and tensions, as they bear fruit and
give life. My hope is that this new edition will help people to live

1 Faith and Light are communities which meet regularly to celebrate life and to
pray. They are composed of parents with their son or daughter who has a mental
handicap and friends. These communities are now spread across the world like a
big family. For more information write to: International Secretariat of Faith and
Light, 90 ave. Suffren, 75015 Paris, France.

better the demands of community life in order to bring more fully the good news of love to this world.

February 1989   *Jean Vanier*

Note

There are some words I have used frequently which sound strange in English. Words such as 'accompaniment', 'formation', 'gratuity', 'fecundity', 'spirituality'. They are often a direct translation from the French. These words are not just l'Arche 'jargon'; they reveal a community experience or reality which cannot be signified in standard English. But I believe language is called to evolve. Over the centuries the English language has assimilated many French words. I hope it can continue to do so where there is no adequate English word. I have, however, taken the precaution of defining these words where they first appear in the text.

Acknowledgements

I wrote the original edition of this book in French. It was Ann Shearer, in London, who with such deep and intimate knowledge of l'Arche, translated it. She did it beautifully and I am deeply grateful to her.

This new edition has been worked on by Olive Peat of Darton, Longman and Todd. I am grateful for her expertise in the English language and her love for this book which have helped this second edition to be more clear and precise.

Introduction

Not too long ago, people lived in homogeneous groups, composed
of families which had more or less the same roots. In these groups
– the tribe, the village – people spoke the same language, with the
same accent, and wore the same type of clothes. They lived by
the same rites and traditions, had the same code of behaviour and
accepted the same authority. There was a solidarity among them,
that came both from their flesh and blood and from the need to
co-operate to meet material needs and to defend the group from
enemy attack and natural dangers. There was a unity among people
of the same group which etched itself deeply on their unconscious.

Times have changed. Contemporary society is the product of the
disintegration of these more or less natural or familial groupings.
Nowadays, people who live in the same area are no longer part
of a homogeneous group. Cities are made up of neighbours who
do not know each other – and this will soon be true of villages
too. People live in a pluralistic society, and many today are the
children of inter-cultural marriages. In the cities, where solidarity
has disappeared, people are afraid, and so shut themselves up in
their own houses, frightened of neighbours and of intruders.
Human community is no longer to be found in the market place,
the neighbourhood or the village. Mobility has brought about a
mixture of people, religions, and philosophies.

People are now drawn toward cities large and complicated
enough to meet our economic desires, and toward families small
and portable (and even disposable) enough to make mobility
possible. Popular sociology portrays us as victims of these
'movements' and 'trends', as if the woes that accompany mod-

ernity had been forced upon us. But no. The destruction of intimate community has been at our own hands. It has corresponded to our own hierarchy of values . . . which stand largely in tension with the value of total and intimate community. As much as we yearn for community, we yearn even more for the social and economic prizes individual mobility can bring.[1]

The breakdown of confidence in community and traditional values pushes people into a desperate form of individualism, with all the struggle that implies, in order to go up the ladder of social success and to be able to stand alone. This has brought a terrible toll on family life. The former extended family has become the nuclear family, with only one or two children and with both the man and woman working in order to obtain the maximum financial income. When the husband or wife asks too much of the other and wants the other to fulfil all their emotional needs, there is serious danger of marital breakdown. And that is what we are witnessing today: families are breaking up. Stark individualism increases and a terrible loneliness sets in which finds a certain relief in working harder for more money and more success, and in more distractions, yet still cut off from relationship. But these ultimately push people into an even deeper loneliness. And so they fall into a vicious circle alternating between inner pain and efforts to escape it.

But of course, people cannot live in isolation and in such extreme individualism; everybody needs friends or companions. A certain togetherness or belonging, be it in groups of friends, in family, in clubs, in gangs, in militant groups orientated to politics and issues, in churches or in groups of all sorts, is an integral part of human nature. Isolated we shrivel up and die.

Today even more than ten years ago, when the first edition of this book was written, people are crying out for authentic communities where they can share their lives with others in a common vision, where they can find support and mutual encouragement, where

1   Parker J. Palmer, *A Place Called Community* (Pendle Hill, Philadelphia, 1977), p. 7–8.

they can give witness to their beliefs and work for greater peace and justice in the world – even if they are also frightened of the demands of community.

When families and tribes were well knit together, people were not lonely. They felt safe and secure, although perhaps parents and those in authority controlled children too much and did not see them as unique and capable of growing towards greater personal freedom. Personal conscience was in some ways sacrificed to group consciousness.

Today the discipline of the family and neighbourhood group, with their sense of belonging, have been lost, and personal freedom has increased. This has led to extreme individualism, but it could also give rise to a deeper search for community and belonging, orientated towards the development of personal consciousness rather than its suppression. But reaction to extreme individualism could also give rise to totalitarian and fanatical forms of power to 'save people from chaos' and preserve the identity of groups. 'I have come to believe,' writes David Clark,

> that without a strong sense of community human beings will wilt and begin to die. Community is the foundation of human society, the zenith of interdependence, the epitome of wholeness; in fact, the end of our journeying. As Parker Palmer writes: 'Community means more than the comfort of souls. It means, and has always meant, the survival of the species.' Without a continuing and enriching experience of community, as well as a vision of its glory to keep us moving forward, all of us eventually perish.[2]

In which direction will humanity evolve? This is the challenge for the last decade of the twentieth century.

When family ties break down, when children come from divorced, separated or single parents, or are adopted, they can suffer from deep insecurity. Children nourished on television, the mass media, and the popularisation of psychology can lack a sense of values

2 David Clark, *Yes to Life* (Collins/Fount, London, 1987), p. 22.

and become rootless. They may have many gifts and talents, opportunities and wealth, but they have difficulty making choices and knowing what direction to take. In many ways they are lost.

The mass media give instant and constant news about the world situation, about wars, oppression, armaments, hunger, catastrophes, the spread of AIDS and inequalities of all sorts. Young people do not know what to do with all this frightening and confusing information; they feel helpless and guilty. The world appears to be chaotic.

Young people today are different from those of the 'sixties and 'seventies who were looking for alternative ways of living, alternative communities, an alternative society. They felt they could do something about things, throw away the old and take the risk of building the new. It was a time of economic expansion. Now in the late 'eighties, young people cannot and do not want to take risks. They feel too insecure, too rootless, unclear as to what they want. They feel helpless and guilty in front of all the pain and the problems. They see no positive way of working towards a better world. Many become apathetic and fall into a world of depression, seeking compensation in gangs, hard rock, drugs, superficial sex; they are desperately seeking to fill the emptiness of their lives. Or else they choose to throw themselves into the established ways, working hard at school, getting a job and trying to forget about all the rest in their search for security and solid ground. And so the pendulum swings from one side to another.

Coming from the insecurity of broken families or from families where there is a lack of warmth and love, young people are in desperate need of communities where they can refind their deeper selves and experience values that give meaning and a certain structure to their lives. They are faced with different alternatives: on the one hand insecurity, with all the anguish that that implies, or the false securities of work or power, of worldly values or closed-up sects; or on the other hand, being part of a community where they can find themselves and grow into openness and universal love.

I doubt whether the leaders in society and in the churches today are sufficiently aware of the changing face of the young and a world which is crying out from its anguish and loneliness for a sense of *belonging*.

But community is an urgent need not only for young people. Their cry is a prophetic sign of what is lacking in the world and in the Church, not only for them but for all.

Of course those who are feeling lonely, confused and lost in the world take a risk when they create or seek communities that may seem at first glance like sects. To overcome the powers of anguish inside them they want something absolute, a strong and all-powerful father- or mother-figure, values that are certain, laws that are rigid. Lacking inner balance, they may throw themselves into extremes of action, prayer, austerity, fundamentalism or even fanaticism. Some people may judge such communities as dangerous, for they lack wisdom and openness and freedom for the individual. And this is true. But we must remember the depth of the pain and the insecurity of the young. Such communities meet their needs.

But communities must be led with wisdom. Young people need help in order to integrate the vision into their own hearts and minds and to develop their own inner freedom and choices, learning little by little to be led inwardly by love, rather than from the outside, by rigid laws. They must be led to *true* community where they can become men and women of prayer and compassion, open to others and to the world, particularly to the poor, the oppressed, the lost, and the vulnerable, and thus become artisans of peace.

Many people today are conscious that they can no longer live isolated from others, nor can each group or country be isolated within its own frontiers. They are becoming more and more conscious that the whole of humanity, fragmented as it is, broken up into so many conflicting groups, is nevertheless one single family. Groups, tribes, and nations have to avoid conflict one with another; war is now too dangerous, and our economies, our lives, our scientific discoveries are intertwined. Through television satellites and radio we know instantly what is happening around the world. We are all interdependent. The days when people could live in isolation off their own land are past. Each people, race and country is part of the vast family of humanity; each one has a gift that can help humanity to live in peace and to be complete. Humanity in its entirety is a body, and in the body each member is important. Groups, nations or races which cut themselves off from others, or seek to dominate by imposing their own culture, ideology and customs by suppressing the identity of another's culture, wound and hurt not only that particular people but the whole of humanity and themselves.

Today, more than ever before, we are called to become more conscious of the fundamental unity of the human family and to help each group of people to find their identity and place in it, and to grow in openness towards others.

The danger for individuals, groups, communities and nations is to close themselves off. This happens to the little child when it feels it is not wanted or loved. Its vulnerable heart is wounded. And because it is so fragile and weak and cannot cope, it closes itself up fearfully behind barriers to protect itself. Inside this little fortress the child feels guilty and angry; it wants to hurt itself because it feels worthless and guilty, or else it wants to hurt others, in revenge for its own inner pain and loneliness. Fear isolates and leads to aggression, conflicts, jealousies, rivalry and competition; communion opens up hearts and leads to unity and peace. Families, communities and nations may experience this same process of closing up behind barriers and frontiers of self-protection. They tend then only to open up from a position of power, in order to dominate, to further their own interests and impose their own ways, rather than from a desire for unity and communion.

There is such fear of difference, such fear of losing one's identity. If an individual, a group or a nation gets too close to others and starts letting down barriers, they can become frightened of losing their own identity and values, their sense of belonging. So, they close up again upon themselves.

The question for every person and community is how to remain rooted in the soil of one's faith and one's identity, in one's own community, and at the same time to grow and give life to others, and to receive life from them. If people in a community live only on the level of the human, rational, legalistic and active aspects and symbols of their faith – which give cohesion, security and unity – there is a serious risk of their closing in on themselves and of gradually dying. If, however, their religious faith opens up, on the one hand to the mystical – that is, to an experience of the love of God present in the community and in the heart of each person – and, on the other hand, to what unifies all human beings, especially the poor, the vulnerable and the oppressed, they will then continue to grow in openness.

This essential rooting through faith and love of God, the source of all life and love, gives immense strength to people and to communities. It is, however, very demanding for it calls for a life of poverty and insecurity, putting one's total trust in God and in his loving protection and providence. And it is precisely this poverty, insecurity and vulnerability which people and communities are frightened of.

This is the fundamental risk of trust, and of belief, taken by the followers of Jesus. Vulnerability, suffering and eventually rejection, appear dangerous and imprudent; they can bring death to the community. This was the fundamental risk taken by Jesus: he accepted vulnerability, insecurity and death, trusting in the power of the Father and of the resurrection. It is the linking of the cross to the openness and radiance of the glory. Followers of Jesus are called to believe that non-violence, poverty, openness and forgiveness are the surest way for them and their communities to receive life from God and to give life, peace and unity to the world. It is in our weakness that the power of God is manifested through the Paraclete, the Holy Spirit.

The paradox for the followers of Jesus is that we can only live and give life if we accept the need to die. 'Truly, truly I say to you, unless a grain of wheat falls into the earth and dies, it remains alone; but if it dies, it bears much fruit' (John 12:24–5).

Today young people are seeking communities – not ones that are closed up and inward-looking but communities that are open to the universal, the international world; that are not limited to their own culture, that are not frightened ghettos but are open to

the pain and injustices of the world. That is why so many flock
to Taizé or join groups that are international. That is why so
many new communities feel called to found sister communities in
developing countries. It is as if a community cannot continue to
exist in its own culture if it is not linked to similar communities
in other cultures. This arises not just from the desire to 'do good'
in the Third World, but also from the discovery and acceptance
of the gifts of these countries, which may be less developed economically but which frequently possess a deep and true sense of
humanity.

For many centuries, communities were linked to institutional churches, but today in many places the influence of these churches is
waning. Many young people see them as irrelevant, cut off from
the reality of the world. But at the same time, with the breakdown of the family or in the face of injustices – particularly in
Third World countries – there is a new cry for togetherness and
community within the Church. This is very evident in the basic
communities in Latin America, but it is also evident all over the
world. The Synod of the Roman Catholic Church, when considering the Laity in 1987, described the parish, for the first time in an
official document of the Roman Catholic Church, as 'a community
of communities'. Yes, there is a new realisation that community
is the place of meeting with God or, as Martin Buber says, 'the
place of theophany'.[3] It is the place of belonging; it is the place of
love and acceptance; it is the place of caring; it is a place of growth
in love. Individualism and materialism lead to rivalry, competition
and the rejection of the weak. Community leads to openness and
acceptance of others. Without community people's hearts close up
and die.

Maybe today some people see opposition between, on the one
hand, a seemingly barren, old, *institutional church*, cut off from the
world, looking after buildings, and worried about membership
and attendance, and on the other hand, *new communities*, filled with

---

3 'We expect a theophany of which we know nothing but the place, and the place
   is called community' (Martin Buber, quoted by Parker J. Palmer, op. cit. p. 4).

life, enthusiasm, risk, openness and welcome, concerned about the big issues of the world – injustice, torture, peace, disarmament, ecology, a better distribution of wealth, the liberation of women, drug addiction, AIDS, people with handicaps, etc. This apparent opposition has always been a question. James, soon after the death of Jesus, cried out against those Christians who had become too institutionalised and who were rejecting the poor.[4] The communities of Francis of Assisi seemed so alive compared to the rich, institutional Church of his time. But we know that every community, with time, risks closing in on itself and becoming an empty institution governed by laws. The new communities of today can become the closed-up, barren institutions of tomorrow.

But no matter how closed up some institutions are, nor how closed up some churches and parishes may appear to be, that does not mean that they are dead and that they should be rejected. The institution is a part of any society. It is like the bones of a body. These bones can be dry; the body can be sick and like a skeleton; but the body needs the bone structure. The institution can be a living and healthy one if it is open to people, to love, and to the inspiration of the Holy Spirit. The institution is there in the Church so that priests and ordained ministers may be shepherds in and for communities, giving the spiritual and sacramental nourishment that they need in order to deepen and grow. As Karl Rahner says so well:

> If . . . basic communities gradually become indispensable – since otherwise in the present situation and that of the immediate future the institutional church will shrivel up into a church without people – the episcopal great church has the task and duty of stimulating and of contributing to their formation and their necessary missionary activity. . . . If the basic community is really Christian and genuinely alive, the result of a free decision of faith in the midst of a secularised world where Christianity can scarcely be handed on any longer by the power of social tradition, then all ecclesiastical organisation is largely at the service of these communities: they are not means to serve the

4 Epistle of St James, ch. 2.

ends of an ecclesiastical bureaucracy defending and wanting to reproduce itself.[5]

And of course if the institution is for people and for communities, then communities are there for the whole body. They give life to the institution. And the institution and the communities together are there, not to be closed in on themselves as warm, prayerful ghettos, but to bring life to the world. John Paul II in his first encyclical to members of the Roman Catholic Church wrote: 'The human person is the first road and fundamental road of the Church.'[6] The Church, like Jesus, is called to announce good news to the poor, liberation to prisoners and the oppressed, and sight to the blind. It is called to bring life and to help people grow to greater freedom and wholeness so that all may be one.

When I use the word 'community' in this book, I am talking essentially of groupings of people who have left their own milieu to live with others under the same roof, and work from a new vision of human beings and their relationships with each other and with God. So my definition is a restricted one. Others would see 'community' as something wider.

This book is above all for those who live, or want to live, in community. But many of its points apply equally to family life. The two essential elements of life in community are also part of life in a family: inter-personal relationship, a sense of belonging and an orientation of life to a common goal and common witness. In the same way, much of the book applies to people who, although they do not live together, are deeply bound to each other and meet regularly in small communities to share about themselves and their ideal, to pray and to find mutual support and encouragement, and to be witnesses of love and hope in this world. And I hope too that much that is said here can be applied to community-building in schools, hospitals, industry and other areas of society. I do not believe that a balance of power between employers and

5 Karl Rahner, *The Shape of the Church to Come* (SPCK, London, 1974), pp. 114–15.
6 *Redemptor Hominis*, p. 14.

employees through trade unions is the only model for the creation of a just society or institution. Today many are seeking to create places of dialogue in industry and a true participation of all in decisions and profits. Is this not the beginning of a search for community?

Almost everything I say here is the result of my own experience of life in l'Arche, the community in which I have been living for nearly twenty-five years. I have also learned a great deal from visiting l'Arche communities across the world and by listening to others who live in other sorts of community.

L'Arche is special, in the sense that we are trying to live in community with people who are mentally handicapped. Certainly we want to help them grow and reach the greatest independence possible. But before 'doing for them', we want to 'be with them'. The particular suffering of the person who is mentally handicapped, as of all marginal people, is a feeling of being excluded, worthless and unloved. It is through everyday life in community and the love that must be incarnate in this, that handicapped people can begin to discover that they have a value, that they are loved and so are lovable.

I began l'Arche in 1964, in the desire to live the Gospel and to follow Jesus Christ more closely. Each day brings me new lessons on how much Christian life must grow in commitment to life in community, and on how much that life needs faith, the love of Jesus and the presence of the Holy Spirit if it is to deepen. Everything I say about life in community in these pages is inspired by my faith in Jesus.

That certainly doesn't mean that there is no community life outside Christianity. To claim that would be to go against all human experience and against common sense as well. As soon as people group together, for whatever reason, a sort of community is created. But the message of Jesus invites his disciples to love one another and to live community in a special way.

Through being close to many people attracted by community and by new ways of life, I have come to realise how great an ignorance there is about community life. Many people seem to believe that creating a community is a matter of simply gathering together under the same roof a few people who get on reasonably well together or who are committed to the same ideal. The result can be disastrous! Community life isn't simply created by either spontaneity or laws. It needs a certain discipline and particular forms of nourishment. Some precise conditions have to be met if this life is to deepen and grow through all the crises, tensions and 'good times'. If these conditions are not met, every sort of deviation is possible; which will lead eventually to the breakdown of the community, or else its members will become enslaved.

This book tries to clarify the conditions which are necessary to life in community. It is no thesis or treatise. It is made up of a series of starting-points for reflection, which I have discovered not through books, but through everyday life, through my mistakes, my set-backs and my personal failings, through the inspiration of God and my brothers and sisters, and through the moments of unity between us as well as the tension and suffering. Life in community is painful but it is also a marvellous adventure and a source of life. My hope is that many people can live this adventure, which in the end is one of inner liberation – the freedom to love and to be loved.

As the Father has loved me, so have I loved you; abide in my love. . . .

This is my commandment, that you love one another as I have loved you. Greater love has no man than this, that a man lay down his life for his friends. (John 15:9, 12–13)

1

One Heart, One Soul, One Spirit

Community as belonging

Community is a place of belonging, a place where people are
earthed and find their identity. Of course, people do not belong
only to communities; some belong to gangs or to sects, to clubs,
to militant groups and other organisations which are not communities. Many also belong to churches and to parishes. The very first
community to which people belong is the family; a child first
belongs to the mother. This initial belonging in the womb is so
deep that some mothers feel they have the right of life and death
over the child, as if the child in the womb does not exist in its
own right.

When a child feels it does not belong to anyone, it suffers terrible
loneliness and this is manifested in anguish. Anguish is like an
inner agitation which affects the whole body, transforming the
digestive and sleep patterns, bringing confusion, destroying all
clarity about what to do, and how to act. It closes the child in on
itself in feelings of uselessness and death, but also of anger and
hatred which are intolerable. A child that feels unloved, knows it
is not lovable; it is not good; it is evil. Loneliness is quickly
transformed into terrible feelings of guilt.

But when a child is loved, seen as precious, listened to, touched
with reverence, then it is at peace. It knows it belongs. It is held,
protected and safe. It opens up without fear.

The deepest yearning in a child is to be in communion with its
mother and father. This is the most fundamental need of every
human being, the source of all other needs and desires.

If that thirst to belong and to be in communion with another is not satisfied, the pain of anguish rises up and with it feelings of guilt, anger, and hate. In fact, this pain can become so unbearable that the child, if it is strong enough, tries to smother it, hide it, cover it up, or forget it by directing its energies into dreams and doing things. Thus, the empty feeling of loneliness and all the pain are pushed down into the secret recesses of its being, into a sort of tomb over which a stone is rolled. All that dirt is hidden away. But with the dirt, the heart itself, the wounded heart craving for communion, is also hidden away. The child can now get on with living, achieving, obtaining success, being admired, seeking independence. Instead of love, the child wants admiration. Other children fall into deep depression and revolt; they are angry with their parents and with the world around them; they seek out companions with whom they can live in an anti-social way. But deep down inside, in all these situations the child continues to be governed by unconscious forces, by those guilt feelings hidden in the tomb of its being.

Each person with his or her history of being accepted or rejected, with his or her past history of inner pain and difficulties in relationships with parents, is different. But in each one there is a yearning for communion and belonging, but at the same time a fear of it. Love is what we most want, yet it is what we fear the most. Love makes us vulnerable and open, but then we can be hurt through rejection and separation. We may crave for love, but then be frightened of losing our liberty and creativity. We want to belong to a group, but we fear a certain death in the group because we may not be seen as unique. We want love, but fear the dependence and commitment it implies; we fear being used, manipulated, smothered and spoiled. We are all so ambivalent toward love, communion and belonging.

According to circumstances and personal needs, according also to childhood needs that were not fulfilled, some people want belonging at almost any price. They feel so lonely that they are prepared to sacrifice personal consciousness and growth in order to be part of a group. Others may be fearful of belonging; it is as if the group stifles and crushes what is most precious in them, their personal conscience and uniqueness, their yearning for communion. This phobia towards all forms of groups prevents these people from living in community. They need their independence, but that does not prevent them from loving people, being compassionate and assuming responsibility for others; it is just that they need a lot of personal space.

There is a great difference between people coming from poorer countries, where the extended family is strong and well-knit, and those coming from Western countries where the family is breaking up and where people are encouraged to live in a very individualistic way, to rise up the ladder of success, and to seek riches, power and the greatest independence possible. The first have a sense of belonging, security and peacefulness, but sometimes their personal conscience, freedom and creativity have not grown; they are in some ways prisoners of the group. The latter are frequently insecure, with little sense of belonging, a confusion of values and a lack of identity. Often they compensate for their insecurity by creating barriers around their hearts and developing their capacities to *do* things, and in this way to be self-sufficient. In both situations, there is a lack of true inner freedom.

When I visit African villages, I realise that through their rituals and traditions they are living community life. Each person has a sense of belonging to the others; men of the same ethnic origin or village are truly brothers. I remember Mgr Agré, bishop of Man, meeting a customs officer at Abidjan airport; they embraced like brothers because they came from the same village, they belonged to each other in some way. Most Africans don't need to talk about community. They live it intensely.

I've heard that Aborigines in Australia want nothing of our technical world except cars, which enable them to visit their clan. The only thing they find important is this link of brotherhood, which they cherish. There is, it seems, such a unity between them that they know – even if they are separated by hundreds of miles – when one of them is dying; they feel it in their guts.

René Lenoir, in *Les Exclus*,[1] says that if a prize is offered for the first to answer a question in a group of Canadian Indian children,

1 R. Lenoir, *Les Exclus* (Editions du Seuil, Paris, 1974).

they all work out the answer together and shout it out at the same time. They couldn't bear one to win, leaving the rest as losers. The winner would be separated from his brothers and sisters, he would have won the prize but lost community.

Our Western civilisation is competitive. From the time they start school, children learn to 'win'. Their parents are delighted when they come first in class. This is how individualistic material progress and the desire to gain prestige by coming out on top have taken over from the sense of fellowship, compassion and community. Now people live more or less on their own in a small house, jealously guarding their goods and planning to acquire more, with a notice on the gate that says 'Beware of the Dog'. It is because the West has lost its sense of community that small groups are springing up here and there, trying to refind it.

We have a lot to learn from the African and the Indian. They remind us that the essence of community is a sense of belonging. This sense of belonging can, however, get in the way of their seeing other groups objectively and lovingly. That is how tribal and religious wars begin. Sometimes too, African community life is based on fear. The group or the tribe give life and a sense of solidarity; they protect and offer security, but they are not always liberating. If people cut themselves off from the group, they are alone with their fears and their own deep wound, facing evil forces, wicked spirits and death. These fears are expressed in rites or fetishes, which in turn are a force for cohesion. True community is liberating.

I love that passage from the Bible: 'And I will say . . . "You are my people"; and he shall say "Thou art my God" ' (Hosea 2:23).

I shall always remember one of Martin Luther King's disciples, saying to a gathering of many thousands of blacks in Chicago, in the early seventies: 'My people are humiliated.' Mother Teresa of Calcutta says: 'My people are hungry.'

'My people' are my community, which is both the small community, those who live together, and the larger community which surrounds it and for which it is there. 'My people' are those who are written in my flesh as I am in theirs. Whether we are near each other or far away, my brothers and sisters remain written within me. I carry them, and they, me; we recognise each other again when we meet. To call them 'my people' doesn't mean that I feel superior to them, or that I am their shepherd or that I look after them. It means that they are mine as I am theirs. There is a solidarity between us. What touches them, touches me. And when I say 'my people', I don't imply that there are others I reject. My people is my community, made up of those who know me and carry me. They are a springboard towards all humanity. I cannot be a universal brother or sister unless I first love my people.

The longer we journey on the road to inner healing and wholeness, the more the sense of belonging grows and deepens. The sense is not just one of belonging to others and to a community. It is a sense of belonging to the universe, to the earth, to the air, to the water, to everything that lives, to all humanity. If the community gives a sense of belonging, it also helps us to accept our aloneness in a personal meeting with God. Through this, the community is open to the universe and to humankind.

We all belong to the universe; we all receive from it and give to it; we are all parts of a whole. The danger for people today is to forget that and to think that they are the centre; that everyone else is there for them. People must die to this form of destructive egoism and be reborn in love, where they learn to receive from others and to give to them.

In many groups of people and clubs of all sorts (political, sports, leisure, liberal professions, etc.) people find a sense of security. They are happy to find others like themselves. They receive comfort one from another, and they encourage one another in their ways. But frequently there is a certain elitism. They are convinced that they are better than others. And, of course, not everyone can join the club; people have to qualify. Frequently these groups give security and a certain sense of belonging but they do not encourage personal growth. Belonging in such groups is not for becoming.

You can often tell the people who belong to a particular club, group or community by what they wear, especially on feast days, or by their hair style, their jargon or accent or by badges and colours of some sort. Grouping seems to need symbols which express the fact that they are *one* tribe, *one* family, *one* group.

Community as openness

People come together because they are of the same flesh and blood or of the same village and tribe; some wanting security and comfort come together because they are alike and have the same vision of themselves and of the world; some come together because they want to grow in universal love and compassion. It is these latter who create true community.

The difference between community and a group of friends is that in a community we verbalise our mutual belonging and bonding. We announce the goals and the spirit that unites us. We recognise together that we are responsible for one another. We recognise also that this bonding comes from God; it is a gift from God. It is he who has chosen us and called us together in a covenant of love and mutual caring. But, of course, a group of friends can become a community, when its sense of belonging grows and it opens to others, and when little by little people begin to feel truly responsible for each other.

Frequently people group together or are grouped together thinking that they are an elite, God's chosen people. Frequently the founder of such a group or 'people' was prophetic and truly chosen by God. This founding figure gave inspiration, laws and traditions which created cohesion and unity, and gave wholeness to the people and a new meaning to their lives. The danger comes when they believe that *only* that particular founding figure was chosen by God and no others.

Our universe is filled with so many species of animals, birds, fish, flowers, fruits and plants; each one is the work of God's hands. It is the same with families, tribes, clans and communities of people. Each one is the work of his love. There is no one family that has all the truth. They are all called to live together in harmony, to share their beautiful gifts and to receive the gifts of others; to discover the height and the depth, the width and the breadth of the wisdom, the beauty and the love of our God.

So often, alas, groupings do not work together for the glory of God. They close themselves off one from another, each one certain that they are the chosen people, the beloved of God, the special community that will renew the face of the earth; that they are the best and they alone have the truth. They do not realise that everyone is special; everyone is called to manifest a particle of the glory of God – in communion with others. When they do not work together, groups create apartheid. Walls are built up between them, rivalry and competition set in. This leads to jealousy which, in turn, leads to hatred and warfare. Thus what began so beautifully ends up so horribly. Religious and political groupings (just as clubs and other groups) become filled with the desire 'to win', to beat others, to prove they are right through powerful means. They become blinded by their own concerns and desire for power (or fear of death); they are unable to see and appreciate the beauty of others.

Communities are truly communities when they are open to others, when they remain vulnerable and humble; when the members are growing in love, in compassion and in humility. Communities cease to be such when members close in upon themselves with the certitude that they alone have wisdom and truth and expect everyone to be like them and learn from them.

The fundamental attitudes of true community, where there is true belonging, are openness, welcome, and listening to God, to the universe, to each other and to other communities. Community life is inspired by the universal and is open to the universal. It is based on forgiveness and openness to those who are different, to the poor and the weak. Sects put up walls and barriers out of fear, out of a need to prove themselves and to create a false security.

Community is the breaking down of barriers to welcome difference.

Community as caring

If community is belonging and openness, it is also loving concern for each person. In other words we could say it is *caring, bonding and mission*. These three elements define it.

In community people care for each other and not just for the community in the abstract, as a whole, as an institution or as an ideal way of life. It is *people* that matter; to love and care for the people that are there, just as they are. It is to care for them in such a way that they may grow according to the plan of God and thus give much life. And it is not just caring in a passing way, but in a *permanent* way. Because people are bonded one to another, they make up one family, one people, one flock. And this people has been called together to be a sign and a witness, to accomplish a particular mission which is their charism, their gift.

So many people enter groups in order to develop a certain form of spirituality or to acquire knowledge about the things of God and of humanity. But that is not community; it is a school. It becomes community only when people start truly caring for each other and for each other's growth.

Esther de Waal writing about the rule of St Benedict says:

It is noticeable how both the abbot and the cellarer are constantly concerned about the brethren, caring for each singly in all their uniqueness rather than with the community *en bloc*, that ideal which seems to haunt so much contemporary ideology. The common life never becomes a piece of abstract idealisation or idealism. St Benedict would probably have appreciated Dietrich Bonhoeffer's aphorism: 'He who loves community, destroys community; he who loves the brethren, builds community.'[2]

A community that is committed to itself – to appearing perfect,

2   Esther de Waal, *Seeking God* (Collins/Fount, London, 1984), p. 139.

stable and secure – rather than to *people*, to their growth and inner freedom, is like a person giving an address who is more interested in the beauty and coherence of the talk rather than in whether the audience can hear and understand it. It is like a beautiful liturgy that nobody can follow and during which people have difficulty praying.

Community must never take precedence over individual people. It is for people and for their growth. In fact, its beauty and unity come from the radiance of each person in their truth, love and union with others.

Some communities – which are more groupings or sects – tend to suppress individual conscience in the interest of a greater unity. They tend to stop people from thinking, from having their own conscience. They tend to suppress whatever is secret and intimate in the individual as if personal freedom cuts across group unity and constitutes a sort of treason. In such a place, everyone must think alike – so there is a manipulation of intelligence, a brainwashing. People become automatons. Unity here is based on fear – the fear of being yourself or of finding yourself alone if you leave the others, the fear of a tyrannical authority, the fear of occult forces and reprisals if you leave the group. Secret societies and sects have a very great attraction for people who lack self-confidence or have weak personalities, because they can feel more secure when they are totally linked to others, thinking what they think, obeying without question and being manipulated into a strong sense of solidarity. The individual submits to the power of the group, and it becomes almost impossible to leave. There is a sort of latent blackmail, individuals are compromised to such an extent that they cannot leave.

In a true community, each of us is able to keep our own deepest secret, which must not be handed over to others, nor may be even shared. There are some gifts of God, some sufferings and some sources of inspiration, which should not necessarily be given to the whole community. Each of us should be able to deepen our own personal conscience and mystical life. It is precisely here that the weakness and strength of the community lie. There is weakness because of the unknown of individual consciences; because they are free, people can deepen in *gratuité*[3] and in the gift which helps build community, or they may betray love, become more egotistical and so give up and harm the community. There is weakness too because, if the individual and his union with God and the truth are paramount, he or she can, if God so calls them, find another place in the community and no longer assume the function that the community finds most useful; he or she can even physically leave. The ways of God for the individual are not always those of the people at the head of the community or what human reason and experience establish. But there is strength too in putting people first. There is nothing stronger than a heart which loves and is freely given to God and to others. Love is stronger than fear.

Belonging is for becoming. A young man or woman leaves the family because it has become stifling; they need something else in order to grow to greater maturity. So it is with community. It is for becoming and for the growth of personal consciousness. If for some reason it becomes stifling, then the person may have to take the risk of moving on, no matter how painful the separation may be. Community as such is never an end in itself. It is people and love and communion with God that are the goal. But, of course, a separation of this kind comes only after mature discernment and not just because being in community is painful or because there is a new leader we do not like!

If community is for growth of the personal consciousness and freedom, and not just for the collective consciousness, with the security it brings, there will be times when some people find themselves in conflict with their community. Some out of fear of this conflict and of loneliness will refuse to follow their personal freedom and inner conscience; they choose not to 'rock the boat'. Others will choose to grow personally but the price they will have

3 *gratuité*: a lovely word meaning giving freely and generously of oneself. Because the English words 'gratuity/gratuitous' have lost this sense and carry negative overtones, the French form is used here.

to pay will be a certain anguish and loneliness as they feel separated from the group.

This happens particularly when someone is called to personal growth and is in a group which has become lukewarm, mediocre and closed in on itself. The loneliness and anguish felt by this person can lead to a more intimate and mystical union with God. The person no longer finding support from the group cries out to God. 'Let those who thirst come to me and drink,' says Jesus. Those who suffer in this way find a new strength and love in the heart of God. Their communion with the Father deepens.

The authenticity of their communion with God is shown as they continually try to love their brothers and sisters with greater fidelity, without judgement or condemnation.

In community, people are called always to *become more*. It can be so easy for some to be stifled and even manipulated by the group, or overcome by a terrible fear of being rejected if they are in contradiction to the group or appear to be different from the others. Belonging should always be for becoming. The right question to ask is: 'Who am I trying to please?' If we are always trying to please Jesus and not just the group, then we will grow, and the community will be *for people*. But, of course, Jesus does want us also to be obedient to a group. That is where discernment and wisdom are necessary.

Workers come together in a factory to produce things and to make a good living wage. Soldiers come together in an army to prepare for war. People come together in community because they want to create a place of caring. Community is not for producing things outside of itself; it is not a gathering of people struggling to win a cause. It is a place of communion where people care for others, and are cared for by others; a place where they become vulnerable to one another.

In community, people let down barriers; appearances and masks disappear. But this is not easy. Many people have built up their personalities precisely by hiding their wounded hearts behind the barriers of independence and of the attitude, 'I know, you don't'. They are highly active and their activity is based on a need to assert, to succeed, to control, to do projects and to be recognised. Others have constructed around their hearts a mask of depression, or of timidity or submission to others; they do not dare allow their true person to rise up inside them.

A community comes about when people are no longer hiding from one another, no longer pretending or proving their value to another. Barriers have come down and they can live together an experience of communion.

Scott Peck talks of this experience as the 'miracle' of community.

An utterly new quietness descends upon the group. People seem to speak more quietly; yet strangely enough, their voices seem to carry better across the room. There are periods of silence, but it is never an uneasy silence. Indeed the silence is welcomed. It feels tranquil. Nothing is frantic any more. The chaos is over. It is as if noise had been replaced by music. People listen and can hear. It is peaceful.[4]

Community and co-operation

In a community, people are called to co-operate together. Work has to be done; food must be bought or cultivated and meals prepared; dishes must be washed and floors cleaned; prayer and work must start on time. People must be welcomed, some turned away. The elderly and the sick must be cared for; younger members must be formed;[5] money must be earned or received as gifts; it must be spent and the accounts must be kept and so on. Obvi-

---

4 M. Scott Peck, *The Different Drum* (Simon and Schuster, New York, 1987), p. 71.

5 form/formation: words used to describe the process of developing a person's inner life, growth and knowledge, understanding and commitment. It has a deeper meaning than the word 'training'.

ously each person will have a job to do and be accountable to someone or to the whole community. There has to be clear organisation and discipline in a community; otherwise there will be chaos and terrible inefficiency.

This is particularly true when people live together, but it is also true – although to a lesser extent – in support groups where people come together only occasionally.

In community, collaboration must find its source in communion. It is because people care for each other and feel called to be with each other, walking towards the same goals, that they co-operate together. Co-operation without communion quickly becomes like a work camp or factory, where unity comes from an exterior reality. And there will be many tensions and strife.

Communion is based on some common inner experience of love; it is the recognition of being one body, one people, called by God to be a source of love and peace. Its fulfilment is more in silence than in words, more in celebration than in work. It is an experience of openness and trust that flows from what is innermost in a person; it is a gift of the Holy Spirit.

Community is above all a place of communion. For this reason it is necessary to give priority in daily life to those realities, symbols, meetings and celebrations that will encourage a consciousness of communion. When a community is just a place of work, it is in danger of dying.

Community, a place of healing and growth

When people enter community, especially from a place of loneliness in a big city or from a place of aggression and rejection, they find the warmth and the love exhilarating. This permits them to start lifting their masks and barriers and to become vulnerable. They may enter into a time of communion and great joy.

But then too, as they lift their masks and become vulnerable, they discover that community can be a terrible place, because it is a place of relationship; it is the revelation of our wounded emotions and of how painful it can be to live with others, especially with some people. It is so much easier to live with books and objects, television, or dogs and cats! It is so much easier to live alone and just *do* things for others, when one feels like it.

As we live with people daily, all the anger, hatred, jealousies and fear of others, also the need to dominate, to run away or to hide, seem to rise up from the wounds of our early childhood when we felt unloved and abandoned or over-protected. All the dirt seems to come up to the surface of our consciousness from the tomb in which it had all been hidden. We begin to experience terrible anguish because people are clutching on to us, asking too much of us, or simply because their presence reminds us of authoritarian parents who did not have time to listen to us.

Community is the place where our limitations, our fears and our egoism are revealed to us. We discover our poverty and our weaknesses, our inability to get on with some people, our mental and emotional blocks, our affective or sexual disturbances, our seemingly insatiable desires, our frustrations and jealousies, our hatred and our wish to destroy. While we are alone, we could believe we loved everyone. Now that we are with others, living with them all the time, we realise how incapable we are of loving, how much we deny to others, how closed in on ourselves we are. And if we are incapable of loving, what is left? There is nothing but despair, anguish, and the need to destroy. Love then appears to be an illusion. We are condemned to inner isolation and death.

So community life brings a painful revelation of our limitations, weaknesses and darkness; the unexpected discovery of the monsters within us is hard to accept. The immediate reaction is to try to destroy the monsters, or to hide them away again, pretending that they don't exist. Or else we try to flee from community life and relationships with others, or to assume that the monsters are theirs, not ours. It is the others who are guilty, not us.

Marriage is not just a honeymoon; it is also a time of loss. Each one loses their individual independence. Each one sacrifices his or her ego for a relationship in which man and woman have become one. That is also the pain of community life. Community is the place where the power of the ego is revealed and where it is called to die so that people become one body and give much life. Jesus said that 'unless a grain of wheat falls into the earth and dies, it remains alone; but if it dies, it bears much fruit' (John 12:24).

As all the inner pains surface, we can discover too that community is a safe place. At last some people really listen to us; we can, little by little, reveal to them all those terrible monsters within us, all those guilt feelings hidden in the tomb of our being. And they can help us to accept them by revealing to us that these monsters are protecting our vulnerability and are our cry for and our fear of love. They stand at the door of our wounded heart. In each one of us there is such a deep wound, such an urgent cry to be held, appreciated and seen as unique and valuable. The heart of each one is broken and bleeding. We want so much an infinite and incarnate love that does not suppress liberty; that does not manipulate us but gives us freedom and creativity. Community life with all its pain is the revelation of that deep wound. And we can only begin to look at it and accept it as we discover that we are loved by God in an incredible way. We are not awful sinners, terrible people who have disappointed and hurt our parents and others. An experience in prayer and the experience of being loved and accepted in community, which has become a safe place for us, allows us gradually to accept ourselves as we are, with our wounds and all the monsters. We are broken, but we are loved. We can grow to greater openness and compassion; we have a mission. Community becomes the place of liberation and growth.

An assistant in l'Arche was telling me how he had felt inferior to his brothers, who were all successful and had wonderful jobs. In his family he had always been seen as a failure. His father seemingly looked down on him, so he felt guilty and had a very broken self-image. He came to l'Arche in a way seeking refuge, but he had not really admitted this to himself when he came. In l'Arche he had some deep experiences in prayer and had known some inner healing, particularly when God revealed to him in the secret of his heart that he was a beloved son. In community, though, it had been quite difficult because he was always wanting to prove himself and was always either angry or depressed, or running away from relationship and dialogue. Little by little, however, he discovered that he was accepted just as he was. Then one day he was able to admit that the wound of his childhood was truly a gift. Through it and through all his inner poverty and pain, he had met community. He had been given something his brothers, with all their success, had no inkling of. He had been given inner joy and liberation and the peace that surpasses all human ideas. In some ways he felt all the joy and exhilaration of the prodigal son. He was loved just as he was, by an eternal love.

The wound in all of us, and which we are all trying to flee, can become the place of meeting with God and with brothers and sisters; it can become the place of ecstasy and of the eternal wedding feast. The loneliness and feelings of inferiority which we are running away from become the place of liberation and salvation.

There is always warfare in our hearts; there is always the struggle between pride and humility, hatred and love, forgiveness and the refusal to forgive, truth and the concealment of truth, openness and closedness. Each one of us is walking in that passage towards liberation, growing on the journey towards wholeness and healing.

As barriers begin to drop, the heart with all its beauty and pain is revealed. The heart, because of wounds and sin, is filled with darkness and the need for revenge. But it is also the place where God resides: the temple of the Spirit. We must not fear this vulnerable heart, with its closeness to sexuality and its capacity to hate and be jealous. We must not run from it into power and knowledge, seeking self-glory and independence. Instead. we must let God take his place there, purify it and enlighten it. As the stone is gradually removed from our inner tomb and the dirt is revealed, we discover that we are loved and forgiven; then under the power of love and of the Spirit, the tomb becomes a womb. A miracle seems to happen. The heart revives in purity. We discover, through the grace of God, a new life, born in the Spirit.

This descent into the heart is a tunnel of pain, but also a liberation of love. It is painful as the barriers of egoism, and of the need to prove ourselves and to be recognised for *our* glory, crack and break. It is a liberation as the child in us is reborn and the selfish adult dies. Jesus said that if we do not change and become like little children, we cannot enter into the Kingdom. The revelation of love is for children, and not for wise and clever people.

As we live truly from the heart, we live from where the Spirit is dwelling in us. We see people as God sees them; we see their wounds and their pain; we no longer see them as problems. We see God in them. But as we begin to live in this way, unprotected by barriers, we become very vulnerable and terribly poor. 'Blessed are the poor in spirit for theirs is the kingdom.' It is this poverty which becomes our wealth, for now we no longer live for our own glory but for love and for the power of God manifested in weakness.

There are more and more groups today oriented towards issues and causes. There are peace movements, ecological movements, movements for oppressed people, for the liberation of women, against torture, etc. Each movement is important and, if they are based in a community life and the growing consciousness that in *each* person there is a world of darkness, fear, and hate, they can then radiate truth and inner freedom, and work towards justice and peace in the world. If not, they can become very aggressive and divide the world between oppressors and the oppressed, the good and the bad. There seems to be a need in human begins to see evil and combat it *outside* oneself, in order not to see it *inside* oneself.

The difference between a community and a group that is only issue-oriented, is that the latter see the enemy outside the group. The struggle is an external one; and there will be a winner and a loser. The group knows it is right and has the truth, and wants to impose it. The members of a community know that the struggle is inside of each person and inside the community; it is against all the powers of pride, elitism, hate and depression that are there and which hurt and crush others, and which cause division and war of all sorts. The enemy is inside, not outside.

> Our burgeoning interest in the existence and source of our prejudices, hidden hostilities, irrational fears, perceptual blind spots, mental ruts, and resistance to growth is the start of an evolutionary leap . . .
>
> The major threats to our survival no longer stem from nature without but from our own human nature within. It is our carelessness, our hostilities, our selfishness and pride and willful ignorance that endanger the world. Unless we can now tame and transmute the potential for evil in the human soul, we shall be lost. And how can we do this unless we are willing to look at our own evil with the same thoroughness, detached discernment and rigorous methodology to which we subject the external world?[6]

John of the Cross says that the love of God and the love of people have the same source and the same goal. If people grow in love for others, then they grow in love for God and vice versa. If they close their hearts to others, then they close their hearts to God.

John, the beloved disciples of Jesus, says the same in his letters:

> If anyone is well off in worldly possessions and sees his brother in need but closes his heart to him, how can the love of God be remaining in him? (1 John 3:17). Whosoever claims to be in the light but hates his brother, is still in darkness. Anyone who loves his brother remains in light . . . whoever hates his brother is in darkness and is walking about in darkness, not knowing where he is going, because darkness has blinded him (1 John 2:9–11).

Community life with all its difficulties is a special place of growth.

In every human being there is such a thirst for communion with another, a cry to be loved and understood – not judged or con-

---

6 M. Scott Peck, *People of the Lie* (Simon and Schuster, New York, 1983), pp. 260, 263.

demned; there is a yearning to be called forth as special and unique. But to have this communion with another involves demands: to come out of one's shell of protection, to become vulnerable in order to love and understand others, to call them forth as special and unique, to share and to give space and nourishment to them. That is where the pain and fear lie, even sometimes the incapacity to love. Jesus calls his followers to love, to love one another as he loves them; not just to love others as one loves oneself. He proposes something new; to love others with the very love of God; to see them with the eyes of the Lord. And we can only see and love them like that if we ourselves have experienced Jesus loving us with a liberating love. It is only then that we can open ourselves and become vulnerable and grow to greater openness to others.

Community is the place where people grow in love and in peacemaking. That is why it is imperative for communities to grow, expand, and deepen; and for many new ones to be founded and supported. Today war has become too dangerous; it could bring an end to our planet and to the human species. We are all called to learn to grow in love and forgiveness.

Sympathies and antipathies

The two great dangers of community are 'friends' and 'enemies'. People very quickly get together with those who are like themselves; we all like to be with someone who pleases us, who shares our ideas, ways of looking at life and sense of humour. We nourish each other, we flatter each other: 'You are marvellous' – 'So are you' – 'We are marvellous because we are intelligent and clever.' Human friendships can very quickly become a club of mediocrities, enclosed in mutual flattery and approval, preventing people from seeing their inner poverty and wounds. Friendship is then no longer a spur to grow, to go further, to be of greater service to our brothers and sisters, to be more faithful to the gifts we have been given, more attentive to the Spirit, and to continue walking across the desert to the land of liberation. Friendship then becomes stifling, a barrier between ourselves and others and their needs. It becomes an emotional dependence which is a form of slavery.

There are also 'antipathies' in community. There are always people with whom we don't agree, who block us, who contradict us and who stifle the treasure of our life and our freedom. Their presence seems to awaken our own poverty, guilt feelings and inner wounds; it seems menacing and brings out in us either aggression or a sort of fear and servile regression. We seem incapable of expressing ourselves or even of living peacefully when we are with them. Others bring out our envy and jealousy; they are everything we wish we were ourselves. Their presence reminds us of what we are not; their radiance and their intelligence underline our own poverty. Others ask too much of us; we cannot respond to their incessant emotional demands and we have to push them away. These are the 'enemies'. They endanger us, and, even if we dare not admit it, we hate them. Certainly, this is only a psychological hatred – it isn't yet a moral hatred, because it is not deliberate. But even so, we just wish these people didn't exist! If they disappeared or died, it would seem like a liberation.

These blocks, as well as affinity between different personalities, are natural. They come from an emotional immaturity and from many elements from our childhood over which we have no control. It would be foolish to deny them.

But if we let ourselves be guided by our emotional reactions, cliques will form within the community. It will become no longer a community, a place of communion, but a collection of people more or less shut into different groups cut off one from another.

When you go into some communities, you can quickly sense these tensions and underground battles. People don't look each other in the face. They pass each other in the corridors like ships in the night. A community is only a community when most of its members have consciously decided to break these barriers and come out of their cocoons of 'friendship' to stretch out their hand to their enemies.

But the journey is a long one. A community isn't built in a day.

In fact, it is never completely finished! It is always either growing towards greater love or else regressing, as people accept or refuse to descend into the tunnel of pain to be reborn in the spirit.

The barriers and walls around communities, as they lock themselves up in fear or elitism, are the mirrors of those barriers and walls that people put around their own wounded hearts.

There is a very significant passage in the letter to the Ephesians where Paul says that Jesus came to break down the dividing walls of hostility between two groups of people to make them both one (cf. Eph. 2:14).

Bill gave as an example of the pain of living in community, where two people live in the same room and one always carefully presses his or her tube of toothpaste from the bottom while the other person borrows the same tube but presses it from the middle!

Scott Peck talks of pseudo-communities. These are where people *pretend* to live community. Everybody is polite and obeys the rules and regulations. They speak in platitudes and generalities. But underlying it all is an immense fear of conflict, a fear of letting out the monsters. If people start truly to listen to each other and to get involved, speaking from their guts, their anger and fears may rise up and they might start hitting each other over the head with frying pans. There are so many pent-up emotions contained in their hearts that if these were to start surfacing, God knows what might happen! It would be chaos. But from that chaos, healing could come. They realise what a terrible mess the community is in, what horrible fears inhabit them. Then they feel lost and empty. What to do; what road to take? They discover that they have all been living in a state of falsehood. And it is then that the miracle of community can happen! Feeling lost, but together, they start to share their pain, their disillusionment and their love, and then discover their brotherhood and sisterhood; they start

praying to God for light and for healing, and they discover forgiveness. They discover community.[7]

Our enemies frighten us. We are incapable of hearing their cries,
of responding to their needs. Their aggression or domination stifles
us. We flee from them – or wish that they would disappear.

But in community we are called to discover that the 'enemy' is
a person in pain and that through the 'enemy' we are being asked
to become aware of our own weakness, lack of maturity and inner
poverty. Perhaps it is this which we refuse to look at. The faults
we criticise in others are often those we refuse to face in ourselves.
Those who criticise others and the community, and seek an ideal
one, are often in flight from their own flaws and weaknesses. They
see the piece of straw in the eye of the other, but seem completely
unaware of the log in their own. They refuse to accept their own
feeling of dissatisfaction, their own wound.

Scott Peck writes that one of the things we know about evil is

the tendency of the evil to project their evil onto others. Unable
or unwilling to face their own sinfulness, they must explain it
away by accusing others of defects . . . [8]

I know that the first task of love is self-purification. When
one has purified oneself, by the grace of God, to the point at
which one can truly love one's enemies, a beautiful thing happens. It is as if the boundaries of the soul become so clean as
to be transparent, and a unique light then shines forth from the
individual.[9]

The message of Jesus is clear:

But I say to you that hear, Love your enemies, do good to
those who hate you, bless those who curse you, pray for those
who abuse you. To him who strikes you on the cheek, offer
the other also. . . . If you love those who love you, what credit

7 cf. Scott Peck's reflections on the movement from pseudo-community to community, through chaos and emptiness, in *The Different Drum*, ch. 5.
8 Scott Peck, *People of the Lie*, p. 260.
9 Ibid., p. 268.

is that to you? For even sinners love those who love them. (Luke 6:27–9, 32)

Of course you don't meet enemies in Carmel, but when all is said and done you do have your sympathies. One sister attracts you; another sister – well, you'd go a good long way round to avoid meeting her. Without knowing it, she is your persecutress. Good; then Jesus tells me this is the sister I've got to love, the sister I've got to pray for. Her behaviour to be sure, suggests that she isn't too fond of me; yes but 'What credit is it to you if you love those you love you? Even sinners love those who love them'. And just loving her isn't enough; you've got to prove it.[10]

The enemy in the community reveals to us the enemy inside us.

Community as forgiveness

As long as we refuse to accept that we are a mixture of light and darkness, of positive qualities and failings, of love and hate, of altruism and egocentricity, of maturity and immaturity, and that we are all children of the same Father, we will continue to divide the world into enemies (the 'baddies') and friends (the 'goodies'). We will go on throwing up barriers around ourselves and our communities, spreading prejudice.

When we accept that we have weaknesses and flaws, that we have sinned against God and against our brothers and sisters, but that we are forgiven and can grow towards inner freedom and truer love, then we can accept the weaknesses and flaws of others. They too are forgiven by God and are growing towards the freedom of love. We can look at all men and women with realism and love. We can begin to see in them the wound of pain that brings

10 Thérèse de Lisieux, *Autobiography of a Saint*, trans. Ronald Knox (Collins, London, 1958), p. 214. Thérèse Martin, frequently called Thérèse of Lisieux, entered an enclosed Carmelite community at the age of 15. She died aged 24. Her autobiography is one of the most enlightening documents about the pain and holiness of community life.

up fear, but also their gift which we can love and admire. We are all mortal and fragile, but we are all unique and precious. There is hope; we can all grow towards greater freedom. We are learning to forgive.

In community it is so easy to judge and then condemn others. We lock people up in a category: 'He or she is like this or like that.' When we do that we refuse them the possibility of growing. Jesus tells us not to judge or condemn. This is the sin of community life. If we judge, it is often because there is something inside us that we feel guilty about and which we do not want to look at or allow others to see. When we judge, we are pushing people away; we are creating a wall, a barrier. When we forgive we are destroying barriers; we come closer to others.

Sometimes I can judge people too quickly, their acts or the way they exercise their authority, not knowing or having assimilated all the facts or circumstances. It is so easy to speak from our wounds rather than from our centre where Jesus is present. It is so easy to see the flaws in others instead of affirming all that is positive in them.

When we speak from our wound, frequently we are trying to prove that we are someone; we are frightened of disappearing and of not being recognised; we are frightened of loss. There can be an unconscious anger or need to dominate and control others in the tone of our voice; there can be also an urgency or compulsion coming from an inner disturbance or anguish. We must not be surprised if we speak from our wound and defence mechanisms and judge others too quickly. That is our broken humanity. Each one of us carries within us wounds and fragilities; we can be quickly frightened by other people and their ideas; we all have difficulty truly listening to others and appreciating them.

However, we must all work on our emotional life and deepen our spiritual life in order to be more centred in truth in love, in God, and in order to speak and act out of that centre and not to judge others.

We can only truly accept others as they are, and forgive them, when we discover that we are truly accepted by God as we are and forgiven by him. It is a deep experience, knowing that we are loved and held by God in all our brokenness and littleness. For me it has been such a grace and a gift over these years in community to verbalise my sins and to ask for forgiveness of a priest who listens and says 'I forgive you in the name of the Father, the Son and the Holy Spirit.' To accept responsibility for our sinfulness and hardness of heart, and to know that we are forgiven is a real liberation. I don't have to hide my guilt anymore.

We can only really love our enemies and all that is broken in them if we begin to love all that is broken in our own beings. The prodigal son, after the discovery that he was loved in such a tremendous way by the Father, would never be able to judge anyone any more. How could he reject someone when he sees how he has been accepted by the Father, just as he is, with all his brokenness. The elder son, on the other hand, did judge, because he had not come to terms with his own brokenness; all this was still hidden in the tomb of his being, with the stone rolled tight against it.

We can only really love with a universal heart as we discover that we are loved by the universal heart of God.

Community is the place of forgiveness. In spite of all the trust we may have in each other, there are always words that wound, self-promoting attitudes, situations where susceptibilities clash. That is why living together implies a cross, a constant effort, an acceptance which is daily, and mutual forgiveness.

Too many people come into community to find something, to belong to a dynamic group, to discover a life which approaches the ideal. If we come into community without knowing that the reason we come is to learn to forgive and be forgiven seven times seventy-seven times, we will soon be disappointed.

But forgiveness is not simply saying to someone who has had a fit of anger, slammed the doors and behaved in an anti-social or 'anti-community' way; 'I forgive you'. When people have power and are well settled in community, it is easy to 'wield' forgiveness.

To forgive is also to understand the cry behind the behaviour. People are saying something through their anger and/or anti-social behaviour. Perhaps they feel rejected. Perhaps they feel that no one is listening to what they have to say or maybe they feel incapable of expressing what is inside them. Perhaps the community is being too rigid or too legalistic and set in its ways; there may even be a lack of love and of truth. To forgive is also to look into oneself and to see where one should change, where one should also ask for forgiveness and make amends.

To forgive is to recognise once again – after separation – the covenant which binds us together with those we do not get along with well; it is to be open and listening to them once again. It is to give them space in our hearts. That is why it is never easy to forgive. We too must change. We must learn to forgive and forgive and forgive every day, day after day. We need the power of the Holy Spirit in order to open up like that.

Have patience

We are not the masters of our own feelings of attraction or revulsion; these come from places in ourselves over which we have little or no control. All we can do is try not to follow inclinations which make for barriers within the community. We have to hope that the Holy Spirit will come to forgive, purify and trim the rather twisted branches of our being. Our emotional make-up has grown from a thousand fears and egoisms since our infancy, as well as from signs of love and the gift of God. It is a mixture of shadow and light. And so it will not be straightened out in a day, but will take a thousand purifications and pardons, daily efforts and above all a gift of the Holy Spirit which renews us from within.

It is a long haul to transform our emotional make-up so that we can start really loving our enemy. We have to be patient with our feelings and fears; we have to be merciful to ourselves. If we are to make the passage[11] to acceptance and love of the other – all the others – we must start very simply, by recognising our own blocks, jealousies, ways of comparing ourselves to others, preju-

---

11 passage: a transition that includes a deeply changed attitude, or a movement from one stage of life to another.

dices and hatreds. We have to recognise that we are poor creatures, that we are what we are. And we have to ask our Father to forgive and purify us. It is good, then, to speak to a spiritual guide, who perhaps can help us to understand what is happening, strengthen us in our efforts and help us discover God's pardon.

Once we have recognised that a branch is twisted, that we have these blocks of antipathy, the next step is to try to be careful of how we speak. We have to try to hold our tongue, which can so quickly sow discord, which likes to spread the faults and mistakes of others, which rejoices when it can prove someone wrong. The tongue is one of the smallest parts of our body, but it can sow death. We are quick to magnify the faults of others, just to hide our own. It is so often 'they' who are wrong. When we accept our own flaws, it is easier to accept those of others.

Here is a word of advice from St John of the Cross: 'Never listen to those who speak of the weakness of another. If someone comes to complain about someone, you can ask that person with humility, not to say anything.'[12]

At the same time, we should try loyally to see the good qualities of our enemies. After all, they must have a few! But because we are afraid of them, perhaps they are afraid of us. If we have blocks, they too must have them. It is hard for two people who are afraid of each other to discover their mutual qualities. They need a mediator, a conciliator, an artisan of peace, someone in whom both have confidence. This third person can perhaps help us to discover the qualities of our enemy, or at least to understand our own attitudes and blocks. When we have seen the enemy's qualities, one day we will be able to use our tongue to say something good about him. It is a long journey, which will end the day we can ask our former 'enemy' for advice or a favour. We all find it far more touching to be asked for help than we do to be helped or 'done good to'.

12 Sayings of St John of the Cross, no. 198.

Throughout this time, the Holy Spirit can help us to pray for our enemies, to pray that they too grow as God would have them grow, so that one day the reconciliation may be made. Perhaps one day the Holy Spirit will liberate us from this block of antipathy. Perhaps he will let us go on walking with this thorn in our flesh - this thorn which humiliates us and forces us to renew our efforts each day. When Paul cried out to be delivered from the thorn in his flesh, Jesus replied: 'My grace is enough for you; my power is manifested in weakness' (2 Cor. 12:9).

We shouldn't get worried about our bad feelings. Still less should we feel guilty. We should ask God's forgiveness, like little children, and keep on walking. We shouldn't get discouraged if the road is long. One of the roles of community life is precisely to keep us walking in hope, to help us accept ourselves as we are and others as they are.

Patience, like forgiveness, is at the heart of community life - patience with ourselves and the laws of our own growth, and patience with others. The hope of a community is founded on the acceptance and love of ourselves and others as we really are, and on the patience and trust which is essential to growth.

There is one sister in the community who has the knack of rubbing me up the wrong way at every turn; her tricks of manner, her tricks of speech, her character, strike me as unlovable. But then, she's a holy religious; God must love her dearly, so I wasn't going to let this natural antipathy get the better of me. I reminded myself that charity isn't a matter of fine sentiments; it means doing things. So I determined to treat this sister as if she were the person I loved best in the world. Every time I met her, I used to pray for her, offering to God all her virtues and her merits. I felt certain that Jesus would like me to do that.[13]

We must pray that God will teach us to love those we do not like and then to like those he is teaching us to love.

To grow in love is to try each day to welcome, and to be attentive

13   Thérèse de Lisieux, *Autobiography of a Saint*, p. 211.

and caring for those with whom we have the greatest difficulty; with our 'enemies'; those who are the poorest, the oldest, the weakest, the most demanding, the most ailing; those who are the most marginal in the community, who have the most difficulty conforming to the rules; and finally those who are the youngest. If people are faithful to these four priorities of love then the community as a whole will be an oasis of love.

Mutual trust

The mutual trust at the heart of community is born of each day's forgiveness and acceptance of the frailty and poverty of ourselves and of others. But this trust is not developed overnight. That is why it takes time to form a real community. When people join a community, they always present a certain image of themselves because they want to conform to what the others expect of them. Gradually, they discover that the others love them as they are and trust them. But this trust must stand the test and must always be growing.

Newly-married couples may love each other a great deal. But there may be something superficial in this love, which has to do with the excitement of discovery. Love is even deeper between people who have been married for a long time, who have lived through difficulties together and who know that the other will be faithful until death. They know that nothing can break their union.

It is the same in our communities. It is often after suffering, after very great trials, tensions and the proof of fidelity that trust grows. A community in which there is truly mutual trust is a community which is indestructible.

I am becoming more and more aware that the great difficulty of many of us who live in community is that we lack trust in ourselves. We can so quickly feel that we are not really lovable, that if others saw us as we really are, they would reject us. We are afraid of all that is darkness in ourselves, we are afraid to face our emotional or sexual problems; we are afraid that we are incapable of real love. We swing so quickly from exhilaration to depression, and neither expresses what we really are. How can we become convinced that we are loved in our poverty and weakness and that we too are capable of loving?

That is the secret of growth in community. It comes from a gift of God which may pass through others. As we gradually discover that God and the others trust us, it becomes a little easier for us to trust ourselves, and in turn to trust others.

To live in community is to discover and love the secret of what is unique in ourselves. This is how we become free. Then we no longer live according to the desires of others, or by an image of ourselves; we become free, free to love others as they are and not as we would like them to be.

The right to be oneself

I have always wanted to write a book called 'The Right to be a Rotter'. A fairer title is perhaps 'The Right to be Oneself'.

One of the great difficulties of community life is that we sometimes force people to be what they are not: we stick an ideal image on them to which they are obliged to conform. We then expect too much of them and are quick to judge or to label. If they don't manage to live up to this image or ideal, then they become afraid they won't be loved or that they will disappoint others. So they feel obliged to hide behind a mask. Sometimes they succeed in living up to the image; they are able to follow all the rules of community. Superficially this may give them a feeling of being perfect, but this is an illusion.

In any case, community is not about perfect people. It is about people who are bonded to each other, each of whom is a mixture of good and bad, darkness and light, love and hate. And community is the only earth in which each can grow without fear towards the liberation of the forces of love which are hidden in them. But there can be growth only if we recognise the potential, and this will never unfold if we prevent people from discovering and accepting themselves as they are, with their gifts and their wounds. They have the right to be rotters, to have their own dark places, and corners of envy and even hatred in their hearts. These jealousies and insecurities are part of our wounded nature. That is our reality. We have to learn to accept them and to live with them without drama, and to walk towards liberation, gradually knowing ourselves to be forgiven.

Many people in community, it seems to me, live with the burden of unconscious guilt; they feel that they are not what they should be. They need to be affirmed and encouraged to trust. They must feel able to share even their weaknesses without the risk of rejection.

There is a part of each of us which is already luminous, already converted. And there is a part which is still in shadow. A community is not made up only of the converted. It is made up of all the elements in us which need to be transformed, purified and pruned. It is made up also of the 'unconverted'.

Thérèse of Lisieux writes that as she meditated on the New Commandment of Jesus, to love people as he loves them, she began to see how imperfect her own love was:

> it was so obvious that I didn't love my sisters as God loves them. I realise now, that perfect love means putting up with other people's shortcomings, feeling no surprise at their weaknesses, finding encouragement even in the slightest evidence of good qualities in them.[14]

To love people is to recognise their gifts and help these to unfold; it is also to accept their wounds and be patient and compassionate towards them. If we see only the gifts and beauty, then we expect too much of people; we idealise them. If we see only the wound,

14 Thérèse de Lisieux, *Autobiography of a Saint*, p. 209.

then we do too much for them and tend to keep them in submission.

Called by God just as we are

We can choose to live in a community because it is dynamic, warm and radiant. We find happiness there. But if a crisis arises, with tensions and turmoil, we begin to doubt the wisdom of our choice: 'Maybe I made a mistake.'

If we *enter* community because of our own choice, we will *stay* only if we become more aware that it was in fact God who chose us for this community. It is only then that we will find the inner strength to live through times of turmoil.

It is not the same thing in marriage? The bond becomes truly deep when husband and wife become conscious that they were brought together by God, to be a sign of love and of forgiveness for one another.

Parker Palmer writes: 'Community is finally a religious phenomenon. There is nothing capable of binding together willful, broken human selves except some transcendent power.'[15] And I would add that no reality can lead us into the heart of forgiveness and open us up to all people, except a loving, forgiving God.

Henri Nouwen says that

> true solitude far from being the opposite of community life is the place where we come to realise that we were together before we came together and that community life is not a creation of human will but an obedient response to the reality of our being united. Many people who have lived together for years and whose love for one another has been tested more than once

15   Parker J. Palmer, *A Place Called Community* (Pendle Hill, Philadelphia, 1977), p. 18.

know that the decisive experience in their life was not that they were able to hold together but that they were held together. That, in fact, we are a community not because we like each other or have a common task or project but because we are called together by God.[16]

God seems pleased to call together in Christian communities people who, humanly speaking, are very different, who come from very different cultures, classes and countries. The most beautiful communities are created from just this diversity of people and temperaments. This means that each person must love the others with all their differences, and work with them for the community.

These people would never have chosen to live with each other. Humanly speaking, it seems an impossible challenge. But it is precisely because it is *impossible* that they believe that God has chosen them to live in this community. So then the impossible becomes possible. They no longer rely on their own human abilities or natural sympathies, but on their Father who has called them to live together. He will give them the new heart and spirit which will enable them all to become witnesses to love. In fact, the more impossible it is in human terms, the more of a sign it is that their love comes from God and that Jesus is living: 'By this all men will know that you are my disciples, if you have love for one another' (John 13:35).

When he created the first community of the apostles, Jesus chose to live with men who were very different from one another: Peter, Matthew (the publican), Simon (the Zealot), Judas, and so on. They would never have come together if their Master had not called them. And when they were together they spent a lot of time squabbling about who was the most important amongst them. Yes, community life is definitely not easy! But it becomes possible because of the call of Jesus.

We shouldn't seek the ideal community. It is a question of loving

16   'Solitude and Community', *Worship*, Jan. 1978.

those whom God has set beside us today. They are signs of God. We might have chosen different people, people who were more cheerful and intelligent. But these are the ones God has given us, the ones he has chosen for us. It is with them that we are called to create unity and live a covenant. We choose our own friends; but in our families, we do not choose our brothers and sisters; they are given to us. So it is in community life.

I am more and more struck by people in community who are dissatisfied. When they live in small communities, they want to be in larger ones, where there is more nourishment, where there are more community activities, or where the liturgy is more beautifully prepared. And when they are in large communities, they dream of ideal small ones. Those who have a lot to do dream of having plenty of time for prayer: those who have a lot of time for themselves seem to get bored and search distractedly for some sort of activity which will give a sense of purpose to their lives. And don't we all dream of the perfect community, where we will be at peace and in complete harmony, with a perfect balance between the outward and the inward, where everything will be joyful?

It is difficult to get people to understand that the ideal doesn't exist, that personal equilibrium and the harmony they dream of come only after years and years of struggle, and even then only as flashes of grace and peace. If we are always looking for our own equilibrium – I'd even say if we are looking too much for our own peace – we will never find it, because peace is the fruit of love and service to others. I'd like to tell the many people in communities who are looking for this impossible ideal: 'Stop looking for peace, give yourselves where you are. Stop looking at yourselves – look instead at your brothers and sisters in need. Be close to those God has given you in community today; and work with the situation as it is. Ask how you can better love your brothers and sisters. Then you will find peace. You will find rest and that famous balance you're looking for between the outward and the inward, between prayer and activity, between time for yourself and time for others. Everything will resolve itself through love. Stop wasting time running after the perfect community. Live your life fully in your community today. Stop seeing the flaws – and thank God there are some! Look rather at your own defects and know that you are forgiven and can, in your turn, forgive others and today enter into the conversion of love, and remember, pray always.'

But to be good instruments of God's love we must avoid being over-tired, burnt-out, stressed, aggressive, fragmented or closed up. We need to be rested, centred, peaceful, aware of the needs of our body, our heart and our spirit. Jesus says that there is no greater love than to give our lives, but let us not give over-tired, stressed and aggressive lives. Let us, rather, give joyful ones!

Share your weakness

One day, Colleen, who had been living in community for more than twenty-five years, told me: 'I have always wanted to be transparent in community life. I have wanted more than anything to avoid being an obstacle to God's love for the others. Now I am beginning to discover that I am an obstacle and I always shall be. But isn't the recognition that I am an obstacle, sharing that with my brothers and sisters and asking their forgiveness, what community life is all about?' There is no ideal community. Community is made up of people with all their richness, but also with their weakness and their poverty, of people who accept and forgive each other, who are vulnerable one to another. Humility and trust are more at the foundation of community life than perfection and generosity.

To accept our weaknesses and those of others is the very opposite of sloppy complacency. It is not a fatalistic and hopeless acceptance. It is essentially a concern for truth, so that we do not live in illusion but can grow from where we are and not from where we want to be or where others want us to be. It is only when we are conscious of who we are and who the others are, with all our wealth and weakness, and when we are conscious of the call of

God and the life he gives us, that we can build something together.
The force for life should spring from the reality of who we are.

The more a community deepens, the weaker and the more sensitive
its members become. You might think exactly the opposite – that
as their trust in each other grows, they in fact grow stronger. So
they do. But this doesn't disperse the fragility and sensitivity which
are at the root of a new grace and which mean that people are
becoming in some way dependent on each other. Love makes us
weak and vulnerable, because it breaks down the barriers and
protective armour we have built around ourselves. Love means
letting others reach us and becoming sensitive enough to reach
them. The cement of unity is interdependence.

Didier expressed this in his own way during a community meeting: 'A community is built like a house, with all sorts of different
materials. Cement holds the stones together. And cement is made
of sand and lime, which are very insubstantial – it takes only a
gust of wind to blow them away in a cloud of dust. The cement
that unites us in our community is the part of us that is weakest
and smallest.'

Community is made by the gentle concern that people show each
other every day. It is made by small gestures of caring, by services
and sacrifices which say 'I love you' and 'I'm happy to be with
you'. It is letting the other go in front of you, not trying to prove
that you are right in a discussion; it is taking small burdens from
the other. 'Do not do anything out of jealousy or vanity; but in
humility count others better than yourselves. Let each of you look
not only to selfish interests, but to those of others' (Phil. 2:3).

If living in community means letting down the barriers which
protect our vulnerability and recognising and welcoming our
weakness, then people who are separated from their community
can sometimes feel terribly vulnerable. Those who live all the time

in the struggles of society have to build an armour around their vulnerability.

People who have spent a long time at l'Arche sometimes discover a whole lot of aggression in themselves when they return to their family, which they find very hard to bear. They had thought that this aggression no longer existed. So they begin to doubt their calling and who they really are. But the aggression is to be expected, because they have been stripped of much of their personal armour by being in community; they cannot live so openly with people who do not respect their vulnerability. They have to defend themselves.

Community is a living body

St Paul talks about the Church, the community of the faithful, as a body where there are many different parts. Every community is a body, and in it all the members belong one to another. This feeling of belonging comes not from flesh and blood, but from a call from God. Each of us has been personally called to live together, to belong to the same community, the same body. This call is the foundation of our decision to commit ourselves with others and for others, responsible for each other. 'For as in one body we have many members, and all the members do not have the same function, so we, though many, are one body in Christ, and individually members one of another' (Rom. 12:4–5).

In this body, each member has a role to play. The foot needs the hand, says St Paul; hearing and sight complement the sense of smell . . .

> The parts of the body which seems to be weaker are indispensable . . . God has so composed the body, giving the greater honour to the inferior parts, that there may be no discord in the body, but that the members may have the same care for one another. If one member suffers, all suffer together; if one member is honoured, all rejoice together. (1 Cor. 12:22, 24–6)

And in this body, each member has a different gift to offer

> . . . according to the grace given to us . . . if prophecy, in
> proportion to our faith; if service, in our serving; he who
> teaches, in his teaching, he who exhorts, in his exhortation; he
> who contributes, in liberality; he who gives aid, with zeal; he
> who does acts of mercy, with cheerfulness. (Rom. 12:6–8)

This body which is community must act and give light for the
work of love, the work of the Father. It must be a body that prays
and a body which is merciful, so that it can heal and give life to
those who are hopeless in their distress.[17]

Using our gifts

Using our gifts is building community. If we are not faithful to
our gifts, we are harming the community and each of its members
as well. So it is important that all members know what their gifts
are, use them and take responsibility for developing them; it is
important that the gift of each member is recognised and that each
is accountable to the others for the use to which this gift is put.
We all need each other's gifts; we must encourage their growth and
our fidelity to them. Everyone will find their place in community
according to their gift. They will become not only useful but
unique and necessary to the others. And so rivalry and jealousy
will evaporate.

Elizabeth O'Connor[18] gives some striking examples of St Paul's
teaching. She tells the story of an old woman who joined the
community. A group of people were discerning her gift with her.
She believed she had none at all. The others were trying to comfort
her: 'Your gift is your presence.' But that wasn't enough for her.
Several months later she discovered her gift; it was to carry each
member of the community by name before God in a prayer of
intercession. When she shared her discovery with the others, she

17 See also 1 Peter 4:10–11 and Ephesians 4:7–16.
18 Elizabeth O'Connor, *The Eighth Day of Creation* (Word Books, Texas, 1971).

found her essential place in the community. The others knew that they somehow needed her and her prayer, if they were to exercise better their own gifts.

When I read that book, I realised how little we at l'Arche help each other to build community by sharing about our gifts. I realised how little sense we have of really depending on each other and how little we encourage each other to be faithful to our gifts.

Envy is one of the plagues that destroys community. It comes from people's ignorance of, or lack of belief in, their own gifts. If we were confident in our own gift, we would not envy that of others.

Too many communities form – or deform – their members to make them all alike, as if this were a good quality, based on self-denial. These communities are founded on laws or rules. But it is the opposite which is important; each person must grow in their gift to build the community and make it more beautiful and more radiant, a clearer sign of the Kingdom.

Nor must we look just at the obvious gift, which is maybe linked to a natural talent. There are hidden and latent gifts, much deeper ones, which are linked to the gifts of the Holy Spirit and to love. They too must flower.

Some people have outstanding talents. They are writers, artists, competent administrators. These talents can become gifts. But sometimes the individuals' personalities are so tied up in the activity that they exercise their talent chiefly for their own glory, or to prove themselves or to dominate. It is better then that these people do not exercise their talents in community, because they would find it too hard to use them truly for the good of others. What they have to discover is their deeper gift. Others, of course, are more open and flexible, or their personality is less formed and rigid. These people can use their abilities as a gift in the service of the community.

There are more and more communities today where there is not
only a variety of gifts but a variety of people in different states of
life. In the communities of l'Arche there are married and single
people; there are also people who are married but are separated;
and others not married but with children. Each situation is so
different, but each one is part of the body and is vital to the life
and growth of the body. Each one must be respected and find
their place and their nourishment and thus be helped to grow. We
can so quickly compare ourselves with others; then jealousy arises.
We truly need the power of the Holy Spirit to accept what we
have been given and to accept what others have been given.

> In a Christian community, everything depends upon whether
> each individual is an indispensable link in a chain. Only when
> even the smallest link is securely interlocked is the chain
> unbreakable. A community which allows unemployed members
> to exist within it will perish because of them. It will be well,
> therefore, if every member receives a definite task to perform
> for the community, that he may know in hours of doubt that
> he, too, is not useless and unusable. Every Christian community
> must realise that not only do the weak need the strong, but also
> that the strong cannot exist without the weak. The elimination
> of the weak is the death of fellowship.[19]

Using our gift means building community. If we are not faithful,
the edifice will be weakened. St Paul emphasises the importance
of charismatic gifts in this building. But there are many others
which are more directly linked to a quality of love. Bonhoeffer[20]
speaks of the different ministries a community needs: holding
one's tongue, humility, tenderness, silence in the face of criticism,
listening, constant readiness to render small services, support of
brothers, forgiveness, proclamation of the Word, speaking truth
and authority.

19 Dietrich Bonhoeffer, *Life Together* (Harper and Row, New York, 1976). Bon-
    hoeffer is not referring here to people without a paid job, but to members of
    the community who refuse a responsibility that is in accord with their abilities.
20 Ibid., p. 90.

The gift is not necessarily linked to a function. It may be the quality of love which gives life to a function; it may be a quality of love which has nothing to do with any function. There are people who have the gift of being able to sense immediately, and even to live, the sufferings of others – that is the gift of compassion. There are others who know when something is going wrong and can pinpoint the cause – that is the gift of discernment. There are others who have the gift of light – they see clearly what is of fundamental concern to the community. Others have the gift of creating an atmosphere which brings joy, relaxation and individual growth. Others again have the gift of discerning what people need and of supporting them. Others have the gift of welcome. Each person has a gift to use for the good and growth of all.

But in each person's heart of hearts there is also the deep and secret union with God, the Bridegroom, which corresponds to their secret and eternal name. We are certainly made to nurture others, each in our own way. But above all we are made to live this unique relationship with our Father and his son, Jesus. The gift is like the radiance of this secret union on the community. It flows from it and strengthens it.

Community is the safe place where all of us feel free to be ourselves and have the confidence to say everything we live and think. Not all communities will get to this point, it's true. But this is the direction in which they should be going. As long as some people are afraid of expressing themselves, for fear of being judged or thought stupid, or of being rejected, there is still a long way to go. There should be a quality of listening at the heart of the community which tenderly respects everything that is most beautiful and true in each other.

Self-expression does not mean simply giving vent to all our frustrations and angers at what is going badly – though sometimes it is good to bring these out. It also means sharing our deep motivations and what we are living. It is often a way of using our gift to nurture others and help them grow.

In nearly every community I know, and especially in older communities, there are marginal people, that is to say, people who do not quite fit into the community, who have difficulty finding their place in the body. Perhaps this is because they have serious fits of anger or depression, or because they are locked up in themselves and refuse all dialogue. They often feel useless, unloved, unaffirmed and persecuted. They feel they are never given any responsibility; but when it is offered to them, they then refuse it. In some way, because they do not feel unique for someone, they are lonely and in anguish. And as they cannot accept the reality of their uneasiness, they have to find fault with someone else; that someone else is the community. The suffering of these people is great. Nature has not endowed them with an easy temperament. But they are children of God, our brothers and sisters. And God can work in and through them with their difficulties and neurosis, for the growth of the community. They too have their gift to offer. Their cry can frequently be prophetic. Others must be attentive and listen to them.

We must not 'psychiatrise' these people too quickly. We are called to learn to love them and to be wise in helping them, and particularly in listening to what they have to say. Some, of course, may need professional help, but this can be sought only if they themselves ask for it. Through the forgiveness of each day, let us help each other to accept those who are marginal in this way. It is a good sign when the body of a community can accept such people without feeling guilty or making them feel guilty. But of course, there has to be a sufficient number of people at ease within the community in order to be able to carry those who are uneasy with it.

Community is a place for *people* and for their growth, before being a place of laws and rules. Leaders must keep a wise balance between respect for individuals, with their hurts and difficulties, and respect for the rules and structures. Rules and structures are necessary; there can be exceptions only if they are there. But rules are for the life of people and the development of their gifts; and not people for the rules!

I often find in communities members who are suffering because they feel they have been put aside; after years of carrying responsibility, they have difficulty finding their new place in the community. They are grieving the loss of responsibility. These people have to discover that we are all in community not because it is wonderful and brings human fulfilment, but because we are called by God. It is to be hoped they will discover that through their pain they are being called by Jesus to a new and deeper intimacy with the Father, and that this is their gift to be lived at this particular time. Is this not finally the ultimate goal for each person? If they do not realise their new gift; if they do not discover the road to resurrection through humility and inner pain, then they may remain simply in the bitterness and humiliation of the cross.

Sometimes when people are taking on responsibility 'successfully', and when they are admired and looked up to, they may forget that communion with Jesus and the Father is our goal, our source of peace. They can in some ways by-pass a certain quality of trust in God; they can replace God by community. Community is then no longer a place of love flowing from God and to God, manifesting his life, but becomes an end in itself. This manifestation of the life of God always flows through our own poverty and feeling of helplessness.

But of course community leaders and councils must not spiritualise their own error and injustice or lack of love by saying that these people who are suffering must obey, bear their cross and pray. No. Leaders must learn to rectify their errors and injustice if they have committed them; they must see that these people find the spiritual help they need, and the opportunity to continue to exercise their gifts. For this, leaders need to be truly compassionate and creative.

From 'the community for myself' to 'myself for the community'

A community is only truly a body when the majority of its members is making the transition from 'the community for myself' to 'myself for the community', when each person's heart is opening to all the others, without any exception. This is the movement from egoism to love, from death to resurrection; it is the Easter, a passage, the passover of the Lord. It is also the passing from a land of slavery to a promised land, the land of inner freedom.

A community isn't just a place where people live under the same roof; that is a lodging house or an hotel. Nor is a community a work-team. Even less is it a nest of vipers! It is a place where everyone – or, let's be realistic, the majority! – is emerging from the shadows of egocentricity to the light of a real love.

Love is neither sentimental nor a passing emotion. It is the recognition of a covenant, of a mutual belonging. It is listening to others, being concerned for them and feeling empathy with them. It is to see their beauty and to reveal it to them.

It means answering their call and their deepest needs. It means feeling and suffering with them – weeping when they weep, rejoicing when they rejoice. Loving people means being happy when they are there, sad when they are not. It is living in each other, taking refuge in each other. 'Love is a power for unity', says Denys the Areopagite. And if love means moving towards each other, it also and above all means moving together in the same direction, hoping and wishing for the same things. Love means sharing the same vision and the same ideal. So it means wanting others to fulfil themselves, according to God's plan and in service to other people. It means wanting them to be faithful to their own calling, free to love in all the dimensions of their being.

There we have the two poles of community: a sense of belonging to each other and a desire that each of us goes further in our own gift to God and to others, a desire for more light in us, and a deeper truth and peace.

It takes time for a heart to make this passage from egoism to love, from 'the community for myself' to 'myself for the community', and to the community for God and those in need. It takes time and much purification, and constant deaths which bring new resurrections. To love, we must die continually to our own ideas, our own susceptibilities and our own comfort. The path of love is woven of sacrifice. The roots of egoism are deep in our unconscious; our initial reactions of self-defence, aggression and the search for personal gratification often grow from them.

Loving is not only a voluntary act which involves controlling and overcoming our own sensibilities – that is just the beginning. It also demands a purified heart and feelings which go out spontaneously to the other. These deep purifications can only come through a gift of God, a grace which springs from the deepest part of ourselves, where the Holy Spirit lives. 'I will give them a new heart, and put a new spirit within them; I will take the stony heart out of their flesh, and give them a heart of flesh' (Ezek. 11:19).

Jesus has promised to send us the Holy Spirit, the Paraclete, to infuse us with this new energy, this strength, this quality of heart which will make it possible for us truly to welcome the other – even our enemy – as he or she is, possible for us to bear all things, believe all things, hope all things. Learning to love takes a lifetime, because the Holy Spirit must penetrate even the smallest corners of our being, all the places where there are fears, defences and envy.

In his last talk with the apostles, Jesus prayed three times that they should be one as he and his Father were one, 'that they should be consumed by unity.' These words are sometimes applied to unity between Christians of different churches, but they apply first and above all to unity between people and within communities. All communities should be working towards this unity - 'one heart, one soul, one spirit'.

It seems to me that we should ask a special gift of the Holy Spirit – the gift of unity and communion in the deepest sense, and with all the implications. This is truly a gift of God to which we have the right and the duty to aspire.

Jesus' prayer is astonishing. His vision goes much further than our imagination or wishes. The union of the Father and the Son is total. Each community should be working towards this union. But it can only reach it in and through the Holy Spirit. As long as we live, all we can do is to walk humbly towards it.

A community is not simply a group of people who live together and love each other. It is a place of resurrection, a current of life:

one heart, one soul, one spirit. It is people, very different one from another, who love each other and who are all reaching towards the same hope and celebrating the same love. This is what brings the special atmosphere of joy and welcome which characterises the true community.

So if there is any encouragement in Christ, any incentive of love, any participation in the Spirit, any affection and sympathy, complete my joy by being of the same mind, having the same love, being in full accord and of one mind. (Phil. 2:1-2)

Now the company of those who believed were of one heart and soul, and no one said that any of the things which he possessed was his own, but they had everything in common. (Acts 4:32)

This atmosphere of joy comes from the fact that everyone feels free to be themselves in the deepest sense. They have no need to play a role, to pretend to be better than the others, to demonstrate prowess in order to be loved. They do not have to hide a whole part of themselves behind barriers and masks. They have become vulnerable one to another because they have become vulnerable to God. They have discovered that they are loved for themselves, not for their intellectual or manual skills.

When we begin to discover and to drop the barriers and fears which prevent us from being ourselves and which prevent the life of the Holy Spirit from flowing through us, we become more simple. Simplicity is no more and no less than being ourselves, knowing that we are loved. It is knowing that we are accepted, with our qualities, our flaws and as we are in the depths of our being. Simplicity is letting the love and the light of God flow and shine through us according to our vocation and gifts.

The wisdom of a true community often seems miraculous . . . and is more a matter of divine spirit and possible divine intervention. This is one of the reasons why the feeling of joy is such a frequent concomitant of the spirit of community. The members feel they have been temporarily – at least partially – transported out of a mundane world of ordinary preoccupations. For the moment it is as if heaven and earth had somehow met.[21]

21 Scott Peck, *The Different Drum*, p. 76.

When the members of a community are living in communion one with another, and when the poor are at the centre of their life, the community is like a sign of the Kingdom of God; a sign of the presence of God. Jesus came to reveal to humanity that God is not a solitary, eternal being, contemplating his own glory; he is not just an extraordinary Creator of a beautiful yet painful universe. God is a family of three; three persons in communion one with another, giving themselves totally one to another, each one relative to the other. And God created man and woman as a sign of the Trinity; he created them to be in communion, one with the other, in this way reflecting his Love. God yearns for community to be a sign of this communion between Father, Son and Holy Spirit: 'That they may be one, as the Father and I are one' (John 17:11).

Beyond human and natural bonds, already so close and strong, there is discerned in the light of faith a new model of the unity of the human race, which must ultimately inspire our solidarity. This supreme model of unity, which is a reflection of the intimate life of God, one God in three Persons, is what we Christians mean by the word 'communion'.[22]

At the heart of the kingdom community lies the divine as well as the human 'Yes' to life, and 'Yes' to life together. If the Trinity is seen in this context, then it is not a static symbol but an attempt to describe the intimate interdependence of three Persons. The encounter and the exchange between Father, Son and Holy Spirit must always have been, and always will be, ongoing, or it can never have been a reality. We are engaged in an exchange of life because God is too; we are involved in a process of becoming as well as being because, in some profound and life-giving way, God is as well.

This continuing exchange of divine life with divine life, of divine life with human life, and of human life with human life, means that the kingdom community is characterised by the

22 John Paul II, Encyclical Letter, *Sollicitudo Rei Socialis* (Vatican City: Libreria Editrice Vaticana, 1987), no. 40.

sharing of all we are and all we have. This involves a sharing of love.[23]

23 David Clark, *Yes to Life* (Fount, London, 1987), p. 54.

2

Walking Toward the Covenant

A birth of hope

I realise more and more how many young people are wounded in
their capacity to live in relationship and remain very immature
emotionally. Perhaps they lacked a warm, emotional environment
when they were young and, above all, genuine and trusting
relationships with their parents. So they are on an emotional quest,
frequently confused and lost, particularly in the area of values and
of the meaning of sexuality. They need a community in which to
grow towards greater maturity and healing and wholeness; they
need a secure and emotionally warm environment where they can
establish the relationships they need without danger. They need
older people who have time to listen to them.

Some young people will find healing and meaning to their lives
in these communities, and then will move on and put their roots
down in another soil. Others will put down roots in one of these
communities, which then becomes the earth in which they grow
and bear fruit. But between the initial call to community and the
final rooting, there are many passages, moments of doubt and
crises of all sorts. The final rooting is the recognition and acceptance of a covenant, a bonding between people that is holy and
sacred because it is given by God. And this covenant between
people is founded on the bonding or the covenant between the
individual person and God.

Our world has more and more need of 'intermediate communities'
– places where young people can stay and find a certain inner

freedom before they make their decision. They either cannot stay in their family or don't want to; they are not satisfied with life alone in an apartment, hotel or hostel. They need somewhere where they can find their inner liberation through a network of relationships and friendships, where they can be truly themselves without trying or pretending to be anything other than they are. It is in these intermediate communities, where they find also meaningful work, that they will be able to shed some of the fears that weigh them down and prevent them from discovering their deep selves. It is only when they discover that they are loved by God and by others, and that they can do beautiful things for others, that they begin to get in touch with what is deepest in them. Only then will they be free to choose a way of life which is truly their own, not that of their parents or the people around them nor something set up in reaction to it, but one which is born of a real choice of life, in response to an aspiration or a call.

For a community to play this 'intermediate' role, it must have a core of people who are really rooted there. Many young people come to l'Arche having left school, university or a job which is no longer satisfying. They are seekers. After a few years they discover who they really are and what they really want. Then they can either go into a more specifically religious community, marry, go back to work or take up studies which now really interest them.

Others choose to stay. The community is no longer simply their place of healing, a place where they feel good and happy, but the place where they have decided to put down their roots because they have discovered the call of God and, in community with handicapped people, a whole meaning to life. Their personal aims melt into those of the community, they no longer feel challenged by other people's plans to leave the community for something else. They too have their personal plan – to stay in the community.

A new hope is indeed being born today. Some people are dreaming of a powerful Christian civilisation as it used to be; they dream of chivalry; they sense that the powers of selfishness, hatred and violence are reaching everywhere and they want to put Christian order and traditional values back into the world. Others want to harness the forces of violence to break up the old world of private property and 'bourgeois' wealth, and then start anew. And finally, some see in the cracks of our civilisation the seeds of a new world, based solidly on gospel values and non-violence, and upon community founded on the love of Jesus. Individualism and technology have gone too far; the illusion of a better world based on economics and technology is evaporating. Across these cracks, many human hearts are being reborn; many young people are discovering that there is a hope within, rather than outside, them – a hope that they can today love and create community because they believe in Jesus Christ. A renaissance is coming. Soon there will be a multitude of communities founded on adoration and presence to the poor, linked to each other and to the great communities of the Church, which are themselves being renewed, and have already been journeying for years and sometimes centuries. A new Church is indeed being born.

In our time, when there is so much infidelity, when there are so many broken marriages, so many disturbed relationships, so many children who are angry with their parents, so many people who have not been faithful to their promise to love each other, more and more communities need to be born as signs of fidelity. Communities of students or friends who come together for a short time can be signs of hope. But the communities whose members live faithfully a life-long covenant with God, among themselves and with the poor, are more important still. They are signs of the fidelity of God.

The Hebrew word *hesed* expresses two things: fidelity and tenderness. In our civilisation we can be tender but unfaithful, and faithful without tenderness. The love of God is both tenderness and fidelity. Our world is waiting for communities of tenderness and fidelity. They are coming.

The call to families

A great hope is growing at this time. I meet more and more families who are discovering that their working life is inhuman. They may be earning a great deal of money, but at the expense of their family life. They get in late at night, their weekends are often taken up with business meetings, their energies are used up by their working world. It is hard for them to find the inner tranquillity they need to live family life. They realise that they are becoming hyperactive and that they are neglecting the deepest parts of themselves.

Some are caught up in the race for professional promotion; they are afraid to change gear because they may not find a decent job and they don't want to lose the material advantages they have. But others realise how serious their situation has become; their love for their family and their desire for God are greater than their desire for possessions and professional prestige. They are looking for a life which is more human and Christian. They dream of living in community.

But it would be useful for them to look more closely at their motives before committing themselves. Is it that they want to leave an inhuman job? Is it that they are looking for a warmer family life? Or are they really looking for community with all its demands? They would do well to start by taking a simpler job, which is less well paid but gives them more leisure, so that they can gradually discover where their hearts are. Perhaps they could get more involved in their parish or neighbourhood or in a community of prayer that meets regularly. Once they have found a new equilibrium in their life, they will be able to think of leaving their jobs and of becoming an integral part of a community. Then it would no longer be a dream but the end of a natural journey.

In many ways communities are like families. But there are clear distinctions. To start a family, two people must choose each other and promise fidelity. It is the fidelity and love of these two people which bring peace, health and growth to the children who are born of their love. When we come into community, we do not promise to be faithful to one person. The parental roles – those of the people at the head of the community – change according to the constitution, and we do not commit ourselves to live always with the same people. It can be wonderful for a community when there are families in it; and it can be wonderful for families to be in community. But it must be clear that a family in itself is a little community. Its own dynamic and originality must be respected. The family must be enabled to forge its own unity. A couple is not the same as two single people living together; it is two people who have become one.

When I meet couples who want to come to l'Arche, I notice that sometimes the husband is enthusiastic and full of idealism, while the wife has more reservations. So I ask her if she too really wants to live at l'Arche. She replies that she loves her husband a great deal and is ready to do what he wants. That sort of situation is not good. For a couple to be able to commit themselves to community, both must really want it and neither must have any doubts. They must be very united and they must have been through the crises that a couple usually go through in the early years of their marriage. If they haven't done this by the time they come into community, they will find any number of ways to avoid resolving their problems. And frequently they will project their difficulties upon the community. If things are not going well for them, they will blame the community.

One of the greatest losses for parents who want to follow Jesus and live in community is to accept a lower income than they might have had elsewhere. This may mean that they will not be able to give their children the financial advantages and opportunities which they themselves had when they were young. Some families want to have their cake and eat it too!

When we follow Jesus, we are called to accept the consequences of our choices. Children of such families may not have the same financial opportunities as others, but they will discover community, and that is an immense gift!

More and more families are being called to community life these days. They want to live with others, as far as they can, and share a certain way of life. They want to live a covenant with the poor and with Jesus Christ.

It is a great richness to have married people at l'Arche. Most of them cannot live in a house with handicapped people, because they need their own place. And because a family is itself a community, it must never be sacrificed to the larger community. But even though families cannot live all the time with handicapped people, their presence in the community is important. Their love, their emotional stability, their children, bring so much to the weaker people – and to us all. The way they live a covenant amongst themselves is a sign of love for the community and for the world. Every loving family is a sign of hope and resurrection.

Other paths

Some people find it hard to live with others. They need a lot of time to themselves, a great sense of freedom and, above all, no tensions. They simply must not feel under pressure, for, if they do, they will become depressed or aggressive. These people are often very sensitive and delicate; they have almost too great a richness of heart. They could not cope with the difficulties of community life. They are called rather to live alone or with a few privileged friends. They must not be made to think that, because community life – in its more limited sense of living together – is not for them, they have no place, gift or vocation. Their gift is different. They are called to be witnesses to love in another way. And they can find a certain community life with friends or groups, with whom they meet regularly to pray and to share.

It is true that some people are called by Jesus to enter and build community in order to radiate love and hope; but, like the rich, young man of the gospels, they turn away, not daring to take the step, unable to give up their way of life or their prosperity.

Others – the vast majority – live community with their family. Sometimes they belong to a larger community which meets periodically; it could be a prayer group, Faith and Light or some other community, or it could be their parish community.

Many others have no family or are separated from them. They feel lonely, they do not belong to any form of community and their parish lacks warmth. Maybe with a few friends, in visiting some old people or those who are sick or who have a handicap and are lonely, they can create bonds which are the beginnings of community.

Finally, I am meeting others who feel lonely and are unable for one reason or another to enter a community; they seem called by Jesus to live a solitary life of prayer. They are the new hermits of today, hidden in small apartments or sometimes in institutions. Their wounded hearts rise up to Jesus as an offering and a call for his presence. It is important that these people find a good spiritual guide who will help them live in the reality of Jesus and not in dream or illusion.

> Many people seek fellowship because they are afraid to be alone. Because they cannot stand loneliness, they are driven to seek the company of other people. There are Christians, too, who cannot endure being alone, who have had some bad experiences with themselves, who hope they will gain some help in association with others. They are generally disappointed. Then they blame the fellowship for what is really their own fault. The Christian community is not a spiritual sanatorium . . . Let him who cannot be alone beware of community. But the reverse is also true, let him who is not in community beware of being alone.[1]

Every person who is alone can try to create community with a few friends; not living together, but in some way being mutually supportive and responsible to one another.

Listening to Thérèse the other day during a retreat, I realised

1 Dietrich Bonhoeffer, *Life Together* (Harper & Row, New York, 1976).

that the availability of some single people could be a mysterious commitment. She read this prayer which she had written:

> We who are not committed to you, Jesus, in either a consecrated celibacy or marriage, we who are not committed to our brothers in a community, are coming to renew our covenant with you.
>
> We are still on the road to which you have called us, but whose name you haven't given us; we are carrying the poverty of not knowing where you are leading us.
>
> On this road, there is the pain of not being chosen, not being loved, not being waited for, not being touched. There is the pain of not choosing, not loving, not waiting, not touching. We don't belong. Our house is not a home; we have nowhere to lay our head.
>
> Even though we have become impatient and depressed when faced with the choice of others, unhappy when faced with their efficiency, we still say 'yes' to our road. We believe that it is the road of our fecundity,[2] the road we must take to grow in you.
>
> Because our hearts are poor and empty, they are available. We make them a place of welcome for our brothers. Because our hearts are poor and empty, they are wounded. We let the cry of our thirst rise to you.
>
> And we thank you, Lord, for the road of fecundity you have chosen for us.

The first call

Commitment in a community is not primarily something active, like joining a political party or trade union. Those need militants who give their time and energy and are ready to fight. A community is something quite different. It is the recognition by its members that they have been called by God to live together, love

2   fecundity: a word, little used in English, that carries within it a sense not just of fruitfulness, but also of potential for growth and fruitfulness. It is the capacity to give life.

each other, pray and work together in response to the cry of the poor. And that comes first at the level of *being* rather than of *doing*. To accept being rooted in a community is more or less preceded by a recognition that you are already 'at home', that you are part of its body. It is rather similar to marriage; couples recognise that something has been born between them and that they are made for each other. It is only then that they are ready to commit themselves to marriage and remain faithful to each other.

So in community everything starts with this recognition of being in communion one with another; we are made to be together. You wake up one morning knowing that the bonds have been woven; and then you make the active decision to commit yourself and promise faithfulness, which the community must confirm.

It's important not to let too much time pass between this recognition that the bonds or the covenant are there and the decision. That's the best way to miss the turning and end up in the ditch!

When people start the journey towards wholeness, the pilgrimage to the promised land, there is a moment when their deepest being is touched. They have a fundamental experience, as if the stone of their egoism has been struck by Moses' staff and water starts to spring from it, or as if the stone which was over the tomb has been lifted and the deep self is able to emerge. It is an experience – and perhaps only a very faint one – of rebirth, of liberation, of forgiveness, of wonder. It is a time of betrothal with the universe, with the light, with others and with God. It is an experience of life in which we realise that we are fundamentally one with the universe and with God, while at the same time entirely ourselves in the most alive, light-filled and profound sense. It is the discovery that we are a spring of eternal life.

This experience at the start of our pilgrimage is like a foretaste of the end, like the kiss which is the foretaste of marriage. This is the call. It guides our steps in revealing our final destiny. There is nothing more deeply personal than this moment of wonder. But it happens very often in a given context. It may be a meeting with a poor person, whose call awakens a response in us; we discover that there is a living spring hidden deep within us. It may be during a visit to a community when we meet people who become models for us; in watching them and listening to them, we discover what we want to be – they reflect our own deepest self and we are mysteriously attracted to them. Or again, the call may be more secret, hidden in the depths of our heart, awakened perhaps by the Gospel or some other writing. It is hidden in our secret part; it makes us feel that we have glimpsed the promised land, found ourselves 'at home', found 'our place'. The experience is often such as to take someone into a community or change the orientation of their life.

The experience can be like an explosion of life, a luminous moment, flooded with peace, tranquillity and light. Or it can be more humble – a touch of peace, a feeling of well-being, of being in 'one's place' and with people for whom one was made. The experience gives a new hope; it is possible to keep walking because we have glimpsed something beyond the material world and beyond human limitations. We have glimpsed the possibility of happiness. We have glimpsed 'heaven'.

The experience has opened our deepest being. Later, once we are in community and on our journey, clouds can obscure the sun and that deepest self can seem to be shut away again. But, nevertheless, the first experience stays hidden in the heart's memory. We know from then on that our deepest life is light and love, and that we must go on walking through the desert and the night of faith because we have had, at one moment, the revelation of our vocation.

When someone visits a community and feels completely at home, in perfect harmony with the others and with the community itself, that is possibly a sign that they are perhaps called to put down roots there. This feeling is often a call from God, which must be confirmed by the call of the community. The covenant is the meeting of two calls which confirm each other.

Many young people don't seem to realise the importance and the depth of this feeling of well-being when they meet a community which manifests a call of God.

Of course doubt can creep in after that first experience. Drawn by the seductions of the wealth and concerns of the world, by fear of criticism, by difficulties and persecution, we can turn away from that revelation of the light. We look for excuses: 'I'm not yet ready; I have to travel, look around, experience the world; we'll see in a few years.' But often we won't hear that call again. We shall be caught up in other affairs; we shall have found other friends to overcome the feeling of loneliness, we shall no longer have the chance of living that fundamental experience of belonging to a community of hope. We shall set off on another road and the meeting with God will perhaps be of another sort, at another moment.

Jesus looked at the young man and loved him. He said to him: 'You lack one thing; go, sell what you have and give to the poor and you will have treasure in heaven; and come, follow me' (Mark 10:21). But the young man didn't trust him; he was afraid because his security was in his wealth. And because he was very wealthy, he went sadly away.

The call is an invitation: 'Come with me.' It is an invitation not primarily to generosity, but to a meeting in love. Then the person meets others who are called and they begin to live community.

I have met quite a number of people who visited a community and knew inwardly and with great certainty that that was the place they were called to be, yet nothing in the community itself attracted them: neither the members, nor the way of life, nor the location. And yet they knew that that was the place!

This type of experience is very often an authentic call of God. Of course, the call has to be confirmed by the community and by a trial period.

Leave your father, your mother, your culture

To enter into a new covenant and belong to a new people, a community with new values, we have to leave another people – those with whom we have lived – with other values and other norms: wealth, possessions, social prestige, revolution, drugs, delinquency, whatever. This passage from one people to another can be a very painful uprooting, and usually takes time. Many do not achieve it, because they do not want to choose or to cut themselves off from their old life. They keep a foot in each camp and live a compromise, without finding their real identity.

To follow the call to live in a community, you have to be able to choose. The fundamental experience is a gift of God, which sometimes comes as a surprise. But this experience is fragile, like a little seed planted in the ground. After the initial experience, you have to know how to take its consequences and eliminate certain values to adopt new ones. So, gradually, comes the orientation towards a positive and definitive choice for community.

Some people flee from commitment because they are frightened that if they put down roots in one soil they will curtail their freedom and never be able to look elsewhere. It is true that if you marry one woman you give up millions of others – and that's a curtailment of freedom! But freedom doesn't grow in the abstract; it grows in a particular soil with particular people. Inner growth is only possible when we commit ourselves with and to others. We all have to pass through a certain death and time of grief when we make choices and become rooted. We mourn what we have left behind.

So many people do not realise that in giving up everything to follow Jesus and live in community, he gives back everything a hundredfold:

> In truth I tell you, says Jesus, there is no one who has left home, brothers, sisters, mother, father, children or land for my sake and for the sake of the gospel, who will not receive a hundred times as much, houses, brothers, sisters, mother, father, children and land – and persecution too, now in this present time, and in the world to come, eternal life. (Mark 10:29–30)

I am sometimes very sad when I feel that people don't take this fundamental experience of the call seriously enough. It is as if they were wasting a treasure. They are going to waste time and perhaps even turn completely away from the light. And yet the earth is ringing with the cry of despair, of the starving, of the parched, with Jesus' cry, 'I am thirsty'. These people do not believe enough in either themselves or the call; they do not know that there is a spring in them waiting to be freed to irrigate our parched world. So many young people do not know the beauty of the life that is in them and which can grow.

Some people dare not make this passage because they are frightened of betraying and hurting their original community, of being unfaithful to them. They are afraid of their family, because to leave them and their way of life seems like judging them. Jesus said: 'Anyone who loves father, mother, brother or sister more than me cannot be my disciple.' To enter a Christian community and universal love, we have to put Jesus and his beatitudes above our own family and friends. Sometimes, it's true, they exercise such pressure, based on fear, that it seems impossible to break away from them.

Some people fear to enter a community because they are afraid of losing their identity. They fear that they will disappear, lose their personality and inner wealth if they become part of a group and accept the principles of community discernment. This fear is not entirely unjustified. When we come into community we give up something of ourselves, and the rougher elements of our personality will have to be left behind. Assertiveness, which enriches an individual, will have to give way to a greater ability to listen; impatience will have to give way to patience. A new strength will be born and new gifts will appear.

Community does not suppress people's identities – far from it. It affirms their deepest identity; it calls on the most personal of gifts, the ones that are linked to the energy of love.

I am sometimes astonished at the way in which parents worry

when their son or daughter becomes as assistant at l'Arche. They come and ask me to persuade their children to 'do something serious'. These parents seem somehow completely bound up in the idea that a university degree or a good marriage brings security; then, they feel, their child will be 'provided for'. Life in a community, especially with handicapped people, seems to them like an insecure folly. They tell themselves that it is an adolescent fancy, that this immaturity will pass.

It is through parents like these that we discover the conflict between the values of community life and those of modern society. Their pressure is sometimes such that their child doesn't dare continue on the community road. Are the parents afraid that their children will judge them? Whatever the reason, it makes me sad to see people who call themselves 'good Christians' crushing the finest aspirations of their children in the sacrosanct name of security.

Perhaps too, parents find it hard to distinguish between a sect which will use psychological pressures to seduce their child and a Christian community which will set them free. They might be comforted if their child were in a well-known religious order.

A hundred years ago it was not too large a leap for many to make the passage from family life, with its rhythm, structures of obedience and traditional values, to the life of a religious community. Today that leap is immense. For today people have been nourished on independence and individualism, the desire to win and go up the ladder; they have seen the possibilities of assuming important and admirable responsibilities in the world; it is harder for them to make this passage into a community. It is easier for those who have not succeeded in school or at work. But there can be a danger there; they may be seeking a refuge and, if so, are unlikely to find their true identity and fulfilment in community. But God also does beautiful things and can help some who felt lost in the world to find truth in community.

Communities need to learn how to welcome those who have succeeded in the world and to give them the right support so they can climb down the ladder into the place of communion;

communities need also to help those who have not succeeded to clarify and deepen their motivations.

Young people, who have let themselves be fed for many years on television, will have difficulty as they enter community and are fed on true relationships. Young people who have become aggressive towards their parents, society and their own selves will have difficulty in learning to trust; young people who have always wanted to do brilliant things, be admired and appreciated will have difficulty with the littleness of everyday life in community. Today, as never before, a special grace of God is needed to make the passage from independence, loneliness and anti-social behaviour to community life.

Sometimes those who have lived warm relationships in a large family and who are in frequent contact with their brothers and sisters say: 'I don't need community.' Perhaps they don't need community, but communities need them. Those who have experienced a healthy family life and relationships have so much to offer to others – and especially to the poorest and the weakest – in a community environment. They must be attentive to the call of Jesus who says: 'Sell all you have, give your money to the poor and then come and follow me.'

There is often an act of faith at the basis of commitment to community – a belief that we will be reborn there. When we live alone or in our families, we build our identity on professional success, the way we use our leisure, and the joys of family life. Community doesn't always – and certainly not straight away – bring the same satisfaction and sense of identity. So we feel we have lost a bit of ourselves. We can only accept this amputation if we are carried by the community and in prayer. We have to know how to wait patiently for the moment of rebirth. The grain of wheat must die before new life can appear. The road can be long and the nights dark; we have to wait for the dawn.

Entering into the covenant is abandoning ourselves trustingly to a new life which is already hidden in the deepest part of ourselves and which – if we give it earth, water and sun – will be reborn with a new strength. And the harvest will come.

I am struck by some people who want to enter community. Their energies are so taken up by this objective that they are unable to hear the cry of the poor and to see those near them who need their attention, their love and their presence. Their desire to enter community seems to blind them. The best way for them to prepare for community life is to love and be present to those near them. Then the passage to life in community will come quite naturally.

There are more and more people today who belong to a community – frequently a religious community – and who feel called by God to join a newly founded community living closer to the poor. They belong then to two communities. This double belonging frequently works very well. The first community is like the mother community with which they keep deep bonds, while they flourish in the new one. It is as if they had needed the formation and growth in the mother community in order to be able to give their lives, and give life, in the new community. Their presence, with all they have learnt in the mother community, is a great source of strength for the new one.

There are dangers and risks too, particularly when people have left the mother community feeling let down, angry or frustrated – even if they do not articulate these feelings – and are looking for a place where they can better live and express their ideal.

The beginning of the journey

When someone enters community, it is important to be clear about what is expected of them, not only from the point of view of work and their daily programme, but even more their inner attitudes. They must understand the position of the community on fundamental issues, such as wealth, sexuality, the use of power and authority. They must know clearly their responsibilities and their rights: what will happen if they fall sick or when they will have time off or what community facilities they can use, etc. They must know how long their trial period lasts. Much confusion comes when these questions have not been looked at. That is why, on entering a community, there must be much discussion with new members. They must be well accompanied,[3] affirmed, encouraged and given the right support.

As people enter into community, they pass from their own culture - their friends and their independence - to the culture of the community. This can be very painful for some, and after a few weeks or months they may experience the terrible pangs of loneliness, doubt and confusion. During this period, they need a great deal of support.

It is important that people entering a community receive adequate spiritual formation, help and nourishment in order to be able to live with all that is painful in community. We cannot ask people to leave behind them the nourishment of their friends, their independence and their leisure ways and not give them new and strong nourishment which will provide them with the energy to live the demands of community life.

3 accompany/accompaniment: an important practice in l'Arche communities is that of 'accompaniment', by which each member of the community is allotted someone who will be with them as a companion to help them grow in freedom and in the spirit of the community (see also chapter 7). There is also spiritual accompaniment carried out by a priest or a spiritual guide; sometimes this is called 'spiritual direction'.

Recognising the bonds

Some people come into community because they are attracted by a simple way of life, in which there is welcome and sharing and where relationships come first. Sometimes too they are afraid of the demands of life in 'open' society. They hope to find their growth in a life of spontaneity and celebration. But they gradually discover that there is more to community life than that. To remain faithful to it means accepting certain disciplines and structures and daily making the effort to come out of the shell of egoism. Then they discover that community is not just a good way of life, but that they have been called by God to carry others in their suffering and growth towards liberation, and to be responsible for them. And that is demanding. Moreover, it is not simply a question of becoming responsible for others and being committed to them; it is also allowing them to carry and love us, and entering into a relationship of interdependence and into a covenant. And that is sometimes even more difficult and demanding, because it implies a revelation of one's own weakness.

This evolution towards a real responsibility for others is sometimes blocked by fear. It is easier to stay on the level of a pleasant way of life in which we keep our freedom and our distance. But that means that we stop growing and shut ourselves up in our small concerns and pleasures.

People enter community to be happy. They stay when they find happiness comes in making others happy.

Almost everyone finds their early days in a community ideal. It all seems perfect. They seem unable to see the drawbacks; they only see what is good. Everything is marvellous; everything is beautiful; they feel that they are surrounded by saints, heroes or, at least, exceptional people who are everything they want to be themselves.

And then comes the period of let-down – generally linked to a time of tiredness, a sense of loneliness or homesickness, some setback, a brush with authority. During this time of 'depression', everything becomes dark; people now see only the faults of others and the community; everything gets on their nerves. They feel they are surrounded by hypocrites who either think only of rules, regulations and structures, or who are completely disorganised and incompetent. Life becomes intolerable.

The greater their idealisation of the community at the start, the more they put the people at its head on pedestals, the greater the disenchantment. It's from a height that you fall down into a pit. If people manage to get through this second period, they come to the third phase – that of realism and a true commitment, of *covenant*. Members of the community are no longer saints or devils, but people – each a mixture of good and bad, each growing and each with their own hope. It is at this time of realism that people put their roots down. The community is neither heaven nor hell, but planted firmly on earth, and they are ready to walk in it and with it. They accept the other members and the community as they are; they are confident that together they can grow towards something more beautiful.

It is important, during the initial months and years that people are in community, that they have regular times of evaluation. It is terribly unjust when a community asks someone to leave after being in the community for a number of years if they have never been told over the years that anything was wrong in their behaviour. How can anyone grow and make efforts to change if they are not helped and if their shortcomings are not pointed out to them?

Choice for rooting

I am more and more struck by the suffering of young people. It doesn't surprise me that some of them find it enormously difficult to accept a rooting in community. Many of them have had more or less unhappy and unstable childhoods. Many have had very

precocious sexual experiences, which can make later commitment
more difficult. And then there is today's tendency to question
everything. People are quick to challenge authority and anyone
who tells them what to think. At the same time, there is the feeling
that our world is changing with a terrible speed; everything is on
the move. Young people can commit themselves for today – but
tomorrow? We have to be very patient with young people who
may in many ways lack inner stability and be incapable of giving
a definite 'yes'. Their world is almost too existentialist. But if they
find someone who is faithful to them, they will gradually discover
what fidelity means and will be able then to commit themselves.

I sense that many people are afraid of committing themselves in
community because they have not yet resolved the questions of
celibacy and marriage – and they could be right to be afraid,
because possibly their time has not yet come. As long as the
question remains unresolved, they cannot put down roots in a
community.

It is good that there are people in a community who have not
yet resolved the question. But it is equally good and necessary that
there are others who have resolved it. For some, settling the question will mean a decision to remain celibate for the rest of their
lives in response to a call from Jesus and the poor. They will
renounce the riches of family life in the hope of a gift from God
and in the desire to be more open to Jesus, the poor and the
Gospel. That does not mean that they will not suffer from their
decision, at least at certain moments, but they put their faith and
their hope in the call to live with Jesus and in community with
the poor.

For others, resolving the question means abandoning themselves
to events and to God and, above all, giving priority to their faith
in and commitment to God and to a way of life. They have
accepted community life fully, committing themselves to the poor,
and putting prayer at the heart of their life. If marriage comes, it
will come only in this context, so that the couple, and then they
and their children, can live these deep aspirations. The best way
of insuring a true marriage is to commit oneself to a way of life,

to be clear about what one wants in life. Then intimacy with another can be built upon this fundamental choice. The two become companions on the same journey of life. When someone seeks intimacy before choosing what they want in life, then there is danger.

It is important that those who do not commit themselves, because they are still asking themselves about marriage and feel incomplete because they have not been uniquely chosen, are honest in their recognition that essentially they are waiting. Some people criticise the community, but their criticisms are only a way of saying, 'I don't want to commit myself' – they are part of a defence system. It would be more honest to say, 'The time hasn't come when I can commit myself, because essentially I want to get married and I put that before my commitment to an ideal of community life.' It is important that people can share at this level and discover the real reason why they do not feel comfortable in the community. Clearly it is their right not to feel comfortable if their time has not yet come. But it is important too that others who hear the call of God or of the poor without shelter, come into community to be there as a sign of the Kingdom, a sign that love is possible and that there is hope.

If a community puts pressure on its members to decide before their time has come, this is because the community itself has not yet found its freedom. It is too insecure; it clings to people. Perhaps it has grown too quickly, forced by an expansionist pride. If our communities are born from the will of God, if the Holy Spirit is at the heart of them, our Heavenly Father will send the people we need. A community has to learn how to be cheerful about letting people leave and how to trust that God will send other brothers and sisters. 'Oh people of little faith! Seek first the Kingdom of God and all the rest will be given in superabundance.'

Some people are able to say a few days after they arrive that they are at l'Arche for life. They feel so at ease, so at home, that they are sure they have found their harbour. For others, it takes longer; they gradually discover that they are at home and that they have no need to seek further. The time it takes to give a definite 'yes' is different for each person.

The final 'Yes'

To be covenanted to others is to be earthed with them. It is God who has called us together to be a sign of fidelity and of love. If we begin to live in covenant as we enter community, it is sealed at a particular moment, maybe a very solemn one.

I once attended the profession of the deaconess sisters of Rueilly. The Mother Prioress put a cross round the neck of each sister as she consecrated herself to God and said to her something which touched me: 'Receive this cross. It is a sign that you belong to God at the heart of our community. From now on, this community is yours. And you are responsible, with us, for its fidelity.'

This is covenant.

You are called to enter into a covenant with God and with your brothers and sisters, especially the poorest among them. You must not hold back.

> I therefore . . . beg you to lead a life worthy of the calling to which you have been called, with all lowliness and meekness, with patience, forbearing one another in love, eager to maintain the unity of the Spirit in the bond of peace. There is one body and one Spirit, just as you were called to the one hope that belongs to your call, one Lord, one faith, one baptism, one God and Father of us all, which is above all and through all and in all. (Eph. 4:1–6)

Without roots we can neither discover where we belong, nor can we grow. Without stability we cannot confront the basic questions of life. Without stability we cannot know our true selves.

Monastic stability means accepting this particular community, this place and these people, this and no other, as the way to God.[4]

It is only as we put our roots down into the earth that we begin to see the fruits. To be earthed is to come alive in a new sense of mission. A new capacity to give life is born, not by myself but in the body of community.

4 Esther de Waal, *Seeking God* (Collins/Fount, London, 1984), pp. 56–7.

3

Mission

Coming together for a purpose

Jesus first of all called men and women to him and told them:
'Leave all: come and follow me.' He chose them, loved them and
invited them to become his friends. That is how it all began, in a
personal relationship with Jesus, a communion with him.

Then he brought together the twelve he had called to become
his friends; they started to live together in community. Obviously
it was not always easy. They quickly began to quarrel, fighting
over who should be first. Community life revealed all sorts of
jealousies and fears in them.

Then Jesus sent them off to accomplish a mission: *to announce*
good news to the poor, *to heal* the sick, and *to liberate* by casting
out demons. He did not keep them with him for long, but sent
them out so that they would have an experience of life flowing
out from them: an experience of giving life to people and an
experience of their own beauty and capacities if they followed him
and let his power act in and through them.

The pains of community are situated between the joy of this
communion and friendship with Jesus and the joy of giving life to
others: the mission.

If people come together to care for each other, it is because they
feel more or less clearly that as a group they have a mission. They
have been called together by God and have a message of love to
transmit to others.

When two or three come together in his name, Jesus is present.

Community is a sign of this presence: it is a sign of the Church. Many people who believe in Jesus are in some degree of distress: battered wives, people in mental hospitals, those who live alone because they are too fragile to live with others. All these people can put their trust in Jesus. Their suffering is a sign of his cross, a sign of a suffering Church. But a community which prays and loves is a sign of the resurrection. That is its mission.

Universal mission to give life

Humanity is one. We are all part of the same human race. However different we may be through culture, race or disabilities, we are all human beings; we are all brothers and sisters.

I remember once when I was in Papua New Guinea, I went up into the mountains. There I met tribal people. The womenfolk wore few clothes, so did the men for that matter! I spoke to them about people with a mental handicap and about l'Arche. Then there was a time for questions. They spoke about their lives and sickness and death, about joys and difficulties in relationships in their families and between families, about the menfolk drinking too much and about violence – all the same questions that could have come up in London or New York. Yes, we are truly of the same race.

The fundamental questions of humanity are always around love and hate, guilt and forgiveness, peace and war, truth and lies (or illusions), the meaning of life and death, and belief in God. Every community wants in some way to manifest a universal truth that they have discovered, like a treasure in a field; they want to announce this good news to other people and to offer some insights on these fundamental questions. They want to live this truth, because they believe it leads to a fuller and more beautiful life: to love, to peace, to truth, to freedom and to an experience of God. They want to communicate to others the beauty they have received.

There is a big difference between a community and a group that is militant for a cause. A community will say 'Come and see'. It wants to manifest the truth in a non-violent way, offering it to others; visitors are encouraged to come, to ask questions, to experience the way of life. A community knows that the fundamental questions of life can only be looked at in a spirit of peace and inner freedom. Nobody can force anyone else to love and to walk to freedom. Militants for a cause will tend to be organised for a struggle which they hope to win; they will seek to impose their way aggressively. Frequently they seek outward change more than inward change. Of course it is very different when those concerned with causes and issues are living in community.

Clubs and closed groups that only accept members on certain criteria of race or of competence are elitist. These clubs demonstrate to themselves and to others their 'superiority'. Consequently, they make others feel inferior and that the good news is not for them. In these groups, humanity is broken down into a system of apartheid – groups separated one from another. There is no universal message of hope or of freedom.

Communities can produce things, make cheese, beer or wine; they can show new and better methods in agriculture: they can build hospitals and schools; they can further culture through their books, libraries or art. However, these things do not necessarily give life; and the mission of a community is to give life to others, that is to say, to transmit new hope and new meaning to them. Mission is revealing to others their fundamental beauty, value and importance in the universe, their capacity to love, to grow and to do beautiful things and to meet God. Mission is transmitting to people a new inner freedom and hope; it is unlocking the doors of their being so that new energies can flow; it is taking away from their shoulders the terrible yoke of fear and guilt. To give life to people is to reveal to them that they are loved just as they are by God, with the mixture of good and evil, light and darkness that is in them: that the stone in front of their tomb in which all the dirt of their lives has been hidden, can be rolled away. They are forgiven; they can live in freedom.

Jesus wants each one of us individually to bear fruit, but he also wants us to bear much fruit in community, and then we become his disciples (John 15).

All living beings give life. Thus from generation to generation we have birds, fish, animals, trees, flowers and fruit – the incredible fecundity of creation as life flows from one being to another. Man and woman together give life, conceiving and giving birth to a child.[1] And that is just the physical and biological aspect of procreation. Once the baby is born, and even before birth, the parents give life to the child, and reveal to him/her its beauty by the way they welcome and love it. Or else they may bring inner death to the child, making it feel ugly and worthless through the way they reject or over-protect it. Through love and tenderness, through welcome and listening, we can give life to people.

Jesus' whole message is one of life-giving. He came to give life and to give it abundantly. He came to take away all the blockages that prevent the flow of life. The glory of God, wrote Irenaeus in the second century, is people fully alive, fully living. Jesus came to announce good news to the poor, freedom to the oppressed and imprisoned, and sight to the blind. He came to liberate, to open up new doors and avenues; he came to take away guilt, to heal, make whole and to save. And he asks his disciples to continue this mission of life-giving, of fecundity and of liberation. That is the mission of every Christian community.

When Jesus sent his disciples out on mission, he told them to be poor, to take nothing with them. And he told them to do things that were impossible for them to do all by themselves. So it is for all missions. Communities and their members are called to be poor and to do impossible things, such as to build community and to bring healing, reconciliation, forgiveness and wholeness to people. Mission is to bring the life of God to others, and this can only be done if communities and people are poor and humble, letting the life of God flow through them.

1 Jean Vanier, *Man and Woman He Made Them* (Darton, Longman and Todd, London; Paulist Press, New York; St Paul Publications, Australia, 1985).

Mission implies this double poverty, but also trust in the call and the power of God manifested through poverty, littleness and humility.

In the degree that people and communities are rich, self-satisfied, proud of their competence and power, and want to do things that they know they are capable of doing, then they can no longer be instruments of the life of God. They give what they have, which is their self-satisfaction.

General and specific mission

This mission of life-giving and of liberation is first of all for the members of the community themselves. It begins with them. People enter community in order to grow in inner freedom, then to give it to others; to radiate it, to offer good news to others. This mission will be accomplished in different ways, places and times. There is the general mission for each community and for each person to give life. However, each community has its specific mission, its specific way of giving life through its particular goals.

The communities started by St Benedict in the sixth century were centred on prayer. Communities founded by Mother Teresa of Calcutta are centred on the lonely, the broken and the dying. The Covenant House community in New York City cares for street kids while the Catholic Worker and Simon Communities are centred on men and women who are down and out. The Taizé Community is centred on prayer and a life dedicated to the unity of all the Christian churches. The community of Lanzo del Vasto (also called l'Arche) is centred on a way of life close to nature and on the principles of non-violence. The basic communities in Latin America are centred on the poor, restoring to them their basic dignity and rights, and their voice and place in the Church and in society.

In each community there is caring, bonding and mission. Each one has different ways of living, and different rules and structures; priorities in daily life are different in each, but there is always the same desire to care for and love one another, to announce the universal good news to all people and to bring greater freedom, life and peace.

Each new community is called forth by God, as he inspires a particular man or woman or a group of people to respond to a specific cry or need of humanity at one particular moment of history. This cry can be very obvious: the cry of the dying in the streets of Calcutta or of the street kids in New York or of people with physical and mental handicaps. Or else it can be a more hidden cry: the need of the sixth-century Church for oases of prayer, the need of the thirteenth-century Church in Assisi for communities close to the poor. There is a cry hidden in the heart of God, of the Church and of the saints to give life. And finally, there are the hidden tears of the rich floundering in their wealth and the pain of their selfishness, emptiness, illusions, error and sinfulness, as they search for meaning. Each new community with its founder has a specific charism, gift and mission, responding to a particular cry for help, for recognition and for love.

A community becomes truly and radiantly one when all its members have a sense of urgency in their mission. There are too many people in the world who have no hope. There are too many cries which go unheard. There are too many people dying in loneliness. It is when the members of a community realise that they are not there simply for themselves or their own sanctification, but to welcome the gift of God, to hasten his Kingdom and to quench the thirst in parched hearts through their prayer and sacrifice, love and acts of service, that they will truly live community. A community is called to be a light in a world of darkness, a spring of fresh water in the Church and for all people. If a community becomes lukewarm, people will die of thirst. If it bears no fruit, the poor will die of hunger.

This sense of urgency, however, does not mean that members are hyperactive, nervous and anguished; it does not conflict with a sense of abandonment, trust, peacefulness and inner relaxation.

It is rather an awareness of the pain and evil in the world, but also of the depth, breadth and universality of the good news.

Clarifying the goals

Some people want to live together, but it is not always clear why. They just want to live in community! If people are not clear about the specific goals of the 'why' of their common life, there will soon be conflicts and the whole thing will collapse. Tensions in community often come from the fact that individuals have not talked about their expectations. They soon discover that each of them wants something very different. (The same thing can happen in marriage. It is not simply a question of wanting to live together. If the marriage is to last, you have to know what you want to do and to be together.) This means that every community must have a charter, which specifies clearly why its members are living together and what is expected of each of them. It also means that before a community begins, its members should take time to prepare for living together and clarify their aims.

Bruno Bettelheim has said: 'I am convinced communal life can flourish only if it exists for an aim outside itself. Community is viable if it is the outgrowth of a deep involvement in a purpose which is other than, or above, that of being a community.'[2]

The more sincere and creative a community is in its search for essentials, and in its efforts to accomplish its goals, the more its members are drawn beyond their own concerns and tend to unite. The more lukewarm a community becomes towards its original goals, the more danger there is of its membership crumbling, and of tensions developing inside it. Its members will no longer talk about how they can best respond to the call of God and the cry of the poor. They will talk instead about themselves and their problems, their wealth or their poverty, the structures of the community. There is a vital link between the two poles of community: its goal and the unity of its members.

2 Bruno Bettelheim, *Home for the Heart* (Thames and Hudson, London, 1974).

The sense of belonging to a people, the covenant, with the commitment that it implies, are at the heart of community life. But that leaves the question: Who are my people? Are my people simply those with whom I live and who have the same outlook as I do, or are they those for whom the community has been created? Let me explain. Three people create community life in a slum, trying to live a welcoming, quiet and loving presence. They come inspired by a universal love, the love of Jesus; they were sent, and they want to witness to the love of God and proclaim the good news of the Gospel by their presence and their life. Are their people the group to which they belong, which sustains them spiritually and perhaps materially, or are they the people of the slum, the neighbours? For whom are they ready to give their lives?

The same question comes up at l'Arche. Is the community made up above all of assistants who freely choose to come, with similar motivations, or is it above all the people in need who did not have this free choice but were placed? We do not want two communities – the helpers and the helped – we want one. That is the theory, but in practice there is a tendency for the assistants to make their own community and be satisfied with that. Truly to make community with the poorest and identify with them is harder and demands a certain death to self. The closer you are emotionally to the assistants, the less chance there is of being close to the poor. Your heart can't be everywhere at the same time.

This can be taken further. Should the community, 'my people', be limited to those – both people in need and assistants – who live under the same roof? Doesn't it also include neighbours, people from the district, friends?

As people grow in love, as their hearts become more open, and as a community in its narrow sense becomes mature, so does the reality of the community, of 'my people', get larger.

But each person who lives in the community must still set their priorities. Where should they concentrate their energies? For whom will they give their life?

In the case of the three people living in the slum, shouldn't the group or mother-community to which they belong become a root, which enables them to be closer to 'their people' in the slum? Then there would be no conflict of influences or loyalty. Roots are there so that flowers and fruits can grow – and it's in the fruit that you find the seeds of tomorrow. In the same way, the unity between assistants at l'Arche is there to encourage them to become closer to the people in need and to create *one* community. Belonging in one sense doesn't rule out belonging in the other – they are there for each other. They are one because love is essentially gift, not possession.

Little Sister Madeleine, who founded the Little Sisters of Jesus, wrote in a letter to them:

> Do not feel obliged, in order to protect your religious dignity and your intimacy with God against exterior dangers, to put up barriers between the lay world and yourself. Don't put yourself on the fringe of human society . . .
>
> Like Jesus, become part of that humanity. Penetrate deeply into and sanctify your environment by the conformity of your life, by your friendship; by your love, by your life totally given to the service of others, like Jesus, by a life so mixed in with everyone else's that you may be one with them, wanting only to be in their midst like yeast that loses itself in the dough in order to make it rise.[3]

Christian communities are there to bring life and hope to people in pain.

We enter community to live with others. But also, and above all, we come to live the goals of the community with them, to respond to a call from God, to respond to the cry of the poor.

> . . . the people of Israel groaned under their bondage, and cried out for help, and their cry under bondage came up to God. And God heard their groaning, and *God remembered his covenant* . . . (Exod. 2:23–4)

3 P. S. Madeleine de Jesus, *Du Sahara au Monde Entier* (Nouvelle Cité, Paris, 1981), p. 410.

Then Yahweh reveals himself to Moses and says:

> I have seen the affliction of my people who are in Egypt and
> have heard their cry because of their taskmasters; I know their
> sufferings and I have come down to deliver them out of the
> hand of the Egyptians, and to bring them up out of that land
> to a good and broad land, a land flowing with milk and honey.
> (Exod. 3:7–8)

And he sent Moses to liberate them. Today as yesterday the covenant between God and the poor remains; he calls people to community to respond to the cry of the poor and the oppressed.

The yearning for God and the cry of the poor

In all ages and in many religions, people have come to live
together, yearning and searching for communion with God. Some
of these communities were founded on the mountain tops or in
desert lands, far away from the hustle and bustle of cities. Life in
these communities is frequently austere, directed essentially toward
a personal relationship with God and to acts of common worship
and work. Other communities – particularly those in the Christian
heritage – were founded to serve the poor, the lost, the hungry
and those in need, in the ghettos and the hustle and bustle of cities.

The quest for the eternal, all-beautiful, all-true and all-pure, and
the quest to be close to the poor and most broken people appear
to be so contradictory. And yet, in the broken heart of Christ,
these two quests are united. Jesus reveals to us that he loves his
Father, and is intimately linked to him; at the same time he is
himself in love with each person and in a particular way with the
most broken, the most suffering and the most rejected. To manifest this love, Jesus himself became broken and rejected, a man of
sorrows and of anguish and of tears; he became the Crucified One.

And so, communities formed in his name will seek communion
with the Father through him and in him; they will also seek to
bring good news to the poor, and liberation to the oppressed and
the imprisoned.

Within the Church, over the ages, one or the other aspect of this double mission has been emphasised, according to the call of God in different times and places, but both are also present. There are those who are called to the desert or the mountain top to seek greater union with God through the Crucified One; and their prayer will flow upon the broken and the crucified ones of this world. And there are those called together to give their lives for and with the crucified and broken ones in the world; and they will always seek a personal and mystical union with Jesus so that they may love as he loves.

Every community and every family are called to live both forms of mission, but in different ways: to pray and to be present in a special way to the smallest and the weakest within their own community or outside it, according to their individual call. God is the fountain from whom we are all called to drink, and this source of life is meant to flow, through each of us, upon all those who thirst: 'As the Father has loved me, so I love you . . . my commandment is that you love one another as I love you.'

Some people drink first of the waters flowing from God and then discover that they are called to give water to the thirsty. Others begin by giving water to the thirsty but soon find that their well is empty; they then discover the sources of water flowing from the heart of God which become in them 'a source of water welling up into eternal life'.

Seen in this way, community life is not something extraordinary or heroic, reserved only for an elite of spiritual heroes. It is for us all; it is for every family and every group of friends committed to each other. It is the most human way of living; and the way that brings the greatest fulfilment and joy to people. As people live in communion with the Father, they enter more and more into communion with one another; they open their hearts to the smallest and the weakest. Being in communion with the smallest and the weakest, their hearts are touched and the waters of compassion flow forth; in this way they enter more deeply into communion with the Father.

Sometimes it is easier to hear the cries of poor people who are far away than it is to hear the cries of our brothers and sisters in our own community. There is nothing very splendid in responding to the cry of the person who is with us day after day and who gets on our nerves. Perhaps too we can only respond to the cries of others when we have recognised and accepted the cry of our own pain.

When we know our people, we also realise that we need them, that they and we are interdependent; they open our hearts and call us to love. We are not better than they are – we are there together, for each other. We are united in the covenant which flows from the covenant between God and his people, God and the poorest.

Jesus is the poor

Jesus reveals an even greater unity between the personal contemplation of the Eternal and the personal relationship and bonding with people who are broken and rejected. This is perhaps the great secret of the Gospels and of the heart of Christ. Jesus calls his disciples not only to serve the poor but to discover in them his real presence, a meeting with the Father. Jesus tells us that he is hidden in the face of the poor, that he is in fact the poor. And so with the power of the Spirit, the smallest gesture of love towards the least significant person is a gesture of love towards him. Jesus is the starving, the thirsty, the prisoner, the stranger, the naked, the homeless, the sick, the dying, the oppressed, the humiliated. To live with the poor is to live with Jesus; to live with Jesus is to live with the poor (cf. Matt. 25). 'Whosoever welcomes one of these little ones in my name, welcomes me; and whosoever welcomes me, welcomes the Father' (Luke 9:48).

People who gather together to live the presence of Jesus among people in distress are therefore called not just to do things for them, or to see them as objects of charity, but rather to receive them as a source of life and of communion. These people come together not just to liberate those in need, but also to be liberated by them; not just to heal their wounds, but to be healed by them; not just to evangelise them but to be evangelised by them.

Christian communities continue the work of Jesus. They are sent to be a presence to people who are living in darkness and despair. The people who come into these communities also respond to the call and the cry of the weak and oppressed. They enter into the covenant with Jesus and the poor. They meet Jesus in them.

Those who come close to people in need do so first of all in a generous desire to help them and bring them relief; they often feel like saviours and put themselves on a pedestal. But once in contact with them, once touching them, establishing a loving and trusting relationship with them, the mystery unveils itself. At the heart of the insecurity of people in distress there is a presence of Jesus. And so they discover the sacrament of the poor and enter the mystery of compassion. People who are poor seem to break down the barriers of powerfulness, of wealth, of ability and of pride; they pierce the armour the human heart builds to protect itself; they reveal Jesus Christ. They reveal to those who have come to 'help' them their own poverty and vulnerability. These people also show their 'helpers' their capacity for love, the forces of love in their hearts. A poor person has a mysterious power: in his weakness he is able to open hardened hearts and reveal the sources of living water within them. It is the tiny hand of the fearless child which can slip through the bars of the prison of egoism. He is the one who can open the lock and set free. And God hides himself in the child.

  The poor teach us how to live the Gospel. That is why they are the treasures of the Church.

In l'Arche, assistants discover that they are called to announce good news to people in need and to reveal to them the immense love God has for them. Sometimes these assistants truly lead people with a handicap over the threshold and into faith. But once over the threshold, people with a handicap truly lead the assistants deeper into faith; they become our teachers.

The cry for love

When I came to Trosly-Breuil, that small village north of Paris, I welcomed Raphael and Philippe. I invited them to come and live with me because of Jesus and the his Gospel. That is how l'Arche was founded. When I welcomed those two men from an asylum, I knew it was for life; it would have been impossible to create bonds with them and then send them back to a hospital, or anywhere else. My purpose in starting l'Arche was to found a family, a community with and for those who are weak and poor because of a mental handicap and who feel alone and abandoned. The cry of Raphael and of Philippe was for love, for respect and for friendship; it was for true communion. They of course wanted me to do things for them, but more deeply they wanted a true love; a love that sees their beauty, the light shining within them; a love that reveals to them their value and importance in the universe. Their cry for love awoke within my own heart and called forth from in me living waters; they made me discover within my own being a well, a fountain of life.

In our l'Arche community in the Ivory Coast, we welcomed Innocente. She has a severe mental handicap. She will never be able to speak or walk or grow very much. She remains in many ways like a child only a few months old. But her eyes and whole body quiver with love whenever she is held in love; a beautiful smile unfolds in her face and her whole being radiates peace and joy. Innocente is not helped by ideas, no matter how deep or beautiful they may be; she does not need money or power or a job; she does not want to prove herself; all she wants is loving touch and communion. When she receives the gift of love, she quivers in ecstasy; if she feels abandoned, she closes herself up in inner pain – the poorer a person is, old or sick or with a severe mental handicap or close to death, the more the cry is solely for communion and for friendship. The more then the heart of the person who hears the cry, and responds to it, is awoken.

Other people we have welcomed in l'Arche are more capable and able to grow in different ways. However, their fundamental need remains the same as Innocente's: communion and friendship, not a possessive friendship but one that gives life and calls them to growth. Love is not something sentimental; it is much deeper than that. It is a power that brings people to greater inner freedom and growth. Love is not opposed to competence. Love is always competent. And, of course, that love is such that it encourages some people to walk on their own, to leave the community, to risk the pain of separation for greater growth.

Inner pain

The cry for love and communion and for recognition that rises from the hearts of people in need reveals the fountain of love in us and our capacity to give life. At the same time, it can reveal our hardness of heart and our fears. Their cry is so demanding, and we are frequently seduced by wealth, power and the values of our societies. We want to climb the ladder of human promotion; we want to be recognised for our efficiency, power and virtue. The cry of the poor is threatening to the rich person within us. We are sometimes prepared to give money and a little time, but we are frightened to give our hearts, to enter into a personal relationship of love and communion with them. For if we do so, we shall have to die to all our selfishness and to all the hardness of our heart.

The cry for love that flows from the heart of people in need is mixed with pain, anguish and sometimes agony. They are so fearful of not being lovable; they have suffered so much from oppression and rejection. If this call for love awakens compassion in the hearts of those around them, their fears and anguish and inner pain can also awaken fears and inner pain in those who hear the cry. That is why it is so hard and so frightening to meet people who are inwardly broken. Their anguish seems to awaken anguish and pain in those around them.

In l'Arche, many assistants have felt this inner pain, which can provoke anger and even hatred for the weak person; it is terrible when one feels surging up inside oneself the powers of darkness and of hate. No wonder some want to run away and others try to forget; some try to cover up, others ask for help from a wise guide. The latter discover then that, in their own brokenness, they are truly brothers and sisters with the people they came to serve. They discover too that Jesus is not only hidden in the poor around them, but in the poor person within their own being.

People come to l'Arche to serve the needy. They only stay if they have discovered that they themselves are needy, and that the good news is announced by Jesus to the poor, not to those who serve the poor

Mission, then, does not imply an attitude of superiority or domination, an attitude of: 'We know, you don't, so you must listen to us if you want to be well off. Otherwise you will be miserable.' Mission springs necessarily from poverty and an inner wound, but also from trust in the love of God. Mission is not elitism. It is life given and flowing from the tomb of our beings which has become transformed into a source of life. It flows from the knowledge that we have been liberated through forgiveness; it flows from weakness and vulnerability. It is announcing the good news that we can live in humility, littleness and poverty, because God is dwelling in our hearts, giving us new life and freedom. We have received freely: we can give freely.

As long as there are fears and prejudices in the human heart, there will be war and bitter injustice. It is only when hearts are healed, and become loving and open, that the great political problems will be solved. Community is a place where people can live truly as human beings, where they can be healed and strengthened in their deepest emotions, and where they can walk towards unity and inner freedom. As fears and prejudices diminish, and trust in God and others grows, the community can radiate and witness to a style and quality of life which will bring a solution to the troubles of our world. The response to war is to live like brothers and sisters. The response to injustice is to share. The response to despair is a limitless trust and hope. The response to prejudice and hatred is forgiveness. To work for community is to work for humanity. To work for peace in community, through acceptance of others as they are, and through constant forgiveness, is to work for peace in the world and for true political solutions; it is to work for the Kingdom of God. It is to work to enable everyone to live and taste the secret joys of the human person united to the eternal.

Mission will always imply struggle: the struggle between the forces of evil that seek to divide – pushing people and groups into isolation and loneliness and then into a closed world of fear, insecurity and aggression – and the force of love and trust, which open up people and groups to forgiveness, humility and understanding, to compassion and mutual acceptance, to unity and peace. This struggle is within each person and each community, and between the community and the world surrounding it. Communities which live this call and mission will always be counter-culture. The world with its false values will try to isolate them, make them look silly or utopian, or else it will try to infiltrate them with its false values so that they lose their spirit and enthusiasm, becoming rich and secure.

Living communities will always be persecuted in one way or another. Their members must be aware of the gravity of the struggle. They must be prepared to live the struggle with courage and in prayer. Satan and the evil spirits do not want loving communities to exist. So they will do everything they can to discourage, wound and ultimately destroy them.

In order to be able to meet Jesus in moments of communion with those who are broken and in need, one must also meet him in prayer and in the Eucharist. 'He who eats my body and drinks my blood, lives in me and I in him.'

Through the years, I am discovering that there is no contradiction between my life with those in need and my life of prayer and union with God. Of course Jesus reveals himself to me in the Eucharist and I need to spend time with him in silent prayer. But he reveals himself too in this life with my brothers and sisters. My fidelity to Jesus is also realised in my fidelity to my brothers and sisters of l'Arche and especially the poorest. If I give retreats, it is because of this covenant, which is the basis of my life. The rest is only service.

Some people in the church consecrate themselves to God in a life of prayer and adoration. Others have a mission to announce the good news or act mercifully in the name of the Church. I sense that my own place in the Church and in human society is to walk with the poor and weak, so that each of us develops and we sustain each other in fidelity to our own deepest growth, on our journey towards a greater internal freedom and sometimes external autonomy.

The waters flowing over humanity

The prophet Ezekiel had a vision (Ezek. 47:1–12) of waters flowing from the Temple. It began as a small stream, but then it grew into a deep river impossible to cross. On each bank of the river there was an immense number of trees constantly bearing fruit; their leaves were medicinal and brought healing. The waters too were healing waters; wherever they flowed, life was abundant and fish were plentiful. John the Evangelist had a similar vision (Rev. 22:1) of crystal clear water, the river of life, flowing from the throne of God and of the Lamb, giving life, bearing fruit.

The Temple – is it not the Body of Christ, the dwelling place of God? Is it not from the wounded heart of the Lamb, on the cross, that living waters flow upon humanity, giving life. The Temple, is it not the Body of Christ that is the Church?

Each community is grafted into the heart of Christ and into his body, the Church. A community is not the initial source; it is part of something very much greater. It is a sign and a revelation and the fruit of the source of life called to flow over humanity, cleansing, healing, giving life and freedom, bearing much fruit.

No community is alone; each one is born from other communities. Each one is born through people of faith who have given life to others over generations, ever since Christ died on the cross. There the water flowed from his heart and he bonded Mary and John together in a covenant of love as he cried out forgiveness. The gift of faith and of universal love, forgiveness and hope have been passed on from person to person, from community to community, from generation to generation. And each community gives birth to other people and other communities. The spirit of community is like a gentle fire giving light and warmth, communicating itself through hearts in communion one with another.

A community is never there just for itself or for its own glory. It comes from and belongs to something much greater and deeper: the heart of God yearning to bring humanity to fulfilment. A community is never an end in itself; it is but a sign pointing further and deeper, calling people to love: 'Come and drink at the source which is flowing from the Eternal and which is manifested in each act of love in the community, in each moment of communion.'

That is why communities must not be isolated one from another. They are called to live in communion and to collaborate one with another. They are all part of a vast body uniting heaven and earth, uniting those who have gone before and those who are present on the earth today. And together they are all preparing the seeds that will flower and bear fruit in the generations to come. They are preparing the ways of tomorrow so that the body of Christ may be fulfilled. Each community is but a sign of the liberating love of God. Some signify this love through contemplative presence and adoration, dwelling in the secret of Love, some through crying out words of truth, some through tenderness poured over broken bodies and hearts, giving life, reconciliation and peace.

Each community needs to be in contact with others. They stimulate and encourage, give support, call forth and affirm each other. Communities that are on the threshold of great pain and warfare, struggling with immense forces of darkness, violence and power, need to be held and nurtured by those secret channels of love – contemplatives rising in the middle of the night to pray, contemplatives who are old people in their homes, and those who are sick in hospitals. A community that isolates itself will wither and die; a community in communion with others will receive and give life. This is the Church, flowing over all of humanity and irrigating it.

And this Church is living not only in believers in the name of Christ, but also in all those who, even centuries before his birth and centuries after are seeking under the guidance of the Spirit the light of universal truth and the mystery of God, the warmth of compassion and the liberation of forgiveness. We are all bonded into one body, the body of humanity which, ever since the Word became flesh and one of us, is the body of Christ. We are called together in love and in compassion to be a witness and a sign of the waters flowing from the heart of God, calling all of humanity to the eternal wedding feast of Love.

And we must always remember that the waters are flowing not just from the heavens and from the places of light, but also from the broken earth: gentle springs of living water are flowing from the broken bodies and hearts of the poor. We must learn to drink from them, for they bring into our presence the wounded and broken heart of Jesus, the Crucified One.

4

Growth

A community grows like a child

Each of us is on a journey – the journey of life. Each of us is a
pilgrim on this road. The period of human growth, from the time
when we are infants in our mother's womb to the day of our
death, is both very long and very short. And this growth is set
between two frailties – the weakness of the tiny child and that of
the person who is dying.

There is a waxing and then a waning in activity. The child and
adolescent are travelling towards adult maturity; it takes many
years for them to reach it and the independence and strength that
it implies. Then come illness and weariness and we become more
and more physically dependent, until that dependence may become
total and we are once again like a tiny child.

While there is a waxing and then a waning in action and
efficiency, growth can be continual at the level of the heart, of
wisdom and of communion with God and with people. There are
some precise stages in the growth of the heart. Tiny children live
by love and presence – the time of childhood is a time of trust.
Adolescents live by generosity, utopian ideals and hope. Adults
become realistic, commit themselves and assume responsibilities;
this is the time of fidelity. Finally, old people refind the time of
confidence which is also wisdom. They cannot be very active, so
they have time to observe, to contemplate and to forgive. They
have a whole sense of the meaning of human life, of acceptance
and of realism. They know that living has not just to do with
action and running; they know that it is also to do with welcome

and loving. They have somehow got past the stage of proving themselves through efficiency.

Between each of these stages, there are steps to be crossed. Each of these demands preparation and education and must bring some suffering, particularly that of grieving for what is lost. Human life is this journey, this growth towards a more realistic and truer love; it is a journey towards wholeness. Tiny children are unified in their weakness and their relationship with their mother. But as they grow, divisions begin to appear between their sexuality and their relationships, between their will and their psychological make-up, between inwardness and outwardness, between what they live and what they say, between their dreams and reality. As they grow towards independence, their fears about their weakness, vulnerability and limitations, about suffering and death, become more conscious, and so do the barriers they throw up around their vulnerability. The journey of each of us is a journey towards the integration of our deep self with our qualities and weakness, our riches and our poverty, our light and our darkness.

To grow is to emerge gradually from a land where our vision is limited, where we are seeking and governed by egotistical pleasure, by our sympathies and antipathies, to a land of unlimited horizons and universal love, where we will be open to every person and desire their happiness.

Just as there are steps to cross in human life, so are there steps in the life of communities. And crossing these also demands preparation, education and a degree of suffering.

There are the steps of foundation and launching, and then there is the time when the community settles down in a peaceful rhythm. It begins to flourish and expand. This is frequently like a period of adolescence; members feel that their community is unique and blessed by God; they are apart from others. They are naive, 'have all the truth' and are very generous and idealistic. Gradually they discover, sometimes through crisis, that they are not perfect and that they have made some serious mistakes; and that there are other communities blessed by God with whom it would be wise to co-operate. Then after a while the number of new members begins to diminish; the mean age of members rises gradually. During this time there can be tensions coming from the clarification of goals and life-style. Then, after the death of the founder, there can be a real crisis if the changeover to new leaders has not been well prepared and thought out. There can be times then when the community appears old and sick.

These steps are less clear than those of human life, but they are still there, and in some ways they are recurring; they never end unless the community dies. Communities are born, grow and give life, grow old and then are reborn. There are different stages in the way authority is exercised, in the evolution of structures of decision making. The community and those responsible for it have to be careful that these transitions are carried out well.

Many tensions in community come from the fact that some people refuse to grow; yet the growth of a community depends on the growth of each of its members. There are always people who resist change; they refuse to evolve; they want things to be maintained as they always were. In the same way, in human life, many refuse growth and the demands of a new stage; they want to remain children, or adolescent, or they refuse to grow old. Community is always in a state of growth.

> The journey towards community is one of continuing discovery. We know little about the route ahead. We are not on an expedition where we carry a detailed map and an itinerary which tells us precisely when we will arrive at scheduled stopping-off points or even at our destination.[1]

The community of Taizé gives an important example of growth and adaptation to events, new circumstances and the inspiration of the Holy Spirit. Kathryn Spink in a particularly inspiring book on the community says:

> From the very beginning of Taizé, Brother Roger accepted that nothing could be accomplished without a process of maturation and that the community must progress one day at a time in the

1 David Clark, *Yes to Life* (Collins/Fount, London, 1987), p. 25.

knowledge that it was only little by little that Christ would become their essential love. They must, he knew, be prepared to love Christ without seeing him and so grow in Spirit. The history of the brothers' life together is characterized by a continual search for the mode of existence which might best make that growth possible. Certain elements within it are constantly changing and evolving.

. . . The search continues as does the creativity. In their different ways, more recent years have been as creative as the first, and perhaps the brothers are still learning how better to integrate their individual creativity into the whole.[2]

It is no easier to live in community after twenty years than it was at the start; on the contrary, in fact. People are always a little naive when they enter community; they have many illusions and they also have the grace they need to pull them away from an individual and egotistical life. People who have been travelling for twenty years in community know that it isn't easy. They are very conscious of their own limitations and those of others. They know the full weight of their own egoism.

Life in community is a little like that journey in the desert towards the promised land, towards inner liberation. The Jewish people only started to murmur against God when they had crossed the Red Sea. Before that, they were caught up in the extraordinary events, by the adventure, by the taste for risk; any burden at all seemed preferable to slavery. It was only later, when they had forgotten what it had been like to be oppressed by the Egyptians and when the extraordinary had given way to the ordinariness of everyday life, that they murmured against Moses and felt they had had enough.

It is easy to keep the flame of heroism burning in the early stages of a community. The struggle with the environment stimulates generosity of heart; no one wants to be beaten. It is much harder when months and years have passed and people find themselves faced with their own limitations. Things from which we think we have detached ourselves come back to tempt us: comfort, the law of least effort, the need for security, the fear of being disturbed.

2 Kathryn Spink, *A Universal Heart* (SPCK, London, 1986), p. 162-3.

And we no longer have the same strength to resist; to control our tongues and to forgive; the barriers come up again and we hide behind them. We are more easily governed by anguish.

Some people say that communities start in mystery and end in bureaucracy; that they start with great enthusiasm and a love that surpasses all frontiers and all difficulties, a yearning for risk, but they end up with a lot of administration and wealth, loss of enthusiasm and fear of risk.

The essence of the challenge to a growing community is to adapt its structures so that they go on enabling the growth of individuals and do not simply conserve a tradition, still less a form of authority and a prestige.

These days, we tend to see spirit and structures as being in opposition to each other. The challenge is to create structures which serve the spirit and the growth of people and which are themselves nourishing. There is a way of exercising authority, of discerning and even of running the finances which is in the spirit of the Gospel and the Beatitudes and so makes these tasks sources of life.

Community means communion of heart and spirit; it is a network of relationships. But this implies a response to the cry of our brothers and sisters, especially the poorest, the weakest, the most wounded, and a sense of responsibility for them. And this is demanding and disturbing. That is why it is very easy to replace relationships and the demands they bring with laws, rules and administrative devices. It is easier to obey a law than to love people. This is why some communities are swallowed up by rules and administration instead of growing in *gratuité*, welcome and gift.

From heroism to dailiness

It is quite easy to found a community. There are always plenty of courageous people who want to be heroes, are ready to sleep on the floor, to work hard hours each day, to live in dilapidated houses. It's not hard to camp – anyone can rough it for a time. So the problem is not in getting the community started – there's always enough energy for take-off. The problem comes when we are in orbit and going round and round the same circuit. The problem is in living with brothers and sisters whom we have not chosen but who have been given to us, and in working ever more truthfully towards the goals of the community.

A community which is just an explosion of heroism is not a true community. True community implies a way of life, a way of living and seeing reality; it implies above all fidelity in the daily round. And this is made up of simple things – getting meals, using and washing the dishes and using them again, going to meetings – as well as gift, joy and celebration; and it is made up of forgiving seventy times seventy-seven.

A community is only being created when its members accept that they are not going to achieve great things, that they are not going to be heroes, but simply live each day with new hope, like children, in wonderment as the sun rises and in thanksgiving as it sets. Community is only being created when they have recognised that the greatness of humanity lies in the acceptance of our insignificance, our human condition and our earth, and to thank God for having put in a finite body the seeds of eternity which are visible in small and daily gestures of love and forgiveness. The beauty of people is in this fidelity to the wonder of each day.

The vision is clarified

After the time of heroism and struggle, after the initial period of wonderment, there comes a time when the vision, the goals and the spirituality of the community are clarified and written down; the community's identity and its place in society, in the Church and in the history of humanity are clarified. It becomes clear how the community is counter-culture, in what way it is prophetic; what are the dangers for it and for its members; what specific formation they need. Vision and intellectual understanding are

important to the life of a community. But intellectual consciousness must always spring from wonder and thanksgiving, which
must remain at the heart of the community.

For us in l'Arche, it took some time to come to the realisation
that our charism was to be with people with a mental handicap
and not with people of all kinds of handicaps or poverty. It was
a number of years before we discovered that we were called into
the pains and joys of community. It is taking time for us to
formulate clearly our spirituality and how we are nourished by
our people. It is taking time to see more clearly what characterises
l'Arche and makes it different from group homes; what makes it
different from religious communities such as the brothers and
sisters of Mother Teresa's Missionaries of Charity, for example.

A community must be clear about its spirituality and help form
its members in it, for it is through the spirituality of the community that its members grow to wholeness and union with God.
Each community brings to light an aspect of the Gospels and the
life of Jesus: Francis of Assisi reveals the beauty and gift of poverty,
while Benedict reveals a life of prayer and work; other communities reveal the role of peace-making and non-violence. The spirituality of a community is its charism and focal point of fidelity. It
is manifested in the way people work, meet, pray and celebrate;
in the routine and rhythm of the day; in the priorities of the
community, and so on. The spirituality of l'Arche is manifested
in the way we live with people who have handicaps and see Jesus
in them. But a spirituality is always oriented to a mystical life; its
finality is always communion with Jesus and his Father in the Holy
Spirit, and in the communion with brothers and sisters.

There is always a temptation, because of the need for security, to
plan a community beforehand, in all its details. Ideas then precede
life and want to govern it. But that is not usually the way the
Spirit works. A community is called to birth and must *live* first
of all; it grows, deepens, evolves with time, under the inspiration
of the Holy Spirit and obviously in a certain direction; but all must

not be planned beforehand. As people join the community they have their say in its development; they bring their insights and inspirations. Events modify the way things are done; little by little a common vision is forged. Too much detailed intellectual planning before a community starts can, in fact, stifle the Spirit, just as a desire to remain open to anything and everything and a refusal to clarify goals, can also prevent growth. There is a time for everything; a time for conception, birth and growth. Then there is a time for reading what has been given and reflecting upon it. God gives us hearts so that we may be inspired by his Love and his Spirit, but he also gives us minds, so that we may understand, clarify, discern and read what he is saying and giving in and through life.

The Latin temperament tends to announce and even impose a vision, and then judge and modify reality according to this vision. It has difficulty sometimes listening, reading and evaluating reality. The vision can become too theoretical. The Anglo-Saxon temperament is more pragmatic; it can listen and evaluate reality, but sometimes it lacks vision. A community needs both; it needs vision, but it also needs to listen and to read reality.

Today, more than ever, people need to understand what community is about – the laws of growth and of deepening in community, the nourishment that is needed and the dangers of community. There must be an intellectual stock-taking. Because we are in a world governed so much by the mass media and by a culture of success, pleasure and independence, people are unclear about the values of community. Many want community and a feeling of being together, but they refuse the demands of community life. They want both freedom and community; freedom to do just what they want when they want, *and* community, which implies certain structures and values. It's like wanting the cake and eating it too! People have to choose. But to be able to choose there has to be clarification.

This is very clear in regards to sexuality. In this area of life people cannot do just what they want when they live in community. Community life implies a common vision of ethics, just as it implies a vision about wealth and the use of power. Some people want community without authority. This might be possible for a few months or years, if there are a few mature people in the community, but it is not possible when a crisis arises. So living in community implies a reflection on all these matters. People in community must reflect on their vision and their way of life; if they do not, then another vision will infiltrate their lives, maybe unconsciously.

In community there is always a danger of people remaining like children, too dependent on good parental figures. They get on with living, doing things and praying, but they do not reflect on what they are living. If people refuse this intellectual stock-taking, remaining only under 'the inspiration of the Spirit' or governed by emotional urges, then the community is in danger.

Of course we must remain like little children, filled with a sense of wonderment, but we must also be wise: wise in knowing how to govern community, how to deepen it and to protect the seed of love against the powers of evil, of seduction and of oppression, that want to crush it.

The more a community grows and puts down roots, the more it must discover its own deep meaning and own philosophy of life, which cannot be cut off from the fundamental questions of the world and of the Church. The more it lives authentic human relationships, and the more it becomes a place to live in rather than a gathering of 'doers', the more it must find answers to the fundamental questions of human life. It must give meaning to suffering and death, to healing and to wholeness, to the place of man and woman in society and in the world, and to sexuality, family and celibacy. It must be clear about the use of power, the role of authority, and about the meaning of growth to freedom and responsibility. It must have a deep sense of the place of God, prayer and religion in human existence. It must have a vision about poverty and wealth, and clarity about the relationship between love and competence.

A community must be aware of its place in the Church of today and in the world; it must be clear how it stands in regards to the terrible pains and injustices of the world. It must also know how it can respond to the cry and despair of the young. Communities must find symbols to express the meaning of these fundamental realities. We cannot grow together in community and deepen in our relationships without looking at these questions. Community traditions in some ways give answers to these questions, but we have also to try to understand intellectually the significance and deeper meaning of these traditions.

From monarchy to democracy

When a community starts, it is the founder who decides everything. But gradually brothers and sisters arrive and bonds are created. Then the founder asks their advice. It is no longer he, or she, who dictates what should be happening; he listens to others. A communal spirit is born. The founder begins to discover the gifts of each of the others. He discovers that others are more able than he is in certain ways, and that they have gifts which he doesn't. So he entrusts more and more to others, learning to die to himself so that the others can live more fully. He remains the link and the person other community members turn to, a co-ordinator who confirms the others in their responsibilities and ensures that the spirit and unity of the community is maintained. At moments of crisis, he will still be called on to assert his authority, because the ultimate responsibility rests with him; he must, when discipline is failing, recall the others to their responsibilities. His authority will become less visible, but will still be very present until the day he disappears and another takes his place. Then his task is done. His work will continue; his role has been to disappear.

There is an analogy with the authority of parents. At the start, they do everything for their children, but gradually they become friends with whom their children can discuss things; they can even become their children's children when they are old. Parents have to guard against a possessiveness which stifles the life that is growing in their children. In the same way, the founder of a community must learn to withdraw gradually and not to cling to his authority.

One of the important passages in a community is when the founder becomes really conscious that the community is not his or her project but the project of God. The founder is but an instrument of God and is called to disappear.

It is important that people in a community have their own projects and responsibilities which allow them to take initiatives. But it is important too that these projects are confirmed by the community, or that they spring from community discernment. Otherwise they will go against the flow of the community; they will be the projects of individuals who either want to prove that they know better than the community or else are saying they do not fit into it.

People in community sometimes believe that they know better than the others, or see themselves as 'saviours'. Community discernment implies that all members, or at least all those with responsibility, try together to discover its direction and the important things it is to do. The vital thing is that discernment is approached without passion, so that no one feels the need to convince others or to impose particular notions. If everyone listens to each other's ideas, the truth will gradually and calmly emerge. This can take a long time, but it is worth while, because once the decision has been made, each member of the community will have a personal commitment to the project.

Some communities have been founded by individuals who need to be leaders, to prove something, to create projects. Founders will always need help to avoid this trap and to clarify their own motives and to die to some of their own ideas. They should not be alone; it is better if a community is founded by two or three people who discern together and share responsibility from the start.

Otherwise founders are in danger of throwing themselves

entirely into their own creation; they do everything and become possessive of 'their' child. They can't bear criticism and listen only to those who agree with them – and they can always find people like that. They think that they alone are inspired and are prophetic. A community will suffocate if its founder stifles the intelligence of the people who have come to join it or mistrusts them and denies them any share in responsibility and creativity.

If people start a community in the desire to prove something through their 'child', there is an unhealthy pride in them which has to die. A community is there for people who live in it, not for its founder. Responsibility is a cross which the founder carries, but which must very quickly be shared so that all the members realise their own particular gift. If the founder doesn't learn to withdraw gradually, the community will either die or be obliged to reject the founder.

From time to time I meet people who want to create a community. After twenty-five years' experience of community life, I wouldn't advise anyone to do so of their own accord. (There are, of course, exceptions, founded on real signs from God.) I advise people instead to go and live in an existing community and then, when the moment is right, that community will send them to found another. If people are to create a community, they need a sense of belonging and a sense of having been sent. We need someone to confirm and support us, to direct and advise us. The first Christian communities were founded by people who were members of the community of apostles and who prayed at Pentecost with Mary the mother of Jesus. They were sent and confirmed by the apostles.

Openness to the neighbourhood and the world

Before starting a community, it is important to make contact with the village or the neighbourhood in which it is to be. Too many communities are born without these initial contacts and, if they welcome people who are handicapped or distressed, that can lead to catastrophe. The neighbours reject them. The community, far from being a sign of hope, becomes an abscess. If the founders had taken time to explain their plans to the neighbours, they would have got a more understanding welcome. And if the community could have welcomed the handicapped people of the village, the community would have been better integrated in it. Time spent over several months creating contacts and forming bonds of friendship with the neighbours, before the community even starts, is never time wasted.

I speak from experience here, for at the beginning of l'Arche I made many mistakes. I welcomed more and more people from the psychiatric hospital; I was burning with zeal for them, and maybe angry about all the injustice that they had experienced. However, I was less aware of what the people in the village were experiencing as we opened new houses. Then, of course, the inevitable happened. The village people – at least some of them – got together and signed a petition against l'Arche. There were several months of tension and of pain which could have been avoided if I had worked more closely with the village people from the start.

For a community to become a sign, its neighbours must see it as bringing something positive to the neighbourhood or village. It is good to have someone in the community who can help people nearby who are old or ill; it is good for the community to be open to welcome people who suffer and are in need.

The more a community deepens and grows, the more integrated it must be in the neighbourhood. When it begins, a community is contained within the four walls of its house. But gradually it opens up to neighbours and friends. Some communities begin to panic when they feel that their neighbours are becoming committed to them; they are frightened of losing their identity, of losing control.

But isn't this what true expansion means? There are times when it is important to knock down the walls of a community. This demands that each person respect the other's commitment and that their rights and responsibilities are clearly explained. Each person must become responsible for the others in a specific way. Each must freely bring something to the others and true bonds must be woven. This is how a small community can gradually become the yeast in the dough, a place of unity for all and between all.

As a community takes root in a neighbourhood and begins to grow, and as its neighbours become involved in it, it will inevitably become aware of social injustices which oppress people and prevent their growth, especially if they belong to disadvantaged minorities. And so the community might have to take a political stand. It will seek to help people and to modify laws and struggle against injustice. Perhaps it will become unpopular with the government, and the opposition parties will try to entice it to join their own political struggle. It is hard for a community in this position to find the middle road between two extremes.

Margarita Moyano, an Argentinian working with young people in Taizé and also on Argentinian evangelisation programmes, reminded us at l'Arche that a butterfly has to break the cocoon if it is to live, and that every child commits a violence when it is born. A new society cannot be brought to birth without some upheaval. But this must spring from, and reinforce, communion and trust.

A community gradually discovers, as it grows, that it is not there simply for itself. It belongs to humanity. It has received a gift which must bear fruit for all people. If it closes in on itself, it will suffocate. When it begins, a community is like a seed which must grow to become a tree giving abundant fruit, in which all the birds of the air can come to make their nests. It must open its arms wide and hold out its hands to give freely what it has freely received. Then seeds fall from the tree and new trees are born, and so life continues to flow and to grow; new communities are born.

A community must always remember that it is a sign and witness to all humankind. Its members must be faithful to each other if they are to grow. But they must also be faithful as a sign and source of hope for all humankind.

A community has to be apart from society and open to it at the same time. To the extent that its values are different from those of society, it must necessarily be apart from it. If it is too open, it will never keep and deepen its own values; it will have no identity or life of its own, and it will tend to seek a compromise with or be influenced by the spirit of the culture and the values of society. It will lose its freedom for truth.

However, if it is too enclosed, it will not grow and it will not see the true values which exist in society and in others outside it. It will become dogmatic: 'I'm right, the others are wrong.' It will become incapable of seeing its own darkness and flaws. A community is called to grow gradually in relationship with others, with its neighbours; each will help the other to grow. It is not a question of one being right and the other wrong; they are there to help each other.

There was a time, it seems, when the religious orders were too shut in on themselves; they were suffocating. They recognised this, and have become more open to society. But some, perhaps, have gone too fast. They discarded their traditional clothing so that they could be closer to people outside; but they threw off their traditions and lost a sense of the initial inspiration as well. They lost their identity; they lost community.

The time when a community feels it is dying is not the time to change externals, like the rule or the habit. If it does this, then there is nothing left to hold people together. This is the time for inner renewal, for a renewed trust in personal relationships and prayer; it is the time to stay close to the poor and those in distress. When the inner life is strong and when love is truly the guiding spirit, then we can reduce the externals, but not before.

Times of trial: a step towards growth

No community grows without times of trial and difficulty; times of poverty, persecution, tensions, and internal and external struggles; times which destroy its balance and reveal its weakness; times of difficulty which are inevitable when a new step has to be taken.

Creating a community means struggling against all sorts of things. But once the community is launched, energies may evaporate and people may seek distractions; they may compromise with other values. This can be very marked in a therapeutic community. At the start, it accepts people who are difficult or depressed, people who break windows. Then gradually everyone settles down and if 'window-breakers' arrive, they are unacceptable. The energies which used to be there to tackle all sorts of problems and to deal with difficult people have dissipated. A time comes when we feel too comfortable together, and that complacency signals a decline in the quality of unity. That is why times of trial are important for a community: they force people to look at themselves and at what is happening in the community, and then to reassess their goals and life of prayer; they oblige them to refind the quality of unity and the energy to face difficulties.

A community which is growing rich and secure, and seeks only to defend its goods and its reputation is dying. It has ceased to grow in love. A community is alive when it is poor and its members feel they have to work together and remain united and dependent upon each other, if only to ensure that they can all eat tomorrow!

It is often when a community is on the verge of breaking up that people agree to talk to each other and look each other in the eye. This is because they realise that it is a question of life or death, that everything will collapse if they do not do something decisive and radically different. Often we have to come to the edge of the precipice before we reach the moment of truth and recognise our own poverty and need of each other, and cry to God for help.

But times of trial will only unite a community if there is enough trust in it to contain these crises. If one member of the community is killed or very seriously injured in an accident, small frictions and interests disappear. A shock like that and brings us up against essentials. A new solid enables us better to bear trials and overco

The times of trial which destroy a superficial security often free new energies which had until then been hidden. Hope is reborn from the wound.

Tensions

Communities need tensions if they are to grow and deepen. Tensions come from conflicts within each person – conflicts born out of a refusal of personal and community growth, conflicts between individual egoisms, conflicts arising from a diminishing *gratuité*, from a clash of temperaments and from individual psychological difficulties. These are natural tensions. Anguish is the normal reaction to being brought up against our own limitations and darkness, to the discovery of our own deep wound. Tension is the normal reaction to responsibilities we find hard because they make us feel insecure. We all weep and grieve inwardly at the successive deaths of our own interests. It is normal for us to rebel, to be frightened and feel tense when we are faced with difficult people who are not yet free from their own fears and aggression. It is normal that our own reserves of *gratuité* run low from time to time, because we are tired or are going through personal tensions or sufferings. There are a thousand reasons for tension.

And each of them brings the whole community, as well as each individual member of it, face to face with its own poverty, inability to cope, weariness, aggression and depression. These can be important times if we realise that the treasure of the community is in danger. When everything is going well, when the community feels it is living successfully, its members tend to let their energies dissipate, and to listen less carefully to each other. Tensions bring people back to the reality of their helplessness; obliging them to spend more time in prayer and dialogue, to work patiently to overcome the crisis and refind lost unity; making them understand that the community is more than just a human reality, that it also needs the spirit of God if it is to live and deepen. Tensions often mark the necessary step towards a greater unity as well, by revealing flaws which demand re-evaluation, reorganisation and a greater humility. Sometimes the brutal explosion of one tension simply reveals another which is latent. It is only when tensions come to a head like a boil that we can try to treat the infection at its roots. I am told that there is a Chinese word for 'crisis' which means 'opportunity and danger'. Every tension, every crisis can become a source of new life if we approach it wisely, or it can bring death and division.

Tensions and stress come from a lack of balance between difficulties that have to be faced and the support or nourishment that is provided. If the difficulties are great and the support minimal, then people will experience great inner stress. This will come out not only in anger and irrational behaviour, which are ways of letting off steam, but also in a great need for compensatory things such as affection, alcohol, coffee, etc. In times of stress people need to be well accompanied if their inner pain is to become a cry for prayer and for God and for wise help, and not just for human comfort and compensations, or a return to values that had been left behind on entering the community. Tensions can break people or bring them back to essentials.

There is nothing more prejudicial to community life than to mask tensions and pretend they do not exist, or to hide them behind a polite façade and flee from reality and dialogue. A tension or difficulty can signal the approach of a new grace of God. But it has to be looked at wisely and humanly. There can be a danger of spiritualising a tension too quickly instead of talking about it with a third person or an external authority.

Tensions and times of trial often come when the community has lost its sense of what is essential, its initial vision, or when it has been unfaithful to the call of Christ and the poor. These tensions then, are a call to a new fidelity. If the community is to refind peace, it must recognise its shortcomings, ask God's forgiveness and beg him to give it new light and strength.

We must accept tensions as an everyday fact, while at the same time trying to resolve them through a search for a greater depth and for truth. And resolution does not mean hasty confrontation. It is not by making a tension explode in the presence of all the people concerned that we will resolve it. People are not necessarily helped to overcome their limitations, fears, egoism, jealousy and inability to enter into dialogue simply by being made conscious of them. In fact, this can sometimes shut people off in even greater anguish, close to despair.

People can generally only become conscious of their limitations if at the same time they are given the strength to overcome these by being helped to discover their own capacities for love, goodness and positive action, and to regain confidence in themselves and the Holy Spirit. People cannot accept their own fears if they do not at the same time feel loved, respected and trusted. They cannot overcome their difficulties and inner darkness if they have not been helped to discover that they are lovable. This is the role of people with responsibility: to perceive the beauty and value of people who are tense and aggressive and to help others in the community to do the same. Then those people, knowing that they are not rejected, but accepted and loved, will gradually be able to allow their positive energies to flourish in the service of others.

And when the fears diminish, when people begin to listen to each other without prejudice and rejection, and to understand why others act the way they do, the tensions disappear. It is a question of accepting others and loving them with all their fears and aggression. This mutual acceptance, which can gradually become a true welcoming of the other, takes time and patience. It can involve many laborious meetings and sensitivity in dialogue, as well as silent, peaceful and tender acceptance.

Tensions should neither be hidden nor be brought prematurely to a head. They should be taken on with a great deal of sensitivity and prayerfulness, trust and hope, knowing that there is bound to be suffering. They should be approached with deep understanding and patience, with neither panic nor naive optimism, but with a realism born of a willingness to listen and a desire for truth even if it is challenging and it hurts.

There are always subjective and emotional elements in situations of tension, but there are also elements of objective truth and real differences of opinion. One must not hide the other. It is dangerous to refuse to look at the truth of a situation that is disturbing, under the excuse that the other person has emotional problems. In the same way, it is wrong not to accept the fact that people can use differences of opinion to express their emotional problems.

Tensions may arise from the fact that some people are too set in their opinions. With time, these people become more open and discover that reality has other dimensions. Their vision is modified and the tensions disappear. That is why we have to be patient with tensions and not always seek a speedy resolution. If we act too quickly, we may push people to exaggerate their position instead of becoming more flexible.

Other tensions in a community come when it contains apparently opposed values. The attempt to harmonise these is the genius of community. We want l'Arche to be a Christian community, but also to work within the structures demanded by the state. We have to be prayerful and loving; we must also be competent. Some people hold to one set of values more strongly than to others, and that is good. But this can sometimes bring tensions between people. These tensions diminish as the community and its members become more mature and reach a certain wisdom.

Yet other tensions come from the fact that the community is evolving and new gifts or realities are appearing, which will gradually demand a new balance or even an evolution in the community's structures. It is vital that we do not panic when faced with these tensions, which cannot always be verbalised. We have to know how to wait for the moment when these questions can be discussed in peace and truth.

The Holy Spirit is always making the new out of the old. I am amazed as I read the history of the Church with its pains and struggles. Always new things unfolding: new prophets, new saints arising to announce the old truths, but in new ways. There is always a tension in the Church between the old and the new: supporters of the old are fearful of the new and see it as a threat, as dangerous and wrong; they condemn it and sometimes even destroy it. The initiators of new ways can also be angry with the old, rejecting it as wrong, as corrupt or evil and then breaking away from it. Similar tensions exist in every community, as each one evolves according to the inspirations of the Spirit and the needs of the time but is reluctant to change.

Leaders can be crucified by these tensions. They are pulled in two directions and often criticised and condemned by both sides. They must try to see the truth in each position, keeping their eyes on essentials, discerning what is prophetic in the new from what is just human desire for change; discerning also what is true in the old and must be retained from what is just fear of change and of insecurity. Leaders need to be patient and to wait until the light of the Holy Spirit is given, and they must call others to be patient.

I am touched by the way tensions in community are so often a gift and a grace. Some tensions are like the pains of childbirth. Different people, holding on to different aspects of the vision which seem to be in contradiction with each other, appear to be opposing one another, but this is not so. It means that a new light or a new reality or new structures, which can harmonise the two, have not yet been given by God. People must continue to bear the pain of these tensions and wait for the resurrection, as Mary waited on that Holy Saturday. The pain keeps each one little and humble; it keeps them calling out to God in prayer; it keeps them also struggling to understand and to love truth over and above their *own* ideas.

Individual growth towards love and wisdom is slow. A community's growth is even slower. Members of a community have to be friends of time. They have to learn that many things will resolve themselves if they are given enough time. It can be a great mistake to want, in the name of clarity and truth, to push things too quickly to a resolution. Some people enjoy confrontation and highlighting divisions. This is not always healthy. It is better to be a friend of time. But clearly too, people should not pretend that problems don't exist by refusing to listen to the rumblings of discontent; they must be aware of the tensions and then learn to work on them at the right moment.

In many communities, there is someone who is more fragile or difficult than the others, who seems to provoke all their aggression and become the butt of their blame, criticism and mockery. All members of a community, in some corner of themselves, feel frustrated and guilty. These feelings can very quickly be felt as a sort of anguish – a sense that we are not comfortable with ourselves. So we project our own limitations and cowardice on to someone weaker than ourselves. This 'scapegoat' for personal and collective anguish can be found in many communities.

Once the aggression, bullying or rejection are unleashed, they are not easy to control. And yet, for the health of the community, they have to be deflected from their target, because no community can live while one of its members is being persecuted. So another person, either consciously, or unconsciously under the inspiration of the Spirit, must absorb the aggression. They may do it by playing the fool. Then the aggression is gradually transformed and the crackle of tension is dissipated in the light of laughter.

Many tensions arise from a refusal to accept that authority has its failings. We are all looking for the ideal mother or father and when we do not find them, we are deeply disappointed. These are good tensions: each person must discover that the people who carry authority are also human beings who can make mistakes, without losing confidence in authority itself. Each person has to grow in maturity to find a true and free relationship with authority. And people with authority have to be ready to evolve and to be less afraid.

Sending people away

Some communities break up under the pressure of internal schism and disruption. It is striking how quickly, after a time of grace and unity, the first Christian communities became divided and partisan. Some, for instance, took Paul's side; others supported Apollos (1 Cor. 3). St John talks of these deep divisions in his first letter. There had been real splits in the community; some people left, refusing to be in communion with the others or to accept the doctrine of the apostles or, in particular, the authority of John (1 John 2:19).

Judas himself lived with the eleven and with Jesus, but his heart was full of malice and jealousy, and long before Satan led him to the final act of betrayal, his heart had become separated from the hearts of the others. Jesus had called him, but very quickly – and for reasons we do not know – he decided to take advantage of his position to further his own glory and personal plan. He did not want to serve Jesus with the other apostles; he wanted to use Jesus for his own ambitions.

At what moment should someone whose heart seems completely separated from the community, who is sowing disruption and trying to use weaker people for personal and destructive ends, be sent away? These people, whose hearts are filled with jealousy, are often extremely intelligent, with a considerable ability to perceive and exploit failings in legitimate authority or the community's life. So they can appear clairvoyant, and to have the ability to redress certain injustices. They can attract some of the weaker people or some who are dissatisfied with community life; they know how to create divisions, sow confusion and sap authority. It seems unreasonable to let them go on dividing the community, especially when all attempts at dialogue with them have failed. But to send them away, especially when they have been in the community for a long time, also seems unbearable.

Jesus is clear:

> If your brother sins against you, go and tell him his fault, between you and him alone. If he listens to you, you have gained your brother. But if he does not listen, take one or two others along with you, that every word may be confirmed by two or three witnesses. If he refuses to listen to them, tell it to the church; and if he refuses to listen even to the church, let him be to you as a Gentile and a tax-collector. (Matt. 18:15–17)

Only the people with responsibility in the community and its long-term members can decide that someone must go. But in doing this, they too must recognise their share of guilt. Perhaps they did not dare to take the person in hand and set up a dialogue as soon as the first inkling of divisions appeared; perhaps they let the situation drag on, hoping naively that everything would sort itself out. Perhaps they even exploited the disruptive individual because they needed him or her for a specific job. But a belated recognition of its mistakes should not inhibit the community from acting firmly. If someone is causing dissension among the members of the community, they must be asked to leave.

At the same time, authority must not be too quick to send people away simply because they dispute it. It is often a refusal to listen to these first disagreements which throws up a barrier of pride. If the points had been heard, if the weaknesses and mistakes of the community had been admitted and if something had been done to try to set them right, perhaps the disputes would have disappeared, or have been converted into positive energy for reform.

A community should not send people away simply because they are disturbing or have a difficult character, or seem to be in the wrong place, or are challenging it. The only people who should be sent away are those who have already cut themselves off from the community in their own hearts, who pose a real threat by influencing others against legitimate authority and sapping confidence in it. These people divide the community and deflect it from its first goals.

In this difficult area of division and schism, there can be no rules except those of patience, vigilance and firmness, and of respect for the community's structures and insistence on dialogue. In fact, as long as people are integrated into a group and have no opportunity to spread discord, there is no reason to send them away. It is rather a question of carrying them, bearing with them and helping them in whatever ways we can. All members of the community must be on their guard against sowing discord, whether consciously or unconsciously. All of them must constantly seek to be instruments of unity. That doesn't, of course, mean that they must always agree with the people at the head of the community. But they must confront them in truth. None of us who lives in community is free from elements of pride, born of bruised susceptibility, which can, if we are not careful, invade our whole being.

It takes much time and wisdom to build a community. But it can take very little time to break and destroy a community if a proud and destructive person seeking power is allowed to become a member, more out of a need of the community to find someone competent than through a real discernment. If there are no strong people in the community to confront him or her, then it is likely that the community will break up and die.

We must never forget that Satan is the adversary of love and communion. He hates communities where people are growing in love and in the knowledge of Jesus. He does everything he can to sow discord, to create tensions and divisions, and finally to destroy community.

The outsider's eye, or external authority

I realise more and more that no community, whether large or small, can cope on its own. Very often its members are not able to resolve their tensions; they are frequently taken up too much by immediate questions and do not have the distance necessary in order to see what is really happening to the community. They need a sympathetic outsider, who is competent and carries a real authority, to help them grasp the way the community is evolving and find new structures for the different stages of growth. Every community seems to need regular visits from someone who listens and asks the right questions about their vision and their life in community, and to whom all its members feel they can talk. Above all there is need for someone who can counsel its leaders, so helping the community to evolve and discover the message of God which is hidden in the tensions.

This outside eye needs to be someone with common sense and an understanding of people, wise in human relationships and community; someone who is committed to the community's fundamental goals and respects its structures.

This person must also help the community to evaluate itself. From time to time, and very freely, we should all evaluate our community life, to see where we should be putting more effort, and sense if we are losing our creativity and falling into habit and routine. We have to evaluate our meetings to see if they are really nourishing and living, or whether they are simply a waste of time. It is so much easier to evaluate with the help of an outside eye.

Yves Beriot, a French educator, has said how important it is for people to visit communities and act as sponges which soak up the anguish. All communities feel far from their ideal, and more or less unable to cope with the violence and anguish of the people they welcome. We are all far from the ideal of the Gospel and this causes a latent anguish and guilt which sap our creative energies and can lead to sadness and despair.

This outsider can also be the community's memory bank. It is always important to have someone coming in who can ask, 'Do you remember?' and reminds us of our origins, history and traditions, of joyful times as well as sad ones. If a community is to be able to make plans for the future, it must have assimilated its past and have a sense of its own tradition. That is one of the reasons why the external authority must not change too often; continuity is important.

The role of this outside authority is a delicate one. It is to see as clearly as possible the positive forces in the community and help them to grow; it is also to point out the negative ones. The outside authority cannot tell people what to do but gives advice, suggestions and ideas for the future. The outside authority encourages, helps to renew hope and take the heat out of things. It must be realised that this role is a passing one; it leaves and the community continues on with the people that are there.

The outside eye is particularly important during the dark winters of community, to call the community to trust, to patience and to prayer.

The external authority has a role also in relation to the leaders; to confirm, give support and encourage them; but also to supervise and challenge them when necessary. It should also be able to intervene firmly and clearly when leaders are incompetent and unable to maintain the spirit and goals of the community or if they start using the community for their own personal interests, or if injustices are being committed.

This external authority is necessary because human beings are weak and fallible, and the forces of evil outside and even within the community are such that if there is no external authority, the community could sooner or later break up or die, or could commit real injustices towards people.

For some therapeutic communities the guarantor may be the state, which has a system of control and evaluation; it can also be a board of directors. Many Christian communities are linked to a bishop. It is he or his representative who approves the community, its charter and constitution; he is its guarantor. Other communities are linked to an authority born out of a network of sister-communities; the person is sometimes called a provincial, a regional superior or servant or a co-ordinator.

I am rather concerned about communities without any traditions which refuse to accept any external authority. They will not outlive their founder for long and, if there is no external control at all, the founder will be in danger of making some serious mistakes.

Growth in individuals and growth in community

Each member of a community who grows in love and wisdom helps the growth of the whole community. Each person who refuses to grow, or is afraid to go forward, inhibits the community's growth. All the members of a community are responsible for their own growth and that of the community as a whole.

Human growth is to do with integrating our capacity for action with our heart. Too often, action springs from fear of relationships, of our own vulnerability, or of love; it comes from fear of dependence, of sexuality and of our own deep and hidden self. Action is too often a flight or a desire to prove something.

When we are at peace, when we have accepted our own deep wounds and weakness, when we are in touch with our own heart and capacity for tenderness, then actions flow from our true selves, and become a source of growth.

True growth comes as members of the community integrate into their hearts and minds the vision and spirit of the community. In that way they choose the community as it is and become responsible for it. When people have not integrated the vision into themselves they tend to imitate others or they are just wanting a place where they can belong. This is dangerous and can prevent growth to wholeness.

Some people come to our l'Arche communities to help people with a handicap. That is good. Others come because they themselves want to grow and sense that they need others to help, stimulate and encourage them; they see the community as the place of their growth and apprenticeship. That is better, as long as they realise that their growth is linked to the growth of others.

Those who come because they feel they have something to offer to people who are weak and poor, often get a shock when they start to become conscious of the weaknesses and limitations in themselves and the other assistants. It is always easier to accept the weakness of people with a handicap – we are there precisely because we expect it – than our own weakness which often takes us by surprise! We want to see only good qualities in ourselves and other assistants. Growth begins when we start to accept our own weakness.

I am always moved when I speak with men and women who have a problem with alcohol. The urge for drink, which is psychological but also biological, is so great in them. And this urge frequently springs from a habit they adopted to fill a terrible emptiness in them and to calm the pain of anguish, loneliness and guilt. But this addiction to a form of sedative is found in all of us. Some addictions can be seen as destructive, like drink or drugs. Other addictions are less obviously destructive, but they are destructive nonetheless. These can be seen in people who calm their anguish by becoming workaholics or by excessive watching of television, or through possessive relationships or compulsive needs, such as always to be in the forefront and applauded. We can all be addicted to something which is disguised in the clothes of virtue and good- ness, but which in reality masks and calms anguish. We are all tempted to relieve our inner pain by letting ourselves be governed by these things. We all have difficulty resisting them, accepting the pain of emptiness and anguish, and walking in truth towards healing, towards communion with God and towards compassion for others.

Some people run from the pain of feeling unlovable by 'doing things' which avoid involvement in deep relationships. But others on the contrary come to community and seek consolation from this pain by responding to whatever demands are made of them. Unconsciously there is a thought pattern: 'If I satisfy your need, then you, or the community, or God, will be grateful, will appreci- ate my existence, will love me.'

Ultimately this can never bring true fulfilment and true growth. It is important that in communities where the needs are often limitless, we are attentive to this false response, so easily disguised by generosity and goodness. We must help each person to live more and more clearly and deeply from an inner confidence of being loved by God just as they are.

I sometimes tend to behave as if everyone could live in community and grow through their own efforts towards universal love. With age and experience of community life, perhaps too with a growing faith, I'm becoming conscious of the limitations and weaknesses of human energy, the forces of egoism and the deep psychological wounds – fear, aggression and self-assertion – which govern human life and raise up all the barriers which exist between people. We can only emerge from behind these barriers if the Spirit of God touches us, breaks down the barriers and puts us on the road to healing.

Jesus was sent by the Father not to judge us and even less to condemn us to remain in the prisons, limitations and dark places of our beings, but to forgive and free us, by planting the seeds of the Spirit in us. To grow in love is to allow this Spirit of Jesus to grow in us.

Growth takes on another dimension when we allow Jesus to penetrate us, to give us new life and new energy.

The hope is not in our own efforts to love. It is not in psychoanalysis which tries to throw light on the knots and blocks of our life, nor in a more equitable reorganisation of the political and economic structures which have their effects on our personal lives. All this is perhaps necessary. But true growth comes from God, when we cry to him from the depths of the abyss to let his Spirit penetrate us. Growth in love is a growth in the Spirit. The stages through which we must pass in order to grow in love are the stages through which we must pass to become more totally united to God.

If we are to grow in love, the prisons of our egoism must be unlocked. This implies suffering, constant effort and repeated choices. To reach maturity in love, to carry the cross of responsibility, we have to get beyond the enthusiasms, the utopias and the naiveties of adolescence. And during this growth we need a friend, a guide, a wise counsellor – someone who accompanies us along the road and through the passages of pain.[3]

3 The whole question of accompaniment is treated in chapter 7.

People in community often ask how they can know if they and it are growing. St Paul gives a clear indication in his Epistle to the Corinthians (ch. 13). Love is not heroic nor extraordinary acts; it is not speaking in tongues, prophesying, knowing all the mysteries and all about science, or even having extraordinary faith, giving all one's goods to the poor or being martyred. Love is being patient, rendering service, not being jealous or proud, not bragging all the time about oneself and exaggerating one's own qualities. Love is doing nothing which bruises others; it is putting the interests of others above our own. It is not being irritable, bitter, aggressive, or searching for the evil in others; it is not rejoicing in injustice but seeking the truth in all things.

And in his letter to Galatians (ch. 5) St Paul says that growth in love is growth in joy and patience, goodness, generosity, fidelity, tenderness and self-control. It is the opposite of all our tendencies to division – hatred, quarrelling, jealousy, rage, disputes, dissension, schism, desire and of all those dark tendencies which lead us to fornication, impurity, debauchery, idolatry, witchcraft, orgies and gluttony.

Perhaps the essential quality for anyone who lives in community is patience: a recognition that we, others, and the whole community take time to grow. Nothing is achieved in a day. If we are to live in community, we have to be friends of time.

And the friend of time doesn't spend all day saying: 'I haven't got time.' He doesn't fight with time. He accepts it and cherishes it.

Losing illusions

The danger for any community and for every person is to live in illusions. We all do that as we shut ourselves off from others. A community that is closed off from others, lives in the illusion that it alone has the truth; or maybe it is fearful of any kind of change or challenge or of being seen as it is, in all its poverty. The leaders refuse to listen to others; they find all sorts of religious reasons and signs to enhance their belief that they alone are filled with the

Spirit and are in direct communication with God. That is perhaps an extreme situation; but in all of us and in every community, there is the fear of challenge; and the danger of covering up tensions and the things that are not going well, or at least refusing to look at them and to confront them.

'Truth is reality,' writes Scott Peck:

> That which is false is unreal. The more clearly we see the reality of the world, the better equipped we are to deal with the world. The less clearly we see the reality of the world – the more our minds are befuddled by falsehood, misperceptions and illusion – the less able we will be to determine correct courses of action and make wise decisions. . . .[4]
>
> Truth or reality is avoided when it is painful. We can revise our maps [i.e our own course of action] only when we have the discipline to overcome that pain. To have such discipline we must be totally dedicated to truth. That is to say that we must always hold truth, as best we can determine it, to be more important, more vital to one's self-interest than our comfort. . . . A life of total dedication to truth also means a life of willingness to be personally challenged . . . but the tendency to avoid challenge is so omnipresent in human beings that it can properly be considered as a characteristic of human nature.[5]

One of the most important things for growth in people and in communities is precisely this dedication to truth, even (and maybe especially) if it hurts. There is no growth when we live in falsehood and illusion; when we are frightened to let the truth be uncovered and seen by ourselves and by others. So often we hide our fears, our injustices, our incompetence, our hypocrisy. We can hide behind religious rules, as did the Pharisees and the Saducees. We must open ourselves up to the truth and let it be revealed, even if it shows our intrinsic poverty and sinfulness. And then let us cry out to Jesus, the Saviour, who will send us his Spirit and guide us, and forgive us. Only then can the truth make us free.

4 M. Scott Peck, *The Road Less Travelled* (Simon and Schuster, New York, 1978), p. 44.
5 Ibid., pp. 52–3.

Peter went through four crises while following Jesus. I imagine it was a crisis when Jesus called him: part of him must have regretted leaving his family and his trade. But his love for Jesus and his hope enabled him to get over this. Then there was the crisis when he discovered that Jesus was not as he would have wanted him. He would have preferred a Jesus who was prophetic and messianic, who didn't insist on washing the disciples' feet, who didn't speak of dying. The greatest crisis was when Jesus became weak and died. Then, Peter denied him – and that was the crisis when he lost all the illusions about himself.

These are the four great crises of community life. The first – which is certainly the least hard – comes when we arrive. There are always parts of us which cling to the values we have left behind. The second is the discovery that the community is not as perfect as we had thought, that it has its weaknesses and flaws. The ideal and our illusions crumble; we are faced with reality. The third is when we feel misunderstood and even rejected by the community, when, for example, we are not elected to a position of responsibility, or do not get a job we had hoped for. And the fourth is the hardest: our disappointment with ourselves because of all the anger, jealousies, and frustrations that boil up in us.

If we are to become totally integrated into a community, we must know how to pass through these crises. They are all new deepenings – movements towards inner freedom. They all imply the losing of illusions and the gradual welcoming of reality as it is.

Losing illusions involves much pain and grieving. We all live more or less on illusions which protect our vulnerability. When these come crumbling down, we are faced with a terrible emptiness; this is rather like death. Elisabeth Kübler-Ross marks the stages before acceptance of death: refusal, revolt, bargaining, and depression. The grieving process can be a long one. But when it is over, we are reborn in truth. And the truth always sets us free.

To grow is to learn to die. Is not this the ultimate meaning of our lives? By the age of twenty-four, each one of us loses daily 100,000 cells in the brain that are not replaced. Fortunately, we have a lot of cells! As we grow, we leave behind us many things. As an adult, we must no longer be attached to childhood ways; we have to learn to be responsible. When married, we lose the freedom of a single person. Ageing, we lose capacities, health and responsibilities. If we spend time weeping over the past, we become imprisoned in that past. We must certainly grieve what we have lost, but we must live freely the new realities of the present and we must wait in hope for new life. And so each one of us will make the final passage of death, not clinging to life, not weeping with guilt because of misspent lives, but trusting, moving forward, waiting for that new gift which we will welcome: the embrace of the eternal.

People are sometimes frightened of following Jesus because they are frightened of *losing* things. To renounce certain values and certain goods that apparently bring human fulfilment is terribly difficult. Many today would rather not choose to follow him. But Jesus tells us (Mark 10: 28–31) that if we do accept the renunciation of father, mother, children, brothers, sisters and land, we will receive these again a hundred-fold, with persecutions, in this life – and in the next, eternal life. That's a good bet! But it calls for belief.

It was easy for Peter to follow Jesus when he was doing miracles and other wonderful things. Then Jesus appeared truly as the Messiah who would give back to Israel the dignity of the chosen people after so many years of humiliation under Roman rule. It is easy to enter a flourishing community that is doing wonderful things. It was more difficult for Peter to follow Jesus when he was beaten and had lost. It is more difficult to remain in a community when it is poor, broken and humiliated. It is *never* easy to lose or to die. And yet, the mystery of growth for a Christian is to accept the pain of littleness and humiliation. It is then that we truly live the mystery of our faith; it is then that the power of God becomes manifest.

It is terrible to see enthusiastic young people becoming disillu-
sioned, wounded and cynical after a few years of community life
where they felt neither welcomed nor understood. After that bad
experience they can lose all taste for giving, and shut themselves
off in political movements or the illusions of psychoanalysis. That
doesn't mean that either politics or psychoanalysis are unimportant. But it is sad when people are totally shut up in them because
they have been disappointed or have not accepted their own limitations. There are false prophets in communities who attract and
stimulate the enthusiastic, but who through lack of wisdom or
pride lead young people towards disappointment. The world of
community can be full of illusions. There are many sects that
attract young people, and it is not always easy to distinguish what
is true from what is false, or to sense if the good grain will flourish
or be stifled by the weeds. Those who are thinking of founding
communities should surround themselves with people who are
wise and know how to discern. I ask forgiveness of all those
who came to my own community or others of l'Arche, full of
enthusiasm, and who felt deceived by our lack of openness, our
blocks, our lack of truth and our pride.

People who enter into a covenant and choose community life are
in danger of losing within a few years the eye of the child and the
openness of the adolescent. They are at risk of shutting themselves
in on their own territory. They tend to want to possess their
function and their community. How, once we are committed to
community life, can we ensure that we never stop growing and
loving? How can we ensure that we keep walking towards an ever
greater human insecurity? Once we have taken root in the ground,
we have to continue to grow and this means being pruned, cut
back, and sometimes even broken so that we can go on bearing
fruit.

There can be danger that we define ourselves entirely by community activity and the responsibilities this brings. We can become
hyperactive and not know either how to stop or how to relax. By
doing things for other people all the time, and devoting ourselves
to them, we become more and more identified with our function

and the privileges this brings; then we cling jealously to these. We have a terrible unconscious fear of letting go because that implies dying and confrontation with the emptiness inside us. Those who carry heavy responsibilities in a community must look at their own inner life: are they blotting it out, or dispersing it in activity, or are they truly trying to nurture it? It is too easy to live on the periphery of ourselves, using our superficial energies instead of constantly working to deepen our inwardness and our contact with the silent places at the heart of our being where God lives.

The more we become people of action and responsibility in our community, the more we must become people of contemplation. If we do not nurture our deep emotional life in prayer hidden in God, if we do not spend time in silence, and if we do not know how to take time to live from the presence and gentleness of our brothers and sisters, we risk becoming embittered. It is only to the extent that we nurture our own hearts that we can keep inner freedom. People who are hyperactive, fleeing from their deep selves and their anguish live on illusions. They quickly become tyrannical, and their exercise of responsibility becomes intolerable, creating nothing but conflict.

The second call

The first call is frequently to follow Jesus or to prepare ourselves to do wonderful and noble things for the Kingdom. We are appreciated and admired by family, by friends or by the community. The second call comes later, when we accept that we cannot do big or heroic things for Jesus; it is a time of renunciation, humiliation and humility. We feel useless; we are no longer appreciated. If the first passage is made at high noon, under a shining sun, the second call is often made at night. We feel alone and are afraid because we are in a world of confusion. We begin to doubt the commitment we made in the light of day. We seem deeply broken in some way. But this suffering is not useless. Through the renunciation we can reach a new wisdom of love. It is only through the pain of the cross that we discover what the resurrection means.

We all carry our own deep wound, which is the wound of our loneliness. We find it hard to be alone, and we try to flee from this in hyperactivity, through television and in a million other ways. Some people think their wound of loneliness will be healed if they come into community. But they will be disappointed. While they are young, they can hide their disappointment behind the dynamic of generosity; they can flee from the present by projecting themselves into the future, into a hope that things will be better tomorrow. But towards the age of forty, the future is past and there are no more great projects; the wound is still there and we can become depressed, especially as we are now carrying all the guilt and apathy of the past. Then we have to realise that this wound is inherent in the human condition and that what we have to do is to walk with it instead of fleeing from it. We cannot accept it until we discover that we are loved by God just as we are, and that the Holy Spirit, in a mysterious way, is living at the centre of the wound.

At the end of a few years in community people often go through a crisis which has to do with this feeling of loneliness. They have believed, more or less consciously, that the community would suffice them in every way. But their wound remains and they feel deceived. Some may think then that the answer is in marriage, hoping that this will heal their wound. But there they are at risk of being disappointed again. No one can really enter marriage unless they are trying to accept their wound and unless they are determined to live for the other.

Old age is the most precious time of life, the one nearest eternity. There are two ways of growing old. There are old people who are anxious and bitter, living in the past and illusion, who criticise everything that goes on around them. Young people are repulsed by them; they are shut away in their sadness and loneliness, shrivelled up in themselves. But there are also old people with a child's heart, who have used their freedom from function and responsibility to find a new youth. They have the wonder of a child, but the wisdom of maturity as well. They have integrated their years of activity and so can live without being attached to power. Their freedom of heart and their acceptance of their limitations and weakness makes them people whose radiance illuminates the whole community. They are gentle and merciful, symbols of compassion and forgiveness. They become a community's hidden treasures, sources of unity and life. They are true contemplatives at the heart of community.

Prayer, service and community life

Some communities start by serving the poor. When they begin, their members are full of generosity – though sometimes a bit aggressive in respect of the rich – and have a rather utopian ideal. Gradually, they discover the need for prayer and an inner life; they realise that their generosity is being burned up and that they are in danger of becoming a collection of hyperactives who put all their energy into external things.

Other communities start with prayer – like many of the communities of the charismatic renewal. But gradually they discover the need to serve the poor and to develop real commitment to them. Opening to God in adoration and opening to the poor in welcome and service are the two poles of a community's growth, and signs of its health. And the community itself must grow towards a stronger sense of its own identity, like a body in which every member can exercise its gift and be recognised for it.

If those communities that started by serving the poor do not discover the deepening of prayer and the bonds of love flowing into celebration, they risk becoming a militant group struggling for justice. If those communities that started with prayer and adoration do not discover the waters of compassion flowing from them upon those in pain, they risk becoming legalistic and sterile.

The three elements of community – prayer, or communion with the Father through and in Jesus, presence and service to the poor, and the consciousness of being bonded in a single body – are always necessary for a community to be healthy and to grow.

Jesus called each apostle into a personal relationship of love with him, then he bonded them together in community and then he sent them out to announce *good news* to the poor.

From doing to listening

Communities which start by serving the poor must gradually discover the gifts brought by those they serve. The communities start in generosity; they must grow in the ability to listen. In the end, the most important thing is not to do things for people who are poor and in distress, but to enter into relationship with them, to be with them and help them find confidence in themselves and discover their own gifts. It isn't a question of arriving in a slum with the money to build a dispensary and a school. It is more a question of spending time with the people who live in the slum to help them discover their own needs and then together building what they want. Perhaps these buildings won't be as beautiful. But they will be more used and loved, because they will belong to everyone and not just to a foreigner who means well. It will take a long time. But all service which is really human takes time. The promise of Jesus is to help us discover that the poor are a source of life and not just objects of our charity. If we are close to them we will be renewed in love and in faith.

Some communities grow by listening more to the needs of their members than to those they are serving. This growth sometimes focuses mainly on the material: better buildings where everyone has more comfort.

Other communities will grow by listening to the cry of the poor. Most of the time this leads them to remain poor themselves, so that they can be closer to the poor people and in communion with them. That does not lessen the fact that the members of a community need to be cared for; they need to have what is necessary for their well-being so that they can be good instruments of God's love and be prepared for the long-haul.

When a community lets itself be guided in its growth by the cry of the poor and their needs, it will walk in the desert and it will be insecure. But it is assured of the promised land – not the one of security, but the one of peace and love. And it will be a community which is always alive.

Signs of sickness and health in community

When people refuse to come to meetings and there is no longer a place of dialogue, when they are afraid to say what they think and the group is dominated by a single strong personality who inhibits the others, when people flee into outside activities instead of taking part in community ones, then the community is in danger. It is no longer home for the people who live there, but an hotel.

When the members of a community are no longer happy to live, pray and work together, but are constantly looking for outside compensations, when they talk all the time about themselves and their problems instead of their ideal of life and their response to the cry of the poor, these are signs of death.

When a community is healthy, it acts like a magnet. Young people commit themselves; visitors are happy to come there. When a community starts to be frightened of welcoming visitors and new people, when it starts to lay down so many restrictions and ask for so many guarantees that practically no one qualifies to come, when it starts to reject its own weakest and most difficult members – the old and the sick – these are bad signs. Then it is no longer a community; it is becoming an efficient place of work.

It's a bad sign too when a community tries to structure itself to ensure total security for the future, when it has a lot of money in the bank. Gradually, it will eliminate all possible risk. It will no longer need God's help. It will cease to be poor.

The health of a community can be measured by the quality of its welcome of the unexpected visitor or someone who is poor, by the joy and simplicity of relationships between its members, by its creativity in response to the cry of the poor. But it is measured above all by the ardour for and fidelity to its own essential goals: its presence to God and the poor.

It is important that communities discover both the signs of

disruption and the signs of deepening. From time to time they should set themselves to find out where they are. It is not always easy, for they have to learn to go through times of trial. But there are signs of life and death which should be discerned.

Openness to others

When a community is born, it is very difficult to know whether it is a real community or a sect. It is only by watching it grow over time that we can know the answer. A true community becomes more and more open, because it becomes more and more humble. A sect seems to be open, but with time in fact becomes more and more closed. A sect is made up of people who believe that only they are right. They are incapable of listening; they are enclosed and fanatical; they find no truth outside themselves. Their members have lost their capacity for individual reflection; only they are elect, saved and perfect; everyone else is wrong. And in spite of the apparent joy and relaxation, there is an impression that these are weak personalities who have been more or less manipulated and who are imprisoned in a false friendship from which they would find it hard to escape. They are governed more by fear than by growth towards inner freedom.

The language of elitism smells bad! It is not healthy to believe that we are the only ones to have captured truth and even less healthy to condemn others. These attitudes have nothing to do with the message of Jesus Christ. A Christian community is based on the recognition that we are all sinners and that we need to be forgiven each day and to forgive seventy times seven. 'Judge not, and you will not be judged' (Luke 6:37). A Christian community should do as Jesus did: propose and not impose. Its attraction must lie in the radiance cast by the love of brothers and sisters.

Communities are also distinguished from sects by the fact that the members of a sect focus more and more on a single authority – their founder, prophet, shepherd, leader or saint. It is he who holds all the temporal and spiritual power and keeps all the members under control. They read only his writings and they live from his words alone. This false prophet refuses to allow anyone but himself to speak to the group; he dismisses anyone who could threaten his all-powerful authority. He surrounds himself with people who are weak, incapable of any personal thought. He is submissive to no one.

At the start of true communities, founders hold spiritual and communal power; they hold authority and are the person others refer to for all decisions. If they are essentially submissive to the Holy Spirit, they must also be submissive to other authorities in their church and to others in the community. They must gradually help the members to make contact with other sources of inspiration and authority, and journey towards their own inner freedom, so that they think freely, while remaining in the spirit of the community.

True Christian communities always have a multiplicity of authorities including the founder, the Gospel, the whole tradition of the Church, the bishop and the Holy Father (if they are Roman Catholic), and other Christians living in the spirit of Jesus. Then, most important of all, each member of the community must learn to take as their authority the Spirit of Jesus living in themselves.

It is fairly natural and perhaps even necessary that a new community is taken up with its own originality and tends to idealise itself. If it didn't believe itself to be unique, perhaps it would never have been founded at all. It's like love, which always starts by idealisation of the other: a baby is always the most gorgeous in the world to its parents, and a bride is always the most beautiful to her husband. With time, both parents and married couples become more realistic; perhaps too they become more committed, more faithful and more loving.

It is understandable that a new community should be turned in on itself, strongly conscious of its qualities and originality, and giving thanks for these. At the start of a marriage, a couple has to take time to forge its unity, this isn't egoism, but a necessary stage in growth. With time, the community must stand back a little to discover the beauty and particular gifts of others, as well as its own limitations. Once it has found its own identity and discovered

how the Holy Spirit is guiding it, it must be very attentive to the
manifestations of the Spirit in others. It should not believe that it
is the only community to have the privilege of being inspired by
the Holy Spirit; it should listen to what the Spirit is saying to
others. This will enable it to rediscover its own gifts and mission
and encourage it to be more faithful to them. This in turn will
enable it to discover its place in the Church and in humanity as a
whole. If it is not attentive, the community risks missing a decisive
turning point in its own growth.

One of the signs of life in a community is the creation of links
with others. An inward-looking community will die of suffo-
cation. Living communities are linked to others, making up a huge
reservoir of love for the world. And as only the one Spirit inspires
and gives life, communities being born or reborn will be alike
without ever even knowing each other; the seeds the Spirit sows
across the world, like prophetic signs for tomorrow, have a
common source. It is a sign of maturity for a community to bind
itself in friendship with others; it knows its own identity, so
doesn't need to make comparisons. It loves even the differences
which distinguish it, because each community has its own gift
which must flourish. These communities are complementary; they
need each other. They are all branches of that unique community
which is the Church, the mystical body of Christ. He is the vine
of which the communities are branches.

I am always amazed by the multiplicity of communities which
exist, from those which go back to St Benedict and have been
revitalised by love, to those which the Holy Spirit is bringing to
birth today. Some are within the churches; others are outside
any institution, bringing together young people with prophetic
intuition who are looking for a new way of life. All these communities are part of the vast invisible Church. Each has its own
spirit, way of life, rule and character. Each is unique.

There are communities founded on adoration and silent and
contemplative prayer – the many Carmels, the Little Sisters of

Bethlehem and all those monasteries whose communication is more non-verbal than verbal, living a tradition that goes back to St Bernard or St Theresa of Avila. Linked to these are the communities of the sisters of Darmstadt in Germany and of the Little Sisters and Little Brothers of Jesus, silent and prayerful, in slums and ghettos across the world, linking contemplation and a presence to the poor.

Then, there are all the communities of prayer which are linked to the charismatic renewal, in which people come together to pray while remaining very rooted in society. There are the 'Foyers de Charité', welcoming retreatants across the world. Madonna House, founded by Catherine Doherty, is yet another example of Christian community based on prayer, manual work, announcing the Word and a very beautiful liturgy. There are all those little communities of Focolari spread around the world. There are ecumenical communities, like Taizé in France. There are communities which have as an immediate goal the welcome and care of the poorest people of all – the Sisters and Brothers, Missionaries of Charity, founded by Mother Teresa and Father Andrew in Calcutta. Some communities are more committed to social action. They aim to bring improvement to the life of oppressed and suffering people, like the communities of the Church of the Saviour and Sojourners in Washington, D.C., the Catholic Worker communities, those of El Minuto de Dios in Colombia, and Father Ted Kennedy's community with the aborigines in Sydney. And there are many others, which are in the world as signs of the Holy Spirit. Personally, I am drawn to the communities whose roots are in the poorest neighbourhoods, or which welcome those who have been deeply wounded, like alcoholics, people coming out of prison, young people who are lost in drugs, delinquents or people with mental illnesses. There is not always much joy and fun in these communities, but there is great fidelity and acceptance of woundedness. The faces of the people who work in them are lined with fatigue. They don't have time for community meetings; they seldom have beautiful liturgies or even celebrations; often, they can only come to snatches of the Mass because their work is so demanding. But in these communities we feel the presence of

Jesus, who is close to the most rejected and wounded people of all.

As I think of all the communities throughout the world, struggling for growth, yearning to answer the call of Jesus and of the poor, I realise the need for a universal shepherd – a shepherd who yearns for unity, who has clarity of vision, who calls forth communities and who holds all people in prayer and in love, who is a guardian of unity and a servant of communion.

How long will it take before people realise this deep need for a universal shepherd? How long will it take for Roman Catholics to understand the depths of their gift and be confounded in humility, and to open themselves up to others in understanding and love? How long will it take them to recognise the beauty of the Ortho-dox Church with its sense of the sacred, and the beauty and gift of the Anglican and Protestant churches, especially with their love of Scripture, of announcing the Word, and their desire to live in the Holy Spirit? And today Protestant churches are discovering more and more the immensity of riches hidden in the Eucharist.

Yes. I yearn for this day of unity.

Roger Schutz, founder of Taizé, has a prophetic passion for unity and I would wish to have the same passion. In the Acts of the Council of Youth 1979 it is written:

A way exists to put an end to the scandal of the divisions among Christians and to allow the churches to join in a common creation: that every local community refer to a ministry of reconciliation at the heart of the People of God. These past few months, the eyes of many men and women have been opened more than ever before to the ministry of a universal pastor: 'attentive to serve humanity as such and not only Catholics, to defend above all and in all places rights of the human person and not only those of the Church'. (John XXIII)

The focal point of fidelity

Communities are born, flourish and then often degenerate and die. You only have to look at the history of communities and of religious orders to see this. The enthusiasm, the ardour, the generosity of their beginnings disappear as they gradually become comfortable; they become mediocre, and rules and law take precedence over spirit. There is nothing attractive about mediocre communities; they disappear.

It is important for communities to discover the focal point of fidelity which enables the spirit to stay strong, and what makes for deviation from it. There seem to me to be two essential – and linked – elements which lead to deviation: the search for security, or a weariness of insecurity, and a lack of fidelity to the initial vision which gave the foundation its spirit.

When a community is born, its founders have to struggle to survive and announce their ideal. So they find themselves confronted with contradictions and sometimes even persecution. These conditions oblige the members of the community to emphasise their commitment; they strengthen motivation and encourage people to go beyond themselves, to rely totally on Providence. Sometimes, only the direct intervention of God can save them. When they are stripped of all their wealth, of all security and human support, they must depend on God and the people around them who are sensitive to the witness of their life. They are obliged to remain faithful to prayer and the glow of their love; it is a question of life or death. Their total dependence guarantees their authenticity; their weakness is their strength.

But when a community has enough members to do all the work, when it has enough material goods, it can relax. It has strong structures. It is fairly secure. It's then that there is danger.

A French civil servant, working in the social services, once said to me, after I had explained in detail what l'Arche was: 'What you are doing is certainly very fine and I'm sure it is the ideal situation for handicapped people. But it depends completely on the motivation of the assistants. Does a government have the right to invest in a place which could disappear completely the day it can't find assistants who want to live that way? What guarantees can you give me?' Of course, I had none. But uncertainty about new assistants arriving and about how long those we have will stay is the insecurity and poverty of our communities. People don't come because of the hours or conditions or pay we offer: they come because of the community's atmosphere. The day we look for material ways in which to guarantee enough assistants, is the day that l'Arche will die. It can be tiring and even agonising to live in insecurity. But insecurity is one of the only guarantees that a community will go on deepening and progressing and remain faithful.

Our focal point of fidelity at l'Arche is to live with people who have a handicap, in the spirit of the Gospel and the Beatitudes. 'To live with' is different from 'to do for'. It doesn't simply mean eating at the same table and sleeping under the same roof. It means that we create relationships of *gratuité*, truth and interdependence, that we listen to our people, that we recognise and marvel at their gifts, and particularly their openness to God and their holiness. The day we become no more than professional workers and educational therapists is the day we stop being l'Arche – although of course 'living with' does not exclude this professional aspect.

Other communities have a different focus of fidelity. For the sisters of Mother Teresa, it is to bring help to the most wounded and rejected people of all. For the Little Sisters of Jesus, it is to live together in small groups, present to the poorest. For contemplative communities, it is to orientate the whole day to silent contemplation. For others, it is to live poverty. Each community must recognise its own focus of fidelity, its own essential vision. If it loses sight of this focal point, it will regress, because the foundation on which it was built has crumbled.

All members of the community have to be watchful that they remain insecure and so dependent on God, and to live in their own way the focal point of fidelity, the essential of the spirit. These two things have to be stressed. Otherwise, the community will fall into routine, doing things by the book. It will end up ossified.

At l'Arche, we have constantly to encourage each other in these two areas. All serious decisions must be seen in their light. Are we deciding this because we are afraid of insecurity? Does this decision reflect the essentials of our life – our faith that Jesus is living in the poor and that we are called to live with them and receive from them?

There is always a prophetic element in the birth of a community. It is a new way of life, set up in reaction to other ways, or to fill a gap in society or the Church. With time, this prophetic element tends to disappear and the community's members are in danger of looking not at the present, or to the future, but to the past, in an effort to maintain the spirit or tradition. But the prophetic spirit must always be there if the community is to remain alive and hopeful. There is a particular tension between the value of the past (spirit and tradition), the needs of the moment (a dialogue with society and its prevailing values), and the pull towards the future (prophecy).

The spirit of a community is more than a way of life. It is a hope, an incarnation of love. It is made concrete, though, in the way authority is seen, in the sharing, obedience, poverty and creativity of communities and their members in the propagation of life, or in the way they emphasise one activity rather than another. The spirit, in effect, decides what is essential in their life. It provides a scale of values.

But with time, this spirit may perhaps be dissipated, stifled and obscured by routine or custom. The job of the responsible people, and indeed all the members of the community, is to try constantly to purify the spirit, clarify it and live it more truly. It is in a way the gift of God to the family, the treasure which he has entrusted to it in a special way; it must always be there at the heart of the community. The community should always live in the spirit of its foundation. That doesn't mean living as it did in its founder's time. But it does mean having the same love, the same spirit and the same courage.

The spirit and spirituality of a community are embodied in particular traditions. It is important to respect these and explain their meaning and origin to new members, so that they do not become routine but are constantly renewed and remain alive.

There are traditions in the way the community lives important events like death, marriage and baptism, in the way birthdays are celebrated and new members welcomed. The songs and actions around these events are not so important in themselves; but they affirm the fact that we are truly members of the same family, with the same heart, soul and spirit. And they have been passed down to us by those who came before us and may now be with the Father. These traditions remind us that the community did not just happen, but was born at a specific moment, that it has perhaps been through some hard times and that what we are living today is the fruit of the work of those who came before us.

It is always good for individuals, communities, and indeed nations, to remember that their present situation is the result of the thousands of gestures of love or hate that came before. This obliges us to remember that the community of tomorrow is being born of our fidelity to the present. We are all links in the great chain of generations which makes up humanity. The fact that our lives are not long in the sum of time gives us a true perspective on our community, and the place of each of us in it. We discover that we are at the same time very insignificant and very important, because each of our actions is preparing the humanity of tomorrow; it is a tiny contribution to the construction of the huge and glorious final humanity.

Generating life

A community cannot remain static. It is not an end in itself. It is like a fire which must spread even at the risk of burning out. A moment comes when a community can only grow through separation, sacrifice and gift. The more it finds unity, the more it must be prepared in some sense to lose it, through the free gift of some of its members who will create other networks of love and communities of peace.

That is the meaning of life. Life reproduces itself. Growth means the appearance of flowers and fruits, which carry the seeds of new life. A community which jealously keeps its members to itself and doesn't take chances in this extraordinary work of procreation is running a far greater risk: the risk of withering away. If the corner isn't turned, if the evolution of a community towards greater giving is not encouraged, its members will become infantile, close to regression. They will become sterile and life will not flow through them. Like dead branches, they will be good only for the fire.

So many communities are dead because the people who carry responsibility in them have not known how to encourage their young members to give life in the procreation of new communities. The time of love has passed and they have come to a stage of sterility and frustration. It will then be hard to refind the forces of love and life.

The moment when life is given is different for each kind and type of community and for each person. For some members, it means leaving for far-off places, with all the risks that this can bring. A community which has reached maturity is able to give a brother or sister to support another community in distress. For others, giving life means more truth and warmth in their welcome of the poor, the marginal person, the stranger. For others again, giving life means taking on the role of shepherd in the community by helping all members see the beauty of life and free themselves from egoism. For yet others, it is discovering and accepting their contemplative role in the community; it is carrying their brothers and sisters and the wounded and rejected of the world in their prayers, bringing them to life in a mysterious and hidden way. Whatever the expression, to give life is to enter into the mystery of the Father. It is to work with him and become his instrument in the extraordinary work of procreation and liberation.

It is sometimes difficult for people who are responsible for distant communities to know what sort of bonds they should have with

the community they came from and the people who hold responsibility there. The important thing is that the distant communities
live deeply their own life and spirit and integrate with their own
neighbourhood. Many members of missionary communities live
a contradiction. They have come from a particular culture and
they have brought their own customs and ways of living, eating,
welcoming and celebrating to a foreign soil. The spirit they want
to transmit is so much born of their own culture that in the end
they transmit more of the culture than of the spirit. And their
neighbours are lost. They are often either shocked or seduced by
what is foreign to their own culture; they do not grasp the spirit.
And those among them who want to commit themselves to the
community are sometimes obliged to adopt customs which are
foreign to their own mentality.

Too often, the anxiety for unity with the 'mother-house', in a
simply material way, takes precedence over the dynamic concern
for love, the spirit and the goals of the community. Unity doesn't
come by ensuring that everyone is living in exactly the same way
across the world. It comes from a harmony of hearts in fidelity to
the initial spirit of the community, with the grace of the Holy
Spirit. Distant communities have to know how to die to some of
the elements of their own culture so that they can better live the
Beatitudes in their new one. They must have a great trust in God
who has sent them so far to make a covenant with a new people.

The concern of the 'mother-house' must be to help the new
community put down roots and so become a source of life where
it is. If the 'mother-house', takes this attitude, it will quickly
discover the grace of rejuvenation and openness which comes from
a multiplicity of communities. The distant communities, which
live in risk and difficulty, can become a source of hope for the
'mother-house', which in turn can offer them the security they
need to establish themselves in hard situations.

Expansion and taking root

The more a community grows and gives life, sometimes by sending some of its members far away, the deeper its roots must grow into its own soil. Expansion has to be accompanied by deepening. The more a tree grows, the stronger its roots must be; otherwise, it will be uprooted by the first storm. Jesus speaks of a house built on sand. A community's solid foundation is in the heart of God. It is God who is at the source of the community, and the more it grows and expands, the more it needs people who stay close to this source.

There is external growth, which is nearly always in expansion. But there is also internal and secret growth, which is a deeper rooting in prayer in Jesus, in greater love and forgiveness between brothers and sisters, and greater compassion and welcome. This growth is not visible but it creates a tangible atmosphere: a lighter joy, a denser silence, a peace which touches people's hearts and leads to a true experience of God.

Born from a wound

There is a mysterious link between suffering, offering and the gift of life – between sacrifice and expansion.

In one of our communities in India, a man with a quite severe handicap, who had only been with us for a short time, drowned in a well. An old friend of his father told us: 'A just man must die if a work of God is to live.'

I'm deeply convinced that people of action and of light can do nothing unless they are in communion and rely on those who accept their own suffering, immobility and prayer, and offer these to bring life. Men and women of prayer, hidden in monasteries and hermitages, sometimes living in great pain, are like hidden pumps irrigating dry land. Some people are like dirty hoses; others are doing the pumping; others are being watered. People who are old or sick and offer themselves to God can become the most precious members of a community – lightening conductors of

grace, secret pumps. There is a mystery in the secret strength of
those whose bodies are broken, who seem to do nothing all day,
but who remain in the presence of God. Their immobility obliges
them to keep their minds and hearts fixed on the essential, on the
source of life itself. Their suffering and agony bears fruit; they
give life.

> Look at your own poverty
> welcome it
> cherish it
> don't be afraid
> share your death
> because thus you will share your love and your life.

Some communities are composed entirely of old people. Their
time of expansion seems to be over and it is probably now too
late for a young person to come into them. The gaiety and peace
of these communities is sometimes astonishing. Their members
know that their community is dying, but they don't mind. They
want to live fully and to the end the grace they have been given.
These communities have a lot to bring to our world: they teach
us to accept setbacks and to die in peace. And it is their acceptance
of their suffering and offering of their sacrifice that brings to birth
new and dynamic communities.

In other communities, by contrast, old people are in terrible
anguish in the face of their sterility. They have not discovered that
this sterility can be transformed into a gift of life by offering and
sacrifice.

Sometimes during a meeting of the International Council of
l'Arche, we speak of one of our communities as a problem. It has
been in crisis for such a long time; assistants do not want to stay
and the people with a handicap are not well, and so on. We forget
that before being a problem, the community is poor and in pain.
If a poor person is a source of life and not just an object of charity,
so too is a poor community. In some mysterious way God is
present there. The cry of a community in pain is also the cry of

the poor. We must approach such a community with great love and respect.

From the wound at the heart of Christ on the cross came water and blood, the sign of the community of believers which is the Church. Life sprang from this cross; death was transformed into resurrection. That is the mystery of life born from death.

The role of Providence

Before they enter community, people feel a call or attraction to a life oriented towards God and the values of love and justice, instead of towards the more egoistical and visible values of possession, comfort, prestige and power. This attraction can be very weak at first, but if we respond to it, it gradually grows and becomes incarnate in a true desire and deep need to give ourselves to God and to our brothers and sisters, especially the poorest among them. This call is already a certain experience of God.

With time and through contact with our brothers and sisters and mutual commitment, there is the discovery of Providence. God has called us not only as individuals, but with others. We have all heard and followed the same call. It is God who has brought us together and inspired us to love each other. It is he who is at the heart of community.

This experience of Providence grows stronger with time, with the discovery that God has watched over the community in times of trial which could have destroyed it. Serious tensions have been resolved, people have arrived exactly when they were needed, there has been unexpected financial or material help, someone has found inner freedom and healing.

With time, the members of the community realise that God is close and is watching over them with love and tenderness. Then the experience of God is no longer personal but communal, and this generates peace and a luminous certainty. It enables the community to accept difficulties, times of trial, need or weakness with a new serenity. It even brings the courage the community needs to keep going through daily setbacks and sufferings, because it knows from experience that God is present and will answer its cry. But this recognition of the action of God in community life demands a very great fidelity.

Nor does the recognition lead to a sort of irresponsibility, a feeling that there is nothing to do because God will provide. Far from it. In fact, the recognition demands that a community cling to the essentials of its vocation, whether this is prayer, welcoming the poor, or openness to the Spirit. God will only watch over us if we try courageously to remain faithful and true in our search for the community's final goals and unity. And God responds to our needs only when we are working, sometimes very hard, to find true solutions. Sometimes he waits until we have exhausted our human resources before he answers our call.

The dangers of becoming rich

At the start of a community, God's action can often be felt very tangibly – in the gift of a house or money, the arrival of the right person at the right time, or other external signs. Because of its poverty, the community is completely dependent on him. It calls and he responds. It is faithful in prayer. It lives in insecurity, it welcomes whoever knocks on the door, it shares what it has with the poor, and tries to take all its decisions in the light of God. In these early days, it is often misunderstood by society. People judge it as utopian or quite simply crazy; to a degree, it is persecuted.

Then with time, people see that this crazy project is working; they discover its values and its radiance. The community is no longer persecuted; it is admired and becomes renowned. It has friends which meet its needs. Gradually, it becomes rich. It begins to make judgements. It becomes powerful.

Then there is danger. The community is no longer poor and humble; it is self-satisfied. It no longer turns to God as it did before; it no longer begs his help. Strong in its own experience, it knows how to go about things. It no longer takes decisions in the light of God; prayer becomes tepid. It closes its doors to the poor and to the living God. It becomes proud. It needs to be jolted and to go through some serious trials if it is to refind its child-like quality and its dependence on God.

The prophet Ezekiel describes the Jewish community as a woman. When she was a child, struggling in her own blood, God rescued her, cared for her and saved her life. He took care of her. Then, at the time of love, he covered her with his shade; he made her beautiful and married her. She became a Queen. And by her union with her King and Bridegroom, she became powerful. Then she turned her eyes from her King; she looked at herself and believed she was the source of life. She found herself beautiful and looked for other lovers. She prostituted herself and was disgraced. But, in the depths of her poverty and despair, God was waiting for her, faithful to his love. He took her back as in the time of her youth, because he is tender and good, slow to anger and full of mercy, because he is the God of forgiveness (Ezekiel 16).

The first sin of a community is to turn its eyes from the One who called it to life, to look at itself instead. The second sin is to find itself beautiful and to believe itself to be a source of life. If it does this, it turns away from God and begins to compromise with society and the world; it becomes renowned. The third sin is that of despair. The community discovers that it is not a source of life, that it is poor, that it lacks vitality and creativity. And so it withdraws into its sadness, into the darkness of its poverty and death.

But God, like the father of the prodigal son, does not cease to wait. Communities which have set aside the inspiration of God to rely on their own power should know how to return humbly to ask his forgiveness.

The risk of growth

When I started l'Arche, we were poor. I remember an old woman who came every Friday night to bring us soup, and others who brought us small gifts of food and money. Now, after twenty-five years, when there is a house for sale in the village, its owners come first to see if we want it – at an inflated price, of course. We are known as the rich people of the village, even though our money comes from state subsidies. In the beginning, professional people ignored us. Now they come to visit us from miles around, even if they still find us a bit crazy. There were five or six of us in the first l'Arche house; now we are over four hundred, not just in Trosly but scattered through neighbouring villages and the town of Compiègne.

Sometimes the assistants complain that l'Arche has become too big, that it is no longer possible to know each other well, as we used to. That is true; there is a danger in growth. But there is also a grace. And I have the feeling that we have followed the signs of Providence at the different stages of our growth. The danger is that we close in on our success, forgetting our first inspiration. The danger is that we become a professionally competent centre which has forgotten *gratuité* and community as a place of communion, that we put so much emphasis on structures and the rights of assistants that we forget that handicapped people need to be with brothers and sisters who give themselves to them and are committed to them. The danger is that we forget how to welcome and no longer see people with a handicap as a gift of God and a source of life.

Some communities should stay small, poor and prophetic, signs of the presence of God in a world which is becoming more and more materialistic. But other communities are called to grow. Their mission is to help not just a few privileged people but a growing number, to show that it is possible to keep a spirit alive in a large centre, to create structures which are sensitive to people and to exercise authority in a way that is both humane and Christian. The mission of the small, prophetic communities is to show a path. Larger communities must live the challenge of this path by creating structures which are just and good for a large number of people.

Personally, I'm happy that l'Arche in Trosly has grown. Each day brings the challenge of trying to live community with a large number of people, of creating structures which allow for the greatest possible participation and give each person the chance to take responsibility and initiatives, while maintaining a unity of spirit. I am happy that we have been able to welcome a large number of people who are wounded and in distress, and that so many of them have been able, after a time with us, to find work and live independently, while keeping in touch with us.

The important thing is to remain open to the signs of Providence while growing, to go on listening to the cry and the needs of handicapped people who are at different stages of their lives, to continue to be welcoming, to be ready to found communities if there seems to be a need for them, and to accept new kinds of poverty each day – for material poverty is not the only one. The danger is that we close in on ourselves and our achievements. We have to pray that we keep going further along the road of insecurity.

One of the only things I regret about the growth of l'Arche is that we have not worked enough with the people of the village; our growth has been rather at their expense and against their wishes. Now there is a good understanding with them, but there is still work to be done if l'Arche is to be integrated into the life of the village. It is important too, that all a community's growth doesn't happen in the same village or neighbourhood.

I was a stranger and you welcomed me

One of the risks that God will always ask of a community is that it welcomes visitors, especially the poorest people, the ones who disturb us. Very often God brings a particular message to the community through an unexpected guest, letter or telephone call. The day the community starts to turn away visitors and the unexpected, the day it calls a halt, is the day it is in danger of shutting itself off from the action of God. Did not Jesus say: 'I was a stranger and you welcomed me'? Staying open to Providence demands a very great availability. It has nothing to do with hiding behind structures, laws, traditions, and what has worked in the past. It demands a quality of attentiveness from each member of the community and an awareness of daily reality with all its unexpected happenings and insecurity. We are too quick to want to defend our past traditions, and so to shut ourselves off from the new evolution that God wants of us. We want human security, not dependence on God.

At the same time it is important that the members of the community remember together, and with the new people who arrive, what Providence has done for them, and that they give thanks for it. The history of a community is important. It should be told and retold, written and repeated. We are so quick to forget what God has done! We have to remember time and again that God is at the origin of everything, and that it is he who has watched lovingly over the community. Thus it is that we refind the hope and the boldness we need to take new risks, and accept difficulties and suffering with courage and perseverance.

The whole of Holy Scripture, as the Jews recognise so well, is a constant reminder of how God has watched over his people. It is when we remember this that we find the confidence to continue without stumbling.

Be zealous and repent!

In the Book of Revelation, the Angel says to the church in Laodicea:

> I know your works; you are neither cold nor hot. Would that you were cold or hot! So, because you are lukewarm, and neither cold nor hot, I will spew you out of my mouth. For you say, I am rich, I have prospered and I need nothing; not knowing that you are wretched, pitiable, poor, blind and naked.

Therefore I counsel you to buy from me gold refined by fire, that you may be rich [in faith], and white garments to clothe you [the clothing of the covenant] and to keep the shame of your nakedness from being seen, and salve to anoint your eyes, that you may see. Those whom I love, I reprove and chasten. (Rev. 3:15–19).

These words can be applied to many of our communities and to each of us, myself first of all.

'Be zealous and repent! Behold, I stand at the door and knock; if anyone hears my voice and opens the door, I will come in to him and eat with him, and he with me' (Rev: 3:19–20). It is sad to see communities which have let fall their first love (Rev. 2:4). We all need to be encouraged and stimulated to repent and set off again with a new enthusiasm and ardour. But for that, we have to reopen the doors of our hearts and let Jesus enter: 'And I will betroth you to me for ever; I will betroth you to me in righteousness and in justice, in steadfast love and in mercy. I will betroth you to me in faithfulness, and you shall know the Lord' (Hos. 2:19–20).

When we are going through difficult times in community, there is a text of Isaiah which I find brings me support and light. The prophet is asking what kind of fasting will be pleasing to God – which has to do not with renouncing food, but with gestures of love towards the poor:

> . . . to loose the bonds of wickedness,
> to undo the thongs of the yoke,
> to let the oppressed go free . . .
> to share your bread with the hungry,
> and bring the homeless poor into your house;
> when you see the naked, to cover him . . .

If we do that, we shall be luminous as the dawn; our deep wound, the inner sores of sin, will be healed.

> Your righteousness shall go before you,
> the glory of the Lord shall be your rear guard,

You will be enveloped in the protection of God.
And in the hard times
the Lord will respond when you call;
If you cry to him from the depths of your poverty,
from your weakness and your weariness,
He will say, Here I am.
He will reveal himself to you.
The Lord will guide you continually,
He will nourish you in the desert,
He will give you water in arid places,
He will give you strength,
He will make your bones strong.   (cf. Isa. 58:6–12)

And then, supported, guided, gathered in by the Lord, we shall
be like irrigated gardens, full of flowers and life. We shall be like
inexhaustible springs of water; we shall be able to spill over a
parched humanity which is dying of thirst.

That is God's promise, if we give ourselves to the hungry, to
those in distress and insecurity, to those who feel alone.

It is when we are close to the poor and defenceless – who need
special protection for precisely that reason – that we are close to
God.

When our communities become tepid, we should open our
hearts and our doors to the poorest and respond faithfully to their
cry.

Then God will always be there to sustain and guide us.

5

Nourishment: Give Us Our Daily Bread

Growth needs nourishment

Human beings need bread if they are to grow. If they don't eat, they die. And if they are to grow spiritually, they, like plants, need sun, water, air and soil. The soil is the community – the place where they are planted, take root, grow, give fruit and die so that others may live.

In the parable of the sower, Jesus says that though we may welcome the word of the Kingdom with joy, this word can be stifled after a time by trials and difficulties, by worldly cares and the attractions of wealth.

We human beings are made up of contradictions. Part of us is attracted by the light and by God, and wants to care for our brothers and sisters. Another part of us wants frivolity, possessions, domination or success; it wants to be surrounded by approving friends, who will ward off sadness, depression or aggression. We are so deeply divided that we will reflect equally an environment which tends towards the light and concern for others, and one which scorns these values and encourages the desires for power and pleasure. As long as our deepest motivation is not clear to us and as long as we have not chosen the people and the place of our growth in its light, we will remain weak and inconsistent, as changeable as weathercocks.

A community reflects the people who make it up. It has energy founded on hope, but there is also weariness, a search for security and a fear of evolving toward maturity of love and responsibility; it often reflects our fear of dying to our personal instincts.

To grow on the journey toward wholeness and a greater radiance of justice and truth, people, like a community itself, need real nourishment. Without it, the energies of hope will waste away. Instead, there will be desire for pleasure and comfort, or a depressed weariness, or aggression, or a legalistic and bureaucratic approach.

Cultures in rich societies are inciting people to an easy way of life. The values of wealth, power and pleasure are seductive. But the gospel values are calling us to love, and to love even our enemies; to be present to the poor and to live poorly, trusting in God; to be peace-makers in a world of war. In order to be able to live these values, we need a new energy, an inner force. This energy and force come from the Holy Spirit. If we cut ourselves off from this energy, if we do not nourish the life of the Spirit within us, we will die to these values. We will be overwhelmed by other forces driving us to comfort, security and pleasure.

Each individual person in a community must be nourished in love. If not, he or she will sooner or later find him or herself in opposition to the life of the community and its demands of love and of forgiveness. These people then become like dead weights. They tend to pull the community down; they criticise decisions; they drain away joy.

But the community as a whole, as a body, must also be nourished in love – not just its individual members. Communities as a whole can also fall into lukewarmness and mediocrity. They can become like hotels, where each person is locked in by him or herself. These communities tend to pull individuals down into sadness and lukewarmness. I remember a sister telling me that after a retreat, she had felt called to spend more quiet time with Jesus in the chapel. The other sisters seemed threatened by her newly found fervour and prayerfulness, by her desire to be closer to Jesus. One of them said to her: 'Who do you think you are, Teresa of Avila?' This community had obviously fallen into mediocrity; the body was sick. Communities like that need a strong form of nourishment to renew their energy and trust, to find new faith and a sense of belonging in love. They need strong moments of grace so that the body may be recreated, renewed and brought back to that which is essential.

To begin with, a community is enthusiastic about living the Beatitudes depending totally on God. The members live poorly and accept insecurity and hard living. Little by little, through fatigue, perhaps ill health or simply growing older or other factors – and frequently after the founder has died – other needs appear, such as security and comfort. There may be an exaggerated way of living the gospels, founded more on human generosity and a desire for heroism; there may be an unhealthy rejection of personal needs and rest, and a lack of respect for one's humanity. If this period of 'heroism' has not really been inspired by the Holy Spirit, and if the members when they were young in the community were not really cared for, then later on, when they are older, there can be a strong reaction by these members towards personal needs and comfort. There can also be a waning in generosity and in accepting poverty and insecurity, through a lack of faith and spiritual nourishment. Communities need wisdom to discern the nourishment they need in order to become truly alive in the Spirit.

Because of our individual richness and complexity, we all need different kinds of nourishment on this journey towards wholeness, and holiness. Some of these feed our heart and ability to relate, some our intellect, others our capacity for generosity and action, others again our search for God and hunger for the infinite. However, some people over-nourish one part of themselves and neglect others; they then grow unbalanced and lack unity.

In some communities, there are very generous and active people, who neglect the richness of their own hearts, the secret part of themselves. Others listen well but need to feed their capacities for generosity and action. Others again seek the presence of God in the secrecy of prayer but have to make an effort to hear the cries of their brothers and sisters and to relate to them.

The journey towards wholeness implies a deepening of personal life in peaceful encounters with God and others, while living community life fully and assuming responsibilities towards society, the Church and the universe. This journey is a long one and we will need plenty of personal and communal nourishment during it – food for the heart, for the mind and for the spirit. What is important is that our deepest motivations be touched, creating in us a renewed spirit of hope.

We are all in danger of living superficially, on the periphery of ourselves. We tend to react to immediate stimuli, to demands from individuals who confront us and to the need for 'urgent' action; we tend to flee from the treasure hidden within us. When for one reason or another, we become aware of it, or when it is touched by an external event, we are nourished. We are nourished by everything that stirs that which is deepest in us and brings it to consciousness. This may be a word, a reading, a meeting or a suffering: all these can reawaken our deepest heart, recentre us, strengthen our faith, and renew our hope. All this can give us a greater desire to live in poverty, in insecurity, putting our trust in God.

Community life demands that we constantly go beyond our own resources. If we do not have the spiritual nourishment we need, we will close in on ourselves and on our own comfort and security, or throw ourselves into work as an escape. We will throw up walls around our sensitivity; we will perhaps be polite and obedient, but we will not love. And when you do not love, there is no hope and no joy. It is terrible to see people living sadly in community, without love. To live with *gratuité*, we have to be constantly nourished.

It is terrible to see people who are living in a so-called community that has become a boarding house for bachelors! It is terrible to see elders in a community who have closed up their hearts, lost their initial enthusiasm and become critical and cynical.

Nourishment is important for growth, but we also have to be

careful not to eat or drink poison. The spiritual life and the life of love and compassion can be severely stifled, if not killed, by some foods. One of these poisons is television, when it is looked at without discernment or just because one has nothing better to do. Television provides images and information and stimulates emotions but cuts people off from relationship. It is possible to look at television with great passivity, just swallowing it in; this maims the capacity to react, which is inherent in relationship. Television may stimulate the imagination but generally does not feed the heart.

Food for each day

If we are to remain faithful to the daily round, we need daily manna. It may be ordinary, a bit tasteless. But it is the manna of fidelity to the covenant, to responsibility, to the small things of everyday life. It is the manna of meetings, of friendship, of looks and smiles that say 'I love you' and warm the heart.

The essential nourishment is fidelity to the thousand and one small demands of each day, the effort to love and forgive 'the enemy' and to welcome and accept community structures, with all this brings by way of co-operation with authority. It is fidelity in listening to the poor of the community, in accepting a simple and unheroic life. It is fidelity in directing personal projects towards the good of the community and its poorest members and in renouncing purely personal prestige.

This fidelity is based on the belief that it is Jesus who has called us to this covenant with the poor, our brothers and sisters. If he has chosen and called us, he will help us in the small things of everyday life. If we accept everyday responsibility, with a humble and trusting heart, he will accompany us and give us strength.

It is sad to see people forced to leave their community to find their nourishment elsewhere. Of course we all have to get away from time to time to rest and refind perspective. But it is essential for all of us to find the nourishment we need in daily life itself. If structures and meetings seem too heavy, and create tension and a sense of oppression, there is something wrong with either the community or the individual. Working structures and meetings should be nourishing. Sometimes organisation and structures are set against *gratuité*, just as professional competence is set against compassion, as if these values were incompatible. In community we have to live structures in *gratuité* and in love, and use professional techniques with compassion.

If we are in community only to 'do things', its daily life will not nourish us; we will be constantly thinking ahead, because we can always find something urgent to be done. If we live in a poor neighbourhood or with people in distress, we are constantly challenged. Daily life is only nourishing when we have discovered the wisdom of the present moment and the presence of God in small things. It is only nourishing when we have given up fighting reality and accept it, discovering the message and gift of the moment. If we see housework or cooking simply as chores which have to be got through, we will get tired and irritable; we will not be able to see the beauty around us. But if we discover that we live with God and our brothers and sisters through what has to be done in the present moment, we become peaceful. We stop looking to the future; we take time to live. We are no longer in a hurry because we have discovered that there is gift and grace in the present of the book-keeping, the meetings, the chores and the welcome.

Every day we ask our Father to give us our daily bread. We are asking then for nourishment for our hearts, so that we will be alerted to the will of the Father and the needs of our brothers and sisters.

Jesus said that his nourishment was to do his Father's will. And it's true that this communion with our Father is the essential nourishment for living our daily life.

Times of wonder and of awe

Many people in community tend to see the times they are alone as times of revitalisation, as opposed to the times of 'dedication' or 'generosity' they spend with the community. This means that they have not discovered the nourishment of community.

This comes in the moments when together we discover that we make up a single body, that we belong to each other and that God has called us to be together as a source of life for each other and for the world. These times of wonder and awe become celebration. They are like a deep, peaceful and sometimes joyful realisation of our unity and call, of that which is essential in our lives and of the way that God is leading us. They are a gift, a message of God in the community which awakens the heart, stimulates the intelligence and gives back hope. We rejoice and give thanks that we are together; we become more conscious of God's love and call for the community.

These times of wonder and awe can come when we are together, at the Eucharist, and in relaxation after meals. A community should be alert to welcome or encourage these times of grace. We have to seize the moment at each meeting to say the word which will create unity or make people relax and laugh, or bring us back to essentials.

These peak moments can come on all sorts of occasions – perhaps a deep warm silence after a brother or sister has shared his or her call, weakness, or need for prayer; perhaps during a celebration when we are singing, playing and laughing together. So every community gathering must be carefully prepared, whether it is a liturgy, a meal, a weekend, a sharing or a Christmas or Easter celebration. Each of these can be an occasion for wonder and awe, a moment of the presence of God. When something unexpected happens during a celebration – as it often does – we become conscious of a moment of grace for the community, a momentary presence of God, a deeper silence; our hearts are touched. We have to know how to make these moments last, savour them and let them deepen us and our unity, and renew our hearts.

When Moses met God in the burning bush and heard his name called out, he hid his face; he was afraid to look at God and to be in his presence. He was struck with awe.

There are special times in community when we too are struck with awe. I have seen this particularly in dramatic circumstances – a serious accident, an unexpected illness or the death of one of the members of the community. Everyone is brought back to essentials; squabblings and tensions disappear or appear so irrelevant. God, in all the pain of the accident, seems to be present, reminding us that he is above us and in us all; that eternity transcends time and that we are all on a journey to God.

An assistant was recently telling me about his struggles. He had felt called to celibacy, and this had been confirmed by a priest and by several years of peace. Then suddenly he fell in love with a girl. He had let this experience deepen without looking too much at the question of celibacy. When he spoke to the priest, and prayed, it seemed evident to him that he had already given his heart to Jesus in celibacy. He and the priest discussed this and decided that he should break the relationship. He was in great inner pain, but he knew that it was right. He came to tell me about what had happened. As I listened to him, I was deeply moved. I felt I was witnessing a special call and presence of God. I was in awe in front of this man who was committing himself to follow Jesus.

We must be attentive to these moments of peace which renew us and create in us a desire to be close to Jesus and to the poor; which call us to greater fidelity. Not only are we called to welcome them, but also to reflect on them, for in themselves and in the circumstances they are given, they constitute a message. Jesus is telling us something through them. He is calling us to change; he is calling us to deeper commitment.

Laughter is an important food. It is healing and nourishing for all the members of a community to burst out laughing until the tears run down their faces. We are not laughing at each other; we are laughing with each other.

Affirmation from outside

Those of us who live all the time in community are in danger of forgetting the special gift which God has given us; sometimes we can be blinkered by daily life. It is very easy to forget that the outside world has its problems too; we tend to see only our own troubles. So we need outsiders to tell us what is unique in our community and remind us of what is positive. Members of a community often need to be encouraged and affirmed, to hear that what they are doing is important for humanity and the Church.

It is good that different types of Christian community meet to share their hope and their vision. It is good too that Christians meet to see how the Spirit is acting among them. It is encouraging and strengthening to discover the network of the Holy Spirit and the marvels of God across the world. We realise then that we are not alone with our problems and that there is a universal hope.

It is important to know what the Spirit is doing in the Church, because he is always raising up, providentially, men and women to show us new ways. The most prophetic are sometimes the most hidden during their lifetime. Few people knew Thérèse of Lisieux or Charles de Foucauld before their deaths.

Today Roger Shutz and his brothers in Taizé are truly prophetic. Their community is bringing forth much fruit. Truly the Taizé community, and Brother Roger's words and gestures, are a sign of God in our broken world. Their yearning for unity amongst Christian churches is a sign of the yearning of God. It is important to listen to such signs and to integrate them into the vision of our own community. The same is true of the vision of Mother Teresa; she also is a sign of the presence of God in our world. She is reminding all our communities that we must be open to the poorest and the weakest of our world, for they are a presence of Christ. Such prophets are showing us a way.

Vatican II announced so clearly that the Holy Spirit is working in all the churches, not just in the Roman Catholic Church. It seems to me that this teaching is not always put into practice. It remains a theory, a doctrine, a vision. Shouldn't we all look at the consequences of it? Roman Catholics are often enclosed within their own groups, their own club, their own community. They are not sufficiently alert to see the signs of the Spirit present in other churches, other communities, or in people of other religions. Yet the Spirit of God is at work there. God is speaking to them; he is revealing himself there. We must be attentive to others, to notice in them the presence of the Holy Spirit. If we confine ourselves only to the workings of the Spirit in 'our' group or in 'our' church, we will miss something; we will be lacking in a gift of the Spirit. Communities have so much to offer to each other. They can offer each other their food, their nourishment.

But of course, in order to really appreciate the Spirit working in the hearts of other communities and churches, we have to be well rooted in our own; we have to belong. Otherwise we risk living in some confusion, without roots.

The Word as bread

Announcing the Word can be a powerful means of piercing armours and routines to let the living waters flow. It can be a nourishment which brings strength, energy and a new hope. But only words that touch the heart can do this. It is these words, not those which are abstract, based on research or reason, which reveal the faith, hope and love of the speaker. It is they which are like a heat-giving flame or water which brings life to parched earth. The logic and content of what is said is less important than the faith and love with which it is conveyed. The tone of voice shows whether the speaker wants to seem brilliant and knowledgeable, or whether he wants to nourish, to give freely and witness humbly to what has been given and freely received. The talks which nourish come from people who allow God to speak through their lips. These talks come from the deep, hidden and silent places where God lives, to nourish those same places in the listeners. The words must arise out of silence and peace and lead back to silence and peace. It makes the call come alive and brings the listeners back to what is essential in the community.

Some people have the gift of speaking to the whole community, others to smaller groups. Those who feel incapable of speaking at all often believe that speaking demands great competence and a wealth of ideas. But people are touched by the simplest words – the ones that come with humility, truth, and love. There is nothing in intellectually complex sermons to nourish hearts; they come from the head and are sterile. Members of a community need people who witness to the Gospel and their own experience, and share their hope as well as their weakness and difficulties.

To listen to a living word flowing from the heart of someone is not the same thing as to read the same message from a book. As we listen to a person, it is a life and a spirit that are communicated. And God uses this living word to give life.

Those who announce the Word must remember this. They are called not to give good ideas to people but to communicate life and reveal communion.

Sometimes it is said that for people with a handicap words should be replaced by music, pictures and mime. It is true that many cannot understand abstract ideas. But many are sensitive to loving words flowing from the heart. I am touched as I watch their attentive faces as they listen to the words of Father Thomas during the Eucharist.

Words can truly become a sacrament bringing the light and the presence of Jesus. Didier, who has a quite serious mental handicap, told me 'when Father Gilbert was talking, my heart was burning'.

The Word of God, of Jesus and of the Gospel are a bread of life of which we can never have enough. They touch our deepest being.

A community – and especially a Christian one – will always be running against the tide of society, with its individualistic values of wealth and comfort and resulting rejection of the people who get in the way of these. A Christian community constantly calls its members to share, welcome, become poorer and go beyond their resources to a truer love.

So a true Christian community will always be a stumbling block, a question mark and a source of unease for society. The people around it will very quickly feel challenged, and the community will either be rejected because it reveals the egoisms in people's hearts, or be attractive because people sense in it a source of life and warmth. A Christian community will often be persecuted or rejected; people may belittle its ideal to make it less of a threat.

The great dangers to a community are the cares of the world and the attraction of wealth. It always needs warm and inspiring talks which remind it of these dangers, bring back hope and strengthen its desire to walk against the tide of society.

Leaders of communities must continually announce the vision and remind members of the call of God; priests and spiritual guides must announce the vision and remind members of the call of God. Each member is called to announce the vision and remind the others of the call of God. Day in and day out, we must remind each other with words of enthusiasm and of love. We forget so quickly and fall into the ways of the world, seeking security, shunning the Beatitudes, refusing to forgive enemies.

In many monasteries the abbot or abbess gives a commentary every morning on the Rule, with applications for daily life. A monk was telling me recently that this daily commentary is essential. 'How could we remain united and loving without it?' he asked. Leaders of communities should take heed.

People need an intellectual understanding of the significance of their community. Individual and communal spirituality are not enough. They need a clear reminder of the meaning and place of the community in today's world and in the history of salvation. It is important too to be reminded of the precise goals of the community, its call and its origins. In too many communities, the essentials are obscured in a thousand and one activities. Their members no longer know why they are together or to what they should be witnessing. They discuss the details but forget what brought them together.

Communities today must be reminded that they are a path to peace. So many in our world today are suffering from isolation, war and oppression. So much money is spent on the construction of armaments. Many, many young people are in despair because of the danger of nuclear war. Today as never before, we need communities of welcome; communities that are a sign of peace in a world of war. There is no point in praying for peace in the Middle East, for example, if we are not peace-makers in our own community; if we are not forgiving those in our community who have hurt us or with whom we find it difficult to live. Young people, as well as those who are older, are sensitive to this vision of peace. It must continually be announced so that hearts and minds are nourished.

Rest and relaxation: 'the Sabbath day'

I often hear talk of people committed to social action or in communities who are 'burned-out'. These people have been too generous; they have thrown themselves into activity which has finally destroyed them emotionally. They have not known how to relax and to be refreshed. Those in responsibility must teach such people the discipline of physical rest and relaxation, and the need for spiritual nourishment and for fixing clear priorities. They must also set an example.

Many people get burned out because, perhaps unconsciously, some part of them is rejecting the need to relax and find a harmonious rhythm of life for themselves. In their over-activity they are fleeing from something, sometimes because of deep unconscious guilt feelings. Maybe they do not really want to put down roots in the community and stay for the long haul. They may be too attached to their function, perhaps even identified with it. They want to control everything, and perhaps also want to appear to be perfect, or at least a perfect hero! They have not yet learned how to live; they are not yet free inside themselves; they have not yet discovered the wisdom of the present moment, which can frequently mean saying 'no' to people.

These people need a spiritual guide to help them look at themselves and discover why they have not the freedom to stop, and what is the cause of their compulsive need to do things. They need someone who can help them stand back and relax enough to clarify their own motives and become people living with other people, children among other children. God has given each of us an intelligence. It may not be very great, but it is great enough for us to reflect on what we need in order to live what we are called to live – community.

These over-active people, it seems, can be fleeing from their own cry for friendship and love, from their own sensitivity and maybe from their inner anguish and agitation. They may be afraid of their emotions, of their own sexuality. They need to reflect on their own deep needs and to refind the child in themselves which is crying because it feels alone. Our bodies need to relax, but so do our hearts, in secure and unthreatening relationships.

Many people are tense because they have not yet entered into the collective conscience of their community; they have not yet surrendered to its gift and call. They have not really made the passage from 'the community for myself' to 'myself for the community', perhaps because their fragility makes them want to prove something to themselves and to others, or because, fundamentally, they have come to the community as a refuge. They will only relax when they have discovered their own gift and put it decisively at the community's service, when they truly desire to die to individualism and to belong to the community.

I once spent an evening with some Franciscans who share an apartment in the black quarter of Chicago. I very much liked their prior, who demanded a real discipline of the novices. They had to sleep for a certain number of hours a night and eat well. 'If we do not care for our bodies, and if we do not find a rhythm of life we can sustain in the years to come,' he said, 'it is not worth us being here. Our job is to stay. It is too easy to come and live among the poor for the experience, to exploit them for our own spiritual ends and then to leave. What we have to do is stay.'

Rest is one of the most important personal resources, and it has a whole discipline of its own. Sometimes, when we are over-tired, we tend to flit about, doing nothing and spending long hours talking into the night when we would do better to get more sleep. We all have to find our individual rhythm of relaxation and rest. A lot of aggression and conflicts have somatic causes. Some assistants in our communities would do well occasionally to take a long hot bath, go to bed and sleep for twelve or fourteen hours!

Before they come into community, many people live the sort of life which allows them to set their own pace of leisure and relaxation. When they arrive in community, they have to be constantly attentive to others. So it isn't surprising that after a time they become tired and even depressed. They will begin to wonder whether they are in the right place; they will become aware of anger in themselves, and often the least frustration becomes intolerable. This isn't surprising, either; they have not found their rhythm of relaxation in their new life; they are too strung up by their wish to do the right thing. They have not found the right nourishment for their hearts. When we come into community we have to take heed of these somatic changes. We have to be very patient with our bodies and learn how to re-create ourselves and how to rest.

It seems strange to say that we have to be disciplined in rest, relaxation and nourishment. So often discipline is equated to work and relaxation to 'no discipline'. If we eat things that make us sick or unable to function well, we are lacking discipline. If we do not choose the nourishment we need or do not get sufficient sleep, we are lacking in discipline.

It is never easy to find the harmony between rest, relaxation and nourishment on one hand, and generosity and availability on the other. Only the Holy Spirit can teach us to love ourselves sufficiently to be able to give our lives as totally as possible. If we are not well, in good shape, joyful and nourished, we will not give life to others; instead, we shall communicate sadness and emptiness.

When we are young we need to *do* lots of things – even for Jesus and the Kingdom. There is so much life and energy in us. And, of course, there is the risk of over-doing and of becoming *too* responsible, of wanting to be the saviours of the world! This has always been a danger for me. In 1976, my body reacted and I fell sick and was in hospital for two months. This sickness was a turning point in my life. It brought me back to the earth of my body; it taught me to slow down, to listen rather than to speak or do; to relax in communion rather than to accomplish.

The more intense and difficult community life becomes, and the more tension and struggles it produces, then the more we need times of relaxation. When we feel strung up, tense and incapable of praying or listening, then we should take some rest – or even get away for a few days.

Some people don't know what to do with free time. They spend hours just sitting about and talking. It is sad if people have no interest outside the community, if they have given up reading, if they don't enjoy simple pleasures like walking and listening to music. We have to help each other keep alive the personal interests which help us relax and re-create us.

It is always good to have a 'grandmother' in the community who can remind its members that they have a body and emotions, that they often turn molehills into mountains and that they could do worse than to take a good rest!

It is easy to be generous for a few months or even years. But to

be continually present to others, and not only present but nourishing, to keep going in a fidelity which is reborn each morning,
demands a discipline of body and spirit. We need a disciplined
spiritual and intellectual nourishment.

The Jewish people honour the Sabbath; it is a day of rest and it is
the day of the Lord.

We all need a sabbath day, a day in the week when we allow
ourselves to be refreshed and reborn; a day when we spend more
time in prayer or a day when we seek more solitude. The more
people live constantly with others in community life, the more
they need this day of solitude. 'Come to me all you who labour
and are heavily burdened, and I will give you rest,' says Jesus.

Food for thought

It is important to feed the intelligence. It is important to understand
nature and the wonders of the universe, and so reach a deeper
understanding of the history of mankind and of salvation. Each of
our minds is made differently; there are a thousand and one doors
into the meaning of things and their mystery.

One of the dangers of our time is that information is reaching
saturation point and we only register superficial knowledge. It is
good to focus our intelligence on a tiny fragment of this huge
body of knowledge which reflects the hugeness of the universe, of
things visible and invisible. If we look more deeply at a particular
aspect – whether this is the growth cycle of the potato or the
meaning of a single word of the Bible – we can touch the mystery
through it. When we turn our intelligence on to a single subject,
we enter the world of wonder and contemplation. Our whole
being is renewed when we touch the light of God hidden at the
heart of things.

We don't read enough in our communities. Sometimes we hit
on a book on psychology, and that is fine. But it could be more
nourishing to read about nature and the mystery of death and

resurrection which is enacted constantly all round us. We shouldn't read only what is useful; we should also try to understand for its own sake, because it is the *gratuité* of the light which is stimulating.

Many people today are living in a world of intellectual confusion. In some ways they have lost trust in the intelligence and in its capacity to know truth. They are suffering from the confusion of values in society propagated by the mass media, but also by a whole world of psychology. They live off their emotions and subjectivity and spontaneous reactions. Many such people gravitate around or enter into communities where emotional life is more recognised. But intellectual knowledge and wisdom are essential components to human growth and earthing in community life. Of course this intellectual discipline will be different according to the needs of each person, but all must reap the benefits of it. There is much danger in people living off dreams and illusions, fearful of reality or unable to reach it. That is where an intellectual discipline is important. This could be in the realm of theology or of Scripture or of the history of the Church and of salvation, or it could be in the area of philosophy or anthropology. People in community need to be helped to reflect and to be grounded more deeply in the certitudes of faith and human thought.

Growth as nourishment

One of the best resources is the feeling that we are growing and making progress. We can get discouraged if we think we are at a standstill. So often we need a shepherd or friend who will remind us that the growth is in fact happening. But we also have to be patient when we feel we aren't growing. We have to trust and remember that it was Jesus who brought us into the community. In winter, it seems that the trees aren't growing; they are waiting for the sun; they have to be pruned. So we need reminding too of the value of waiting and sacrifice.

I am personally helped a lot by seeing, in people with disabilities, the light come into their eyes and a smile to their lips as they gradually come out of anguish and spiritual death – by seeing life rising in them. The rebirth of a human being makes all the weight of daily life in community seem worthwhile.

When we meet people who are dying of sorrow in a huge, institutional ward, or who are aggressive and closed up, we find the courage to continue and to create new communities which will welcome people with handicaps. These visits give us the nourishment we need to go on living with our brothers and sisters at l'Arche. When we understand the purpose and usefulness of a community, we find strength.

Dawn was explaining the other day that she found problems stimulating. 'When everything is too easy, I close in on myself and my own concerns. When a handicapped person is calling out or there are problems in the community to which I must respond, I feel a strength growing in me. I need this stimulus.'

The friend

A real friend, to whom we can say exactly what we feel, knowing that we will be listened to, encouraged and confirmed in love and tenderness, is an essential resource. When friendship encourages fidelity, it is the most beautiful thing of all. Aristotle calls it the flower of virtue, it has the *gratuité* of the flower. On the dark days, we need the refuge of friendship. When we feel flat or fed up, a letter from a friend can bring back peace and confidence. The Holy Spirit uses small things to comfort and strengthen us.

Bernard of Clairvaux wrote the following to a friend in 1127 (Letter 90):

While I write this letter, you are present to me as I am sure I shall be present to you when you read it. We wear ourselves out scribbling to each other, but is the Spirit ever weary of loving? We find rest in those we love and we provide a resting place in ourselves for whose who love us.

Letters can be a real nourishment.

When some assistants at l'Arche are very tired, they need to talk and talk and talk. They need a friend who will listen to them and take in a whole mass of words, sufferings and fears. They will only be at rest when they are freed of all this and the friend has accepted it.

All of us in community – and especially, perhaps, the people with responsibility – may carry a load of frustration which cannot always be expressed in a group without endangering the community itself. The more sensitive we are, the more we are weighed down by these feelings of frustration, anger, anxiety, incompetence, sadness, and apathy. We have a tremendous need to pour all this out to someone with whom we feel secure. We may need to say how much we detest someone who challenges us, without being accused of a 'lack of charity'. We may need this outlet for our emotions if we are to refind peace. But the person who becomes our 'dustbin' has to have the wisdom to collect all this without getting worked up about it, without trying to set everything right and without judging it; nor should they encourage bad feelings.

When we feel loved and appreciated for who we are, when we feel trusted and loved by people, we are nourished in the depths of our hearts. And to be nourished by the love of others is a call to become a nourishment for those who suffer and are alone in distress. So we learn to become good 'bread' for others.

We should not be afraid of loving people and telling them that we love them. That is the greatest nourishment of all.

Sharing

Sometimes in our communities we share about why we came to l'Arche, and how, and about what seems vital to us. And in listening to each other, in discovering the routes we have taken, the ways in which God has led us and made us grow, we feel nourished. Hope is reborn out of this sharing in community.

I am struck by how sharing our weakness and difficulties is more nourishing to others than sharing our qualities and successes. There is a fundamental tendency to become discouraged in community. We either believe that others are better than we are, or that they don't have to cope with the same problems. The discovery that we are all in the same boat and all have the same fears and weariness, can help us to continue. People are nourished by humility, because humility is truth; it is a sign of a presence of God.

One of the greatest sins of a community is perhaps a sort of sadness and moroseness. It is easy to spend our time with a few friends, criticising others, saying that we are fed up and that nothing is like it was in the good old days. This state of spirit, which you can read on people's faces, is a real cancer which can spread right through the body. Sadness, like love or joy, comes in waves which immediately spread. We are all responsible for the atmosphere of the community. We can nourish people with trust and love or we can poison them with sadness and all sorts of criticism.

The eyes of the poor

Sometimes the greatest resource of all can be a small gesture of kindness from someone who is poor. It is often a gentle look from someone who is vulnerable which relaxes us, touches our heart and reminds us of what is essential. One day I went with some sisters of Mother Teresa to a slum in Bangalore where they were looking after people with leprosy. The sores stank and, humanly speaking, it was revolting. But the people there had light in their eyes. All I could do was hold the instruments the sisters were using, but I was glad to be there. The expressions and smiles of the people seemed to reach right into me and renew me. When I left, I felt an inexplicable joy, and it was they who had given it to me. I remember too an evening in a prison in Calgary, in Canada, where I spent three hours with the members of 'Club 21' – the men who are serving more than 21 years for murder. They touched me and recharged my spirit. They changed something in me.

My heart is transformed by the smile of trust given by some people who are terribly fragile and weak. They call forth new energies from me. They seem to break down barriers and bring me a new freedom.

It is the same with the smile of a child: even the hardest heart can't resist. Contact with people who are weak and are crying out for communion, is one of the most important nourishments in our lives. When we let ourselves be really touched by the gift of their presence, they leave something precious in our hearts.

If we remain at the level of 'doing' something for people, we can stay behind our barriers of superiority. We have to welcome the gift of the poor with open hands. Jesus says: 'What you do for the least significant of my brothers [the ones you don't notice and reject], you do for me.' It's true.

We ask God each night in the l'Arche prayer to help us see in the sufferings of our wounded brothers and sisters the humble presence of the living Jesus.

The poor are always prophetic. As true prophets always point out, they reveal God's design. That is why we should take time to listen to them. And that means staying near them, because they speak quietly and infrequently; they are afraid to speak out, they lack confidence in themselves because they have been broken and oppressed. But if we listen to them, they will bring us back to the things that are essential.

Father Arrupe, formerly General of the Jesuits, said in a talk to American religious:

> Effective solidarity of the religious with those who are truly poor will be accompanied by solitude among the poor. . . . We will feel ourselves alone when we see that the labourer's world does not understand our ideal, our motives and our methods. In the depths of our soul we find ourselves in complete solitude. We need God and his power to be able to keep working in the solitude of our solidarity . . . and, in the last analysis, misunderstood and alone.
>
> This is why we see that many religious men and women who are inserted into the world of the labourer have found a new experience of God. In the experience of finding themselves alone and misunderstood, their soul is ripe for the fulness of God. In this simple experience, they feel themselves very small and yet open to value in a new way how God speaks to them through those with whom they stand in solidarity. They see that those people, the marginal ones, even though not often believers, have something divine to tell them through their suffering, their oppression, their abandonment.
>
> Here one understands true poverty; one rediscovers awareness of one's own incapacity and ignorance; one opens one's soul to receive very profound instruction in the lives of the poor, taught by God himself, by means of those rough faces, these half-ruined lives. It is a new face of Christ discovered in 'the little ones'.[1]

When I feel tired, I often go to La Forestière. This is a house in my community which welcomes very handicapped people; none of the ten who live there can talk, several can't walk, and in many ways they have only their hearts and the relationships they express through their face and bodies. The assistants who feed, bathe and care for them have to do this, not at their own rhythm, but at that of the people with a handicap. Things have to go at a pace which can welcome their least expression; because they have no verbal

1 'A New Service to the World of Today', 20 December 1977.

skills, they have no way of enforcing their views by raising their voice. So the assistants have to be the more attentive to the many non-verbal communications, and this adds greatly to their ability to welcome the whole person. They become increasingly people of welcome and compassion. The slower rhythm and even the presence of the people with severe disabilities makes them slow down, switch off their efficiency motor, rest and recognise the presence of God. The poorest people have an exraordinary power to heal the wounds in hearts. If we welcome them, they nourish us.

Communities, if they close themselves off from the poor, close themselves off from God. That does not mean that every contemplative monastery should open its doors to the poor. No. But every contemplative monastery, every Christian, must be concerned by the poor and broken of the world. Every one must be close to the poor who are close by and who are calling us to love - these might be the sick and the old in a monastery; they might be those who hunger and ask for food and shelter for a few days. It might be those who are close by and who are in pain, calling out for a word of comfort. Every follower of Jesus is called to compassion and to walk with the poor and the broken and to pray for them.

It is not possible to eat the broken Body of Christ in the Eucharist and to drink his blood shed for us through torture, and not open our hearts to the broken and the crucified people in our world today.

If at l'Arche we no longer live with the poor and the broken and celebrate life with them, we as a community will die; we will be cut off from the source of life, from the presence of Jesus in them. They nourish us and heal our wounds daily. They call forth the light and love within us. But, of course, if we cut ourselves off from the broken body of Christ in the Eucharist and in prayer, we will not be able to see them as a source of life and as a presence of Christ. We would also die spiritually.

Personal prayer

When we live in community, and everyday life is busy and difficult, it is absolutely essential for us to have moments alone to pray
and meet God in silence and quietness. Otherwise, our activity
motor will become overheated and whizz around like a chicken
without a head.

The Little Sisters of Jesus have a whole rhythm in their rule of
prayer and solitude: an hour a day, a half day a week, a week a
year and a year each 10 years. Interdependence grows in community, but we have to avoid an unhealthy dependence. We have
to take time alone with Our Father, with Jesus. Prayer is an attitude
of trust in Our Father, seeking his will, seeking to be a presence
of love for brothers and sisters. Each of us must know how to
rest and unwind in silence and contemplation, heart to heart with
God.

> Do not be afraid that your momentary withdrawal will be
> detrimental to the community; and do not be afraid that an
> increase in your personal love for God will in any way diminish
> your love for your neighbour. On the contrary, it will enrich
> it.[2]

Sometimes when I am alone, a light is born within me. It is like
a wound of peace in which Jesus lives. And through this wound,
I can approach others without barriers, without the fears and
aggression I often feel, without everything that stands in the way
of dialogue, without the waves of egoism or need to prove something. I can remain in the presence of Jesus and the invisible
presence of my brothers and sisters. I discover more and more
each day my need for these times of solitude in which I can
rediscover others with more truth, and accept, in the light of God,
my own weakness, ignorance, egoism and fear. This solitude does
not separate me from others; it helps me love them more tenderly,
realistically and attentively. I begin to distinguish too between the
false solitude which is a flight from others to be alone with egoism,

2   Carlo Carretto, *In Search of the Beyond* (Darton, Longman & Todd, London,
    1975.)

sadness or a bruised sensitivity, and the true solitude which is communion with God and others.

We all have to find our own rhythm of prayer. For some of us, this will mean praying for hours at a time, for others, for fifteen minutes here and there. For all of us, it is being attentive to God's presence and will throughout the day.

Some of us need the stimulus of the Word of God or saying the Our Father; others need to repeat the name of Jesus or Mary. Prayer is like a secret garden made up of silence and rest and inwardness. But there are a thousand and one doors into this garden and we all have to find our own.

If we do not pray, if we do not evaluate our activities and find rest in the secret part of our heart, it will be very hard to live in community. We will not be open to others, we will not be makers of peace. We will live only from the stimuli of the present moment, and we will lose sight of our priorities and of the essentials. We have to remember too that some purifications come only with the help of the Holy Spirit. Only God can shed light on some corners of our feelings and unconscious.

To pray is to surrender our whole being to God, letting him take over the rudder of our existence. To pray is to trust, saying to God: 'Here I am. Behold the handmaid of the Lord; may it be done unto me according to Thy word.'

'We must learn to trust, refusing to set any value on what is felt, whether it be consolation or suffering.'[3] To trust that God is calling us to grow in our community and calling our community to become a source of refreshment in a parched world.

Prayer is a meeting which nourishes our hearts. It is presence and communion. The secret of our being is in this kiss of God by

3 Ruth Burrows in *Guidelines for Mystical Prayer* (Sheed and Ward, London, 1976).
   Her other books: *Before the Living God, To Believe in Jesus* and *Ascent to Love*
   are also important.

which we know we are loved and forgiven. In our deepest selves, below the levels of action and understanding, there is a vulnerable heart, a child who loves but is afraid to love. Silent prayer nourishes this deep place. It is the most important nourishment of all for people who live in community, because it is the most secret and personal.

Carlo Carretto[4] speaks of finding the desert wherever we are, in our own room, in a church, even in the middle of a crowd. I sometimes find that desert in the streets between l'Arche's houses in Trosly; then I recollect myself and rediscover this tabernacle in which Jesus lives. But I also need longer times.

Often at l'Arche or elsewhere, when I am waiting for someone who is late, I get irritable. I hate wasting time. My inner motor goes on running, but isn't getting anywhere. My energy is revving up but is not directed. I get worse on a journey! I still have a lot to learn about using these apparently wasted moments to relax and rest, to find the presence of God, to live more totally in the presence of others, or simply to look around like a child and wonder. I need to discover patience and, even more, how to live in the moment given by God.

Two dangers lie in wait for members of a community. Either they build a protective wall for themselves – in the name of their union with God, their health or their private life – or they throw themselves helter-skelter into meetings, spilling out all their emotions in the name of dialogue and sharing. The first group tend to live for themselves in a false solitude; the second tend to become dependent on others and lose their own identity. The balance between solitude and community is difficult to find.

At one time, we tended to ignore the gift of community and of sharing; now we are in danger of forgetting the gift of the inner

4 *In Search of the Beyond.*

life and the needs of the heart. To live fully in community, we must first know how to keep going and to love. The community is a spring-board, not a refuge. People who marry just because they need to are in danger of having problems. The real reason for getting married is that you love each other and want to live and journey together through life, and to make each other happy. In the same way, we enter community in response to a call from God, to be what we should be, to live with others, and to build something with them. But this demands that we have our own roots. Otherwise, we will not have the inner consciousness that helps us distinguish the will of God and the true needs of the community from our own instincts, fears, and needs. We will speak not to give life, but to free ourselves or to prove something; we will act with and for others, not for their growth, but because we need to be doing something. To grow in human ways and inner freedom, we need both sharing and communal prayer, and solitude, reflection, inwardness, and personal prayer.

Henri Nouwen shows that some people find conflict between solitude and community. Either solitude is equated with private life, which must be protected from the life of 'generosity' which is community; or solitude is there to enable us to live community life more fully, a necessary resource if we are to become more to others.

But it is not simply that solitude is 'for me' and community 'for others', says Nouwen:

> Solitude is essential to community life because in solitude we grow closer to each other. In solitude we discover each other in a way which physical presence makes difficult, if not impossible. There we recognise a bond with each other that does not depend on words, gestures or actions and that is deeper and stronger than our own efforts can create.
>
> Solitude and community belong together; each requires the other as do the centre and circumference of a circle. Solitude without community leads us to loneliness and despair, but community without solitude hurls us into a 'void of words and feelings' (Bonhoeffer). [5]

5 Henri Nouwen, 'Solitude and Community', in *Worship*, January 1978.

Community life, with all its complexity, implies an inner attitude. Without this, it very quickly ossifies and we seek all sorts of compromises to avoid growth. This attitude is that of a trusting child who knows that he is only a tiny part of the universe and that he is called to live in gift and oblation where he is. All this implies a total confidence in God, seeking his will and good pleasure at each moment. When we no longer have the heart of a child who seeks to be an instrument of peace and unity among all people, we either become discouraged or want to prove ourselves. In either case, we destroy the community.

How can we nourish this child's heart? That is the essential question for everyone who lives in community. Love can only feed on love. The only way to learn to love is to love. As soon as the cancer of egoism takes hold, it spreads very quickly through everyday activities. When the love that is sacrifice begins to grow, words, gestures and flesh itself are permeated with gift and communion.

The heart is nourished if it remains faithful to the heart of God. Prayer is no more than the child resting in his Father's arms and saying 'Yes'.

The heart finds its nourishment in fidelity to the poor, listening to them and allowing itself to be disturbed by their prophetic presence. It finds its nourishment in fidelity to the collective conscience and structures of the community, in its continual, loving and patient 'yes' to these.

Sometimes when I pray, resting close to Jesus and in him, another person, a brother or a sister, comes into my heart – not as a distraction which separates me from Jesus, but as an icon that reveals his love to me more totally and calls me into the heart of the Trinity. It is there that we live a gentle ecstasy together.

In a mysterious way, our own suffering and pain can become a nourishment. Like our poverty and helplessness, they can become a sacrament, a place where God resides. When we are successful and feeling on top of the world, we can so easily turn away from

God; when we are in pain, we call out to him. And he responds: 'Here I am.' There is a presence of God in suffering which can nourish the deepest part of our being.

Becoming bread

Some people, who cannot see what nourishment they could be bringing, do not realise that they can become bread for others. They have no confidence that their word, their smile, their being, or their prayer could nourish others and help them rediscover trust. Jesus calls us to give our lives for those we love. If we eat the bread transformed into the Body of Christ, it is so that we become bread for others.

Others find their own nourishment is to give from an empty basket! It is the miracle of the multiplication of the bread. 'Lord, let me seek not so much to be consoled as to console.' I am always astonished to discover that I can give a nourishing talk when I feel empty, and that I can still transmit peace when I feel anguished. Only God can perform that sort of miracle.

Sometimes I meet people who are aggressive towards their community. They blame it for their own mediocrity, claiming that it isn't nourishing enough and doesn't give them what they need. They are like children who blame their parents for everything that goes wrong. They lack maturity, inner freedom, and above all trust in themselves, Jesus, and their brothers and sisters. They want a banquet with a nicely written menu, so they reject the crumbs they could have all the time. Their 'ideal', their idea of the spiritual nourishment they feel they need, prevents them from seeing and eating the food God is giving them in their daily life. They cannot accept the bread that the poor people, their brothers and sisters, are offering them through their look, their friendship or their words.

At the start, community can be a nourishing mother. But with time, we must all discover our own nourishment in its thousand

and one activities. We may find the strength from God to discover our own wound and solitude, our cry of distress. Community can never comfort this distress; it is inherent in the human condition. But community can help us to accept it, and remind us that God responds to our cry and that we are not entirely alone. 'And the Word became flesh and dwelt among us' (John 1:14). 'Fear not, for I am with you' (Isa. 43:5). To live in community is to learn to walk alone in the desert, at night and in tears, putting our confidence in God the Father.

When the original vision of the community gets lost, when we are far from the focal point of fidelity, we can stuff ourselves with a diet of spiritual practices but get no nourishment from it at all. We have to become re-converted, become again like little children, and rediscover our original call and that of the community. When we question this call, doubt spreads like a cancer which can undermine us entirely. We have to know how to nourish our trust in the call.

Communal prayer and Eucharist

Communal prayer is an important nourishment. A community which prays together, which enters into silence and adoration, is bound together by the action of the Holy Spirit. God listens in a special way to the cry which rises from a community. When we ask him, together, for a gift of grace, he listens and grants our request. Jesus says that the Father will give whatever is asked in his name; all the more reason for him to give when it is a community that asks. It seems to me that we do not yet have enough recourse to this communal prayer at l'Arche. Perhaps we are not yet simple or child-like enough. In spontaneous community prayer we sometimes feel a bit lost. It is sad, to me, that we do not use the very beautiful texts of the Church, that we do not know the Scriptures better. It is true that a text can lose its savour if it is used every day. But spontaneity can lose its savour too. We have to find a harmony between the texts that tradition gives us and the spontaneous prayer which springs from the heart.

Often a community stops crying to God when it has itself stopped hearing the cry of the poor, when it has become self-satisfied and found a way of life which is not too insecure. It is when we are aware of the distress and misery of our people, and of their oppression and suffering, when we see them starving and sense our own inability to do anything about it, that we will cry loudly to God: 'Lord, you cannot turn a deaf ear to the cry of your people; listen then to our prayer.' When the community makes a covenant with poor people, their cry becomes its own.

A community must be a sign of the resurrection. But a divided community, in which everyone goes their own way, preoccupied with their own sanctification and personal plans, and without tenderness for the other, is a counter-witness. All the resentment, bitterness, sadness, rivalries, divisions, refusals to hold out a hand to 'the enemy' and whispered criticisms, all the division and infidelity to the gift of the community, are profoundly wounding to its true growth in love. Divisions also show the bruises of sin, the forces of evil which are always in our hearts, ready to erupt. It is important that a community sometimes takes stock of all its infidelities. Penitential ceremonies in the presence of a priest can be important, if they are well prepared: the community's members become conscious of both their call to unity and their sin, demanding forgiveness of God and each other. It can be a moment of grace which brings hearts together.

The Eucharist links communal and personal nourishment, because it is itself both at the same time. The Eucharist is celebration, the epitome of the communal feast, because in it we relive the mystery of Jesus' gift of his own life for us. We relive in a sacramental way his sacrifice on the cross, which opened up a new life for people, which liberated hearts from fear and for love and union with God, and for community. The Eucharist is the time of thanksgiving for the whole community. That is why the priest says, after the consecration: 'Grant that we, who are nourished by his body and blood, may be filled with his Holy Spirit and become one body, one spirit in Christ.'[6] There we touch the heart of the mystery of community.

But the Eucharist is also an intimate moment when each of us is transformed through a personal meeting with Jesus. 'He who eats my flesh and drinks my blood abides in me, and I in him' (John 6:56). At the moment of consecration, the priest repeats Jesus' words: 'Take this all of you and eat it, this is my body which will be given up for you.' It is the 'given up for you' which is striking. It is only when we have eaten this body that we can give ourselves to others. Only God could invent something like that. This sacrifice, which is also a wedding feast, calls us to offer our lives to the Father, to become bread for others, and to rejoice in the wedding feast of love.

Being in l'Arche, I am very sensitive to the reality of the body. Many of our people cannot speak, but all express love and fear through their bodies. The body is more fundamental than the word. The Body of Christ is more fundamental than his Word. Many handicapped people cannot understand the Word but they can eat his Body. And they seem to have a deep understanding of what communion means. They live off communion between people, so they are eminently prepared for communion with Christ.

Communities are becoming more and more aware of the central aspect of the Eucharist in their lives. Jesus came into the world to give us a new bread of life, a new nourishment, his word and his body; and the word is for the body; it is for communion. Jesus told his apostles to do the Eucharist in his memory. It is at his command that the priest celebrates the Eucharist which renders Jesus present in a sacramental way.

When the Eucharist is celebrated in a community, all the mem-

6 Third Canon of the Mass.

bers are gathered together in communion one with another, offering themselves to the Father with and in and through his Son, Jesus, so that the whole community may be a place of the presence of the Kingdom on this earth and may be life-giving with the love of the Holy Spirit.

The Word is essential in bringing about *co-operation*. Symbols and touch are vital to bring about *communion*, which is the essence of community. The celebration of the Body of Christ and the Eucharist are powerful symbols and signs to create communion.

The gospels, however, and the writings of the saints over the ages, show clearly the polarity within the Church between *the Body of Christ* and *the poor*. Jesus became poor and he announced that the poor are himself. The broken body of Christ in the Eucharist is only clearly understood when it is seen in relation to the broken bodies and hearts of the poor; and their broken bodies and hearts find the meaning in the broken Body of Christ. The two are so intimately linked that St John in his gospel does not mention the Eucharist at the Last Supper, but only the washing of the feet. The washing of the feet of the poor is Eucharist.

Unfortunately, over the ages the priest, because he presided over the Eucharist, has come to preside over the church community. He became *the* authority, as if lay people had not received the Holy Spirit and were unable to think and assume responsibility in the Church. The Church became terribly clerical; priests carried all the power. Forgotten was the mystery of the Church as a community, as a body where each person has a place.

With the priest assuming *all* the power somehow the poor have been forgotten. The Church remained centred upon the Eucharist and worship, but lost sight of its other pole: the broken body of the poor and the community of believers called together to welcome them. For this reason the Church has become rich; it has lost a lot of its credibility; frequently it is no longer a visible sign of the Kingdom of love.

When the vulnerable body becomes central in community, there is a specific place for Mary, the Mother of Jesus. She was the first to welcome the body of Jesus, the Word made flesh. The apostles and disciples were sanctified by the word of Jesus; Mary was sanctified by his Body, by his real presence. And she was there, at the foot of the cross, close to his broken and dying body, when the others had fled.

All Christians are perhaps called to make the passage from the light and beauty of the Word to the poverty and littleness of the body. Mary, before the Word became flesh in her, was filled with grace, filled with light. She loved the words of the prophets which united her to the light of the Invisible God. When the Word became flesh in her; when Jesus was born; her heart was touched by a deeper, more hidden, more mystical presence and communion. God became visible in the poverty of the body of a little child needing to be held, nourished and loved; a little child seeking and giving communion.

The day Joseph and Mary presented their child, Jesus, in the temple has become a precious feast day for communities of Faith and Light. Simeon, the high priest, said to Mary that a sword would pierce her heart. Many parents of children with a handicap have had their hearts broken and pierced with pain. But in some mysterious way, their son or daughter is called to renew the Church and society. But they, with all their brokenness and weakness, will only be able to renew the Church if people within the Church listen to them and live in communion with them.

The bread of pain

Many of our l'Arche communities are interdenominational, that is to say, where Roman Catholics, Anglicans and Protestants live together. In these times of division and of anguish, such communities are an immense grace. They come from a very particular call of God. Jesus thirsts for unity; before he died, he prayed: 'May they be one, as the Father and I are one.' But while there is a real gift and grace in these communities, there is also much pain.

Four people were living in an apartment belonging to our London community. One of them was Nick, who has a mental handicap. He himself has come from a family where the parents have separated. He found it intolerable on Sundays when everyone in the apartment went off to separate communion services. He could not bear the separation. On Sunday evenings, each one would take their turn in preparing the supper. One Sunday, it was Nick's turn, and when he called the others to the table, they were surprised to find only bread and water. Nick then took the bread and said, 'This is my body.' He handed a piece to each one and then passed the glass of water. Then he said: 'Now we have all been to communion *together*'. Yes, the pain of separation is difficult to bear when we live together.

An interdenominational community does not want to become another church with its own services and sacraments. There are enough already! No, an interdenominational community is called to bring people together and, through them, their churches. Its role is to help people discover each other more deeply, their beliefs and their beauty, and to help people discover that the things that unite are far deeper than the things that divide.

This means that people in the community must be rooted each in their own parish and religious traditions. Today however – and this is a real problem and I am not sure what the answer is – there are more and more young people who wish to follow Jesus but who are not affiliated to any specific church; they have no spiritual roots. They too must be helped to deepen and to grow in a sense of belonging.

We did not plan to be ecumenical in l'Arche; it was *given to* us through our people. We discovered that we were ecumenical when we started welcoming people with a mental handicap from institutions; they needed a place to live, a new family. We did not, of course, ask them what their religious affiliation was; we received them because we saw their need. So, once they were with us, we had to see how to help them grow also in their faith. That implied contacts with the local priests and ministers. Then, of course, we realised that we could not all participate in the same Eucharist or communion service. And then the pain began!

Some people felt we should just go ahead and have intercommunion. Then there would be no pain. It would be much easier. Were not handicapped people prophetic? And anyway, how would they be able to understand all the differences? How could they ever understand why they would be refused communion at one service and given it at another? Those arguments were very real. And yet, how can we belong to a church, a parish, if we refuse to abide by the ways, traditions, theology and rules of the particular church? For the Roman Catholic and Orthodox Churches intercommunion, except in very special cases, is not allowed. Were we to refuse to obey these rules because people with a mental handicap are prophetic? No matter what decision we made, there would be pain. We chose to live the pain in the community and not to separate people from their church.

Does that mean that we can never have the Eucharist in the community or at community gatherings? For Roman Catholics, Anglicans and the Orthodox the Eucharist is at the centre of a Christian community. It creates and nourishes community, because it is the real presence of Jesus. And l'Arche cannot live if its members are not rooted and grounded in a deep spiritual life, united to Jesus, nourished by him. L'Arche is not just a nice group home; it's much more than that; it is a new way of living Christian community with the poor at the heart and centre.

Sometimes communities which have welcomed only people from one religious tradition feel guilty because they are not ecumenical enough. No, that is not our way. Ecumenism is a gift. It is also a beautiful gift to welcome people coming from the same church and to be able fully to live the Eucharist together. Each one of us is called to have an ecumenical heart, but not all communities are called to be interdenominational.

If Jesus called l'Arche into being, then he will guide it through and with the pain. I believe our communities are precious to his heart, for he yearns for unity, and every gesture for unity is

inspired by his love. So, if he is calling us, he will give us the
wisdom and the strength to follow the right road, in face of
misunderstanding, difficulties, criticism and sometimes even persecution. Of course, we will make mistakes, but we will learn
from them.

If the Eucharist, which is at the heart of community for many
Christians, cannot be at the heart of interdenominational communities, then we must discover the bread of pain at the heart of these
communities. When the Eucharist is not there, or when it is there
but we cannot eat from the same table, the division in the Church
becomes terribly present in broken hearts. But in this bread of
pain there is a nourishment and a hope. For many in our world
today, the division in our churches is not a source of pain; it is
simply a historical and theological fact. When this pain becomes
anguish and agony – as it did in the heart of Christ – then we can
offer ourselves up in sacrifice, for unity. We crave for unity; we
work for unity.

In the chapels of Mother Teresa's Sisters there is always a cross
on the wall and under one of the arms of the cross are the last
words of Jesus: 'I thirst'. In those communities of l'Arche which
are interdenominational, I would like to see the words, 'I thirst
for unity'. Jesus is saying to each one of the members: 'Are you
prepared to suffer for unity? Will you follow me along the road
and carry the cross of this pain?'

With all the suffering of a divided Eucharist and of divided
churches, we can be nourished by this bread of pain. We know
the road is uncharted and painful, but we are walking with Jesus;
we are walking towards unity.

However, all of us hate pain. We try to flee from it; we do
everything to avoid it. So, time and time again in our communities, the question of intercommunion comes up, sometimes in
quite an aggressive way, especially as new assistants arrive. It is
not easy to keep walking on the right path, particularly as we do
not always receive the necessary encouragement from the clergy
in the different churches. Each priest or minister belongs to a
particular church, where they have their own problems; they are

not always concerned about an interdenominational community. To whom does such a community belong? Perhaps to all the churches involved, but only as long as they are yearning for unity as Christ does.

The danger for interdenominational communities is that the people in them begin to see religion and the churches as a source of division. It is so easy to slip away then from all spiritual values and religious activities, and to put all our energy into leisure activities and community celebrations where we can be united. But such activities are not sufficient for building and sustaining community. L'Arche communities could easily become good group homes and forget they are communities, with all that that implies.

To live ecumenism, each person is called to live and deepen what is essential to their faith in Jesus: to be in communion with the Father and to grow in love for others. But they must live and deepen what is specific to their own church too. True ecumenism is not the suppression of difference; on the contrary, it is learning to respect and love what is different. The members of the community must then be grounded in their own tradition and love it. It means also that they feel truly called by Jesus to eat the bread of pain in order to further that unity. In such communities each person must be truly nourished spiritually, in order to grow in wholeness and in holiness.

The bread of unity anticipated

If interdenominational communities cannot be nourished by the Eucharist, there must be other moments when the presence of Jesus is signified to bring about communion. Communities, as I have said, are places of communion before being places of co-operation. This communion must be nourished. Members of interdenominational communities are called to deepen their prayer life together. They are called to celebrate all that unites Christians of different traditions: in particular baptism; the Word of God; the cross of Jesus and carrying our cross; living in the Holy Spirit, prayer and the presence of Jesus. Together, all the members are called to holiness and love. If they cannot celebrate the Eucharist together, they can celebrate the washing of each other's feet; living it as a sacrament.

In l'Arche, if we cannot eat at the same eucharistic table, we can all eat together at the table of the poor. 'When you give a banquet,' says Jesus, 'invite the poor, the crippled, the lame and the blind, not your friends or relations or rich neighbours' (Luke 14:13–15). If we cannot drink together from the same eucharistic chalice, we can all drink together from the chalice of suffering (cf. Matt. 20) caused by division amongst Christians and by the rejection of the poor and the weak. These are the specific gifts of l'Arche.

We can discover also the intimate link between the broken body of Christ in the Eucharist and the broken and suffering bodies of our people. We can discover that the poor are a path to unity. As we are called to love them, and to be loved by them, we are in some mysterious way brought together in the heart of Christ.

What I have said of interdenominational communities can also be said, but in a different way, about inter-religious communities. Here the bread of pain is perhaps even greater. We have to discover how to celebrate our common humanity. We must discover the cycles of nature and the presence of God in all the beauty of our universe. We must learn how to celebrate a common prayer to God, the Father of us all.

In all this, we must discover that l'Arche is called to be a prophetic place of peace and reconciliation. That is our call and our gift. And our beloved God will give us the nourishment we need as he gave it to his people in the desert with the manna and the waters springing from the rock. If we cry out in our pain he will feed us.

6

Authority as a Gift[1]

Authority

The role of authority can only be understood if it is seen as one of the many gifts or ministries which we need to build community. It is, of course, a very important gift, because the community's well being and growth depend to a great extent on the way it is exercised. But too often authority is seen as the only gift; the role of everyone else in the community is seen simply as obedience to it. This, however, is an industrial or military model of authority. In a community authority needs to be exercised in a completely different way. The leaders do not have a monopoly of insights and gifts; their role, on the contrary, is to help all the community's members to exercise their own gifts for the good of the whole. A community can only become a harmonious whole, with 'one heart, one soul, one spirit', if all its members are exercising their own gifts fully. If the model of their relationship to authority is worker to boss, or soldier to officer, then there is no understanding of what community means.

When I speak of 'authority' in the following pages, I do not mean only the leader of a community, but all those who are giving direction, support and formation to others. At l'Arche that means those in charge of the workshops, the houses and the garden teams, as well as anyone in the administration, the kitchens and the service of welcome, who has charge over the work of others. Each person has to learn how to exercise authority.

1 I was greatly helped in writing this section by the many valuable insights into authority of Robert K. Greenleaf, in his book *Servant Leadership* (Paulist Press, New York, 1977).

A child's first models of authority are the mother and father. Both are necessary, not only for the conception of the child, but also for its growth. Together, in unity, they are responsible for the child and its development. Authority is linked to growth. The word itself comes from the Latin *augere* to grow. This is very far from the way many people see authority: the guardian of the law; the person who punishes and who stifles growth towards freedom and fulfilment.

The mother cherishes and envelops, holds and comforts the child. She is close to bodily needs and is presence. It is in her womb that the child begins to grow. It is her body that nourishes it.

But authority must also encourage the child to advance, to make efforts and to be equipped to leave the family. This is essentially the father's role[2] (obviously in unity with and not in opposition to the mother). He encourages his son or daughter to go forward; he 'authorises', that is to say, opens up new doors and new avenues. He affirms: 'Go, you can do it. Take the risk, move on!' And the father can encourage in that way because he himself has attained a certain fullness and wholeness in his humanity and inner freedom. He urges the child not to remain a prisoner, frightened and closed up in itself, but to walk forward towards maturity, wholeness and freedom, the freedom to give oneself and to love.

There is much confusion today about the role of the father. The mother's role is somewhat clearer. Many children, particularly during their adolescence, suffer from a lack of presence and attention from their father. They are craving for a father and angry with him at the same time. They lack affirmation. They are not sure where their gifts lie. They lack confidence in themselves. They do not know what direction to take. In fact, even with a very affirming father, most children need to meet another father-figure, a spiritual father or teacher, or someone to whom the child is attracted and whom it sees as a model.

A man who serves as a father-figure must love the person in a

2 Of course, one cannot categorise and generalise too much concerning the mother's role and the father's role. Both are important. According to different temperaments, situations, cultures and so on, these two aspects of *comfort and confirmation* or *encouragement* are shared.

unique and personal way. A relationship of trust is born between them. The father-figure recognises the gifts of the young person even if they are only in the seed stage, and so he is able to affirm, encourage, teach, give support and counsel and, if necessary, correct in order to help the person to have trust in him or herself and to grow to greater maturity, wisdom and freedom. This form of authority is not necessarily attached to a function. It is something more fundamental.

To exercise authority is to feel truly responsible for others and their growth, knowing too that the 'others' are not their property, are not objects but people with hearts in whom resides the light of God, and who are called to grow to the freedom of truth and love. The greatest danger for someone in authority is to manipulate people and to control them for his or her own goals and need for power.

Many people seem to have a strange concept of authority. They are afraid of it and of taking it on. To them authority seems to lack tenderness and relationship. They see it only as bad and bullying. Perhaps they had an authoritarian father who was neither tender nor trusting. Perhaps too, this is one of the ills of our times; the tendency everywhere seems to be to separate authority from love and to make it legalistic.

True authority is exercised in the context of justice for all, with special attention to the weakest people, who cannot defend themselves and are part of the oppressed minority. This is an authority ready to give its life, which does not accept any compromise with evil, deceit, and the forces of oppression. A family or community authority, as well as having this sense of justice and truth, needs personal relationships, sensitivity in its action and the ability to listen, trust, and forgive. None of this, of course, excludes moments of firmness.

At the same time, and perhaps for the same reasons, many people confuse authority and the power of efficiency, as if the first role of people with responsibility is to take decisions, command effectively and so exercise power. But their role is first of all to be a person to whom others can turn to for help and advice, to provide security, to affirm, to support, to encourage and to guide.

In biblical language authority is a *rock*; it is solid and gives support. It is a *source of water*, giving life, cleansing, forgiving, nourishing. It is the *shepherd* leading the flock to green pastures. It is a *gardener* watering seeds so that they may bear fruit.

In the tenth chapter of St John's gospel, Jesus talks of himself as the good shepherd. The qualities he gives to this good shepherd are truly those every shepherd of a community needs. Shepherds lead the flock and give direction. They must also 'know each one by name'. In the biblical vision the *name* signifies the gift and the call or the mission of a person. Shepherds must have a personal relationship with each one, know their specific gifts in order to help them grow; know their wounds in order to give strength, comfort and compassion, especially in times of pain. Shepherds must be bonded to people with bonds of love and be ready to give their lives for them, sacrificing thir own personal interests.

Leaders of communities need *to organise* the community so that each member is in the right place and things work smoothly. They need to *animate it*, so that it continues to be alive and the eyes of all are fixed on the essential goals. They need *to love each person* and be concerned about their growth. Members can sense very quickly if those with responsibility in the community love and trust them and want to help them to grow, or if they are there just to prove their authority, impose the rules and their own vision, or else are seeking to please.

To lead is to judge situations and make wise decisions. And judgement is always in respect to certain criteria; these criteria are the goal or objectives of the community. That is why the leader must continually keep the goal in view; even more, they must *live it* and *love it*. The Abbot of a contemplative monastery must be a man of prayer, a contemplative himself. Leaders of l'Arche communities must enjoy the company of people with a handicap and find in them a source of life. The leader is always *a model*, and teaches more by the way he or she lives than by what he or she says.

A mission from God

The people who carry responsibility in a community have received a mission which has been bestowed on them either by the community, which has elected them, or by a superior (or some other external authority) who has appointed them and to whom they are accountable. But the mission is always received from God. We cannot assume responsibility towards other people without his call and help, for, as St Paul says:

'There is no authority except from God, and those that exist have been instituted by God' (Rom. 13:1). Anyone who carries authority which comes from God must be accountable to God. That is the limitation and the scope of human authority.

Authority is there to help the freedom and growth of individuals. It is a work of love. Just as God watches over his children to see that they grow in love and truth, so the people responsible for a community must be at the service of God and individuals, so that they too can grow in love and truth.

To carry authority is a huge responsibility. But it is also beautiful, because people set in authority have the assurance that God will send the insight, strength and gifts they need to accomplish the task. That is why those in authority have to do more than refer to those who appointed them, as the secretary of an association would do. They must refer to God and discover the divine light in their own hearts. I am a great believer in the grace that is given to carry out a mission or to assume a function. God will always come to the aid of people in authority if they are humble and try in truth to serve. To really understand that becomes very liberating for leaders, who then do not have to carry all the worries of the world. God is there; it is he who has called them to leadership, and he will give them the strength and wisdom they need. They can remain peaceful and relaxed. They must just do their best and then leave everything in God's hands, and go to bed with a smile.

Cardinal Danneels, the Archbishop of Bruxelles, sharing with all the leaders of l'Arche communities, said:

When I get home after a long day, I go to the chapel and pray. I say to the Lord, 'There it is for today; things are finished. Now let's be serious, is this diocese mine or yours?' The Lord says, 'What do you think?' I answer, 'I think it's yours.' 'That is true,' the Lord says, 'it is mine.' And so I say, 'Listen, Lord' it is your turn to take responsibility for and direct the diocese. I'm going now to sleep.'

Then he added, 'This principle is just as valid for parents as for a person responsible for a diocese' . . . or for a community!

The people who carry final authority in communities are always, in a sense, alone. Even if there is a community council, they will have to take some decisions by themselves. This loneliness is their cross, but it is also the guarantee of presence, light and the strength of God. That is why they, more than anyone else in the community, must have time to be alone with God. It is in these moments of solitude that inspiration is born in them and they will sense what direction to take. They must have confidence in these intuitions, especially if they are accompanied by a deep peace. But they must also confirm them, by sharing them with some people in whom they have real trust and then with the community council.

Faced with difficult decisions about the future, they must of course reason and reflect, using all the information available. But at the end of the day, because of the complexity of the problems and the impossibility of foreseeing every detail, they must, having assimilated everything, rely on the deep intuitions which come to them when they are alone. This is the only way that people with authority can acquire the freedom which will allow them to go forward and take decisions without fearing the consequences.

I discover more and more the marvellous way in which responsibility leads to spiritual growth. Of course it is a cross, and some people mope and groan under it. Others see responsibility as something deserved which brings prestige and advantages. But if we are aware of the gravity of responsibility and what it means to carry people, and if we accept the cross with all its implications, this is a marvellous way to grow.

But if we are to carry our cross lightly, with patience and wisdom, we have to cling to the Spirit of God. More than anyone else, we need time with our God. Otherwise, we will lose peace; we will lose the light if we do not have time to listen.

We always need to remember the words of Jesus to Peter: 'Feed my flock.' Yes, the community is essentially the flock of Jesus. We are but his instruments. So, if we have been called to assume leadership, Jesus will always be there to help us nourish the flock and to guide us and give us the necessary strength and wisdom.

Sometimes at l'Arche I feel a bit overwhelmed by problems. A member of the community may be in a state of crisis. One of the houses may be struggling. A group of assistants may be united against something which I feel to be essential. There may be divisions in the community, especially between the professionally-oriented, who want more competence, and the spiritually-oriented, who want a more religious life. Things like these can upset me.

But it doesn't do for me to take myself too seriously or to dramatise things. I have to be aware of situations and not hide from them or pretend they do not exist. But I have to remember too that I don't have to solve all problems single-handed. First of all, there are several of us who share responsibility. But, most important, God has promised to help us. So, we shouldn't get too worked up. We have to be aware of what is going on and discern calmly what has to be done and act accordingly, taking small steps forward, even if the horizon is blurred.

People with responsibility will be faced by many complex problems. They must keep the heart of a child, confident that Jesus will always come to their help in their weakness. They have to put their worries into God's hands and then do whatever they can.

No one will be happy in the community if the people in authority are always preoccupied, anxious, serious and closed in on themselves. Responsibility is certainly a cross which has to be picked up each day. But we have to learn to carry it lightly. The secret is to stay young, open, and capable of wonder. And the best way to do that is to stay open to the Holy Spirit who will keep us young.

Leaders should remember that God chose as leaders men who were very broken: Moses, who had murdered an Egyptian; Peter, who had denied Christ; Paul, who had participated in the killing of Stephen. Maybe because they were broken and not really trustworthy from a human point of view, they were more humble and thus better instruments of God.

People in authority must take heed of what others think. But they must not be imprisoned by these views. They have a responsibility before God and so have no right to compromise, deceive, or be instruments of injustice.

Being a servant

There are different ways of exercising authority and command: the military model, the industrial model and the community model. The general's goal is victory; the factory manager's goal is profit. The goal of the leader of a community is the growth of individuals in love and truth.

Leaders of a community have a double mission. They must keep their eyes and those of the community fixed on what is essential, on the fundamental aims of the community. They must give direction, so that the community doesn't get lost in small wrangles, which are secondary and incidental. At l'Arche, those with responsibility have always to remind people that the community exists essentially to welcome people with handicaps and help them grow, in the spirit of the Beatitudes. The members of a community of prayer have always to be reminded that the demands of work are subordinate to those of prayer. The mission of people in authority is to keep the community in touch with essentials. That is why they must clearly and frequently announce the vision and see that others announce it. A community needs continually to be nourished in this respect.

But the leaders' mission is also to create an atmosphere of mutual love, confidence, sharing, peace and joy among the community's members. Through their relationship with individuals, through the trust shown in them, they will lead each member to trust the others. Human beings grow best in a relaxed environment built on mutual confidence. When there is rivalry, jealousy, and suspicion, and where people are blocked against each other, there can be no community, no growth, and no life of witness.

The Brothers in the Taizé community no longer call their leader 'the Prior', but 'the Servant of Communion'. This touches me deeply. Yes, the leader's role is to facilitate communion; a community is fundamentally more a place of communion than a place of collaboration.

If the leader or prior is a servant of communion, then he or she must be a person of communion, seeking communion with the Father and communion with people. Then the leader will create space for communion in the community.

We must remember that all of us, and not only the leader, are called to be servants of communion.

Jesus is the model of authority for Christians. On the night before he died, he washed the feet of his disciples like a common slave. Peter was shocked out of his wits by this gesture. And then Jesus told his disciples they should do likewise: 'Blessed are you if you do what I have done.' This is such a different way of exercising authority and goes against our wish to be superior and above others. Jesus leads by going lower than others. We truly need the Spirit of Jesus to teach us to be humble servants of communion.

Different people exercise authority in different ways, according to their own temperaments. Some people are leaders and have a creativity which gives them a vision of the future: they lead from the front. Others are more shy and humble: they walk among the others and make excellent co-ordinators. The essential, for all people with authority, is that they are servants before they are bosses. People who assume responsibility to prove something, because they tend to be dominating and controlling, because they need to see themselves at the top or because they are looking for privileges and prestige, will always exercise their responsibility badly. They must first want to be servants.

Some communities choose their leaders for their administrative ability or ascendancy over others. But leaders should be chosen because they have shown that they put the interests of the community above their own. People who are humble and who want to serve the community and others, and who know how to seek advice from the right people, are worth more, even if they are shy and lack certain abilities, than people who know they are 'capable' but are caught up in themselves and lack humility. But, of course, a leader has to have some areas of competence and some natural abilities.

The people who carry responsibility best are those who receive it as a mission of God and lean on his strength and the gifts of the Holy Spirit. They will feel poor and incapable, but they will always act humbly for the good of the community. They will have the community's confidence, for it will sense that they trust not in themselves and their own vision, but in God. The community will sense that such leaders have no need to prove anything, that they are not seeking anything for themselves and that their vision isn't

clouded by their own problems. It will sense that they are willing
to disappear when the moment comes.

People who assume responsibility should remember that, in the
perspective of the Gospel, it is the poorest people who are the
most precious and close to God, not the leaders. It is they whom
God has chosen to confound the strong and who are at the heart
of Christian community. The whole ministry of government must
be concerned for them and their growth in love.

People with responsibility must always be concerned for the minorities in a community and those who have no voice, listening to
them, and interpreting for them. The leaders must defend individuals because the interests of the individual must never be sacrificed
to those of the group. A community is always built around people;
people should not be shaped to suit community.

The leader is the guardian of unity. He or she must thirst for unity
and work for it day and night. For this, the leader must not fear
conflict, but rather accept it and strive to be an instrument of
reconciliation; the leader must be in contact with all the different
elements in the community, and particularly with those who are
in pain or who are angry with the community.

To be a servant leader is to be more concerned for *people* than for
the *institution*. There is always an institutional aspect to a community: things have to be done, work must go on, the accounts
must be wisely administered, the cows must be milked, etc. It is
a bad sign when leaders become more preoccupied by the institutional aspect than by the growth of people. Sometimes people
for their growth and well-being should leave the community or
work less, at least for a short while – even if that involves difficulties for the institution.

At l'Arche there is a whole institutional aspect around the needs and the growth of people with a handicap. Leaders can become so preoccupied with that aspect that they forget the growth and well-being of assistants. They must seek wisdom and harmony here. Obviously leaders must be concerned by the institutional aspects, but they must never forget the needs and growth of assistants.

The danger of pride

I see increasingly how difficult it is to exercise authority in a community. We are so inclined to want authority for the honour, prestige and admiration that comes with it. Inside each of us is a little tyrant who wants power and the associated prestige, who wants to dominate, to be superior and to control. We are frightened of criticism. We feel we are the only ones to see the truth – and that, sometimes, in the name of God. We interfere with the work of others, taking charge of everything and jealously guarding our authority. The others are reduced to simply carrying out our ideas, as if they were incapable of making judgements themselves. We only allow freedom when it doesn't challenge our own authority and we can control it. We want our ideas to be put into action, and straight away. So the community becomes 'our' project.

All these tendencies can very easily filter into the exercise of authority, to one degree or another. And Christians can sometimes hide these tendencies behind a mask of virtue, doing what they do for 'good' reasons. There is nothing more terrible than a tyrant using religion as his or her cover. I know my own tendencies towards this and I have to struggle against them constantly.

It is important that the limits of individual power in a community are clearly understood and even written down. A father can so quickly go beyond his proper power over his children, wanting them to turn out according to his own ideas; he so quickly fails to take their freedom and their wishes into account.

It is not easy for people in authority to find the mean between too much command and too little. The dangers of pride and the desire to dominate are so great for all leaders that they need limits set to their power, and systems of control which help them to be objective and remain truly at the service of the community.

There is often the danger of failing to take a decision because we are afraid of making the wrong one, afraid of being unpopular, afraid of entering into conflict with others. And some people just have difficulty in making decisions. They like analysing a situation, seeing all the pros and cons, but they have trouble in deciding to make changes.

But not to take a decision is in fact to take one. People with responsibility certainly need patience; they should not act in the flush of anger. They have to know how to listen, find out the facts and take their time. But, after prayer and discussion, they also have to be able to take decisions and not let themselves be controlled by circumstances or past events.

Some people in authority, because they want to be close to everyone, tend to say 'yes' to everyone. They frequently lack a sense of the community as a whole and do not like working through the structures. This can lead to chaos!

Rivalry for power between members of the community and jealousy of the others' radiance is a terrible force for destruction. A united community is like a rock; a community which is divided against itself rapidly destroys itself.

Even the apostles around Jesus, sometimes behind his back, argued about who was the greatest among them (Mark 9:34; 10:35–41). St Luke says they were talking about this during the Last Supper. Is that why Jesus got up from the table and washed their feet?

Rivalry between members of a community often becomes more apparent when there is a vote for a position of responsibility. There can also be rivalry over who is the most spiritual and intellectual. Such struggles for power and influence are deeply rooted in our human hearts. We are afraid for our very existence if we do not win the vote, or a certain position. We are so quick to equate function with person, and popularity with quality of being.

No authority is free from over-hasty judgements which hurt people and get them caught up in a vicious circle of anger and sadness. Unity grows from the soil of humility, which is the safeguard against schisms and division. The spirit of evil is powerless against humility. And it is the spirit of evil which creates deceit, illusion, a partisan spirit producing internal feuds, struggles, unhealthy criticism, and provoking pride.

Sharing responsibility

People with responsibility must always share their work, even if others do it less well than they do or in a different way. It is always easier to do things ourselves than to teach others to do them. People with responsibility who fall into the trap of wanting to do everything themselves are in danger of becoming isolated, and overstressed, and of losing the vision.

Even very limited and fragile people, if they can work with a leader who has vision, compassion and firmness, can do marvellous things. They participate in the leader's vision and they benefit from his gifts. The wealth of a community lies in the fact that all its members can share the qualities and gifts of the others.

It is sometimes difficult for those who carry responsibility at a lower level to fit harmoniously into the whole. They are answerable to those immediately above them – as indeed is everyone who carries responsibility, up to the director who is accountable to the Board of Directors. But it is not always easy for people in the middle range of responsibility to see when they can take initiatives on their own, and when they need to refer to their immediate superior, get his opinion and recognise his authority. Some people refuse to consult with their immediate superior, feeling more free to do what they want without this control; they act as if they were in sole charge. Others take the completely opposite line: they are so afraid of accepting authority and unsure of themselves that they refer the last detail upwards, becoming servile and taking no real responsibility themselves. We have to find the middle way between these two extremes, assuming our responsibility fully before God and referring truthfully to him and to the next person up the line. This demands an open heart, which is not trying to prove anything.

The superior authority can err in the same way: either letting the intermediate authority do everything without any dialogue or accountability; or, on the other hand, telling the intermediate authority everything that has to be done and how. True authority enters into dialogue, gives general directions and ideas, and then leaves others to fulfil their responsibility and get on with the job. But, of course, there must be dialogue also after the job has been done – whether it has been well done or not – in order to confirm and support or maybe correct.

Leaders must take great care of those who have been given responsibility in the community and who for one reason or another (health, tiredness, lack of certain qualities, etc.) cannot exercise it well. Sometimes they must be relieved of their responsibility; in other cases, the leader must be more demanding and encourage them to do better. Much wisdom is needed here.

Obviously there must be dialogue, unity and love between those carrying responsibility. If there are barriers between them and they are criticising each other, there is danger for the community. If there is no communion and sharing between leaders, how can they become servants of communion? They risk becoming agents of division and thus of death.

In the community of l'Arche in Ouagadougou in Burkina Faso, West Africa, we welcomed Karim from a local orphanage, where he had been put after the death of his mother. Soon afterwards he fell sick with meningitis and was isolated from the other children. The consequences of his sickness were serious: he could neither walk nor talk. Unfortunately he was kept for many years in isolation. When we welcomed him at the age of seven, he was in terrible anguish and would hit his head frequently.

After a number of years in the community, he became peaceful, able to walk and to do some work; he belonged to a new family and felt safe. However, whenever there were tensions between assistants and they were unable to communicate with each other or to share, Karim felt this and anguish would rise up in him; he would begin again to hit his head. There was no point in seeking a psychologist to help Karim to stop hitting himself. The need was for a reconciler to bring the assistants together again in love.

Of course to be in communion one with another does not mean there are no differences of opinion. One can still appreciate and love others and be determined to struggle for the same goals, without always having the same ideas.

At the start of communities, founders base their actions on their own vision. Gradually the people who join them become one body with all the life and inevitable tensions that that must bring. Then founders can no longer behave as if they were the only ones to have the vision. They must listen to the community and respect its life and vision. The role of founders is to understand the life of the community and allow it to flourish under their guidance.

Perhaps the hardest thing founders have to do is to accept that the vision of others may reflect the community and its fundamental goals more clearly and truly than does their own.

One of the most important things for people in authority is to be clear about their priorities. If they lose themselves in a thousand details, they are in danger of losing the vision. They have to keep their eyes fixed firmly on essentials. The best authority is the one which does very little itself but reminds others of these essentials in their activities and their life, calls them to assume responsibilities, supports them, confirms them, and directs them.

Good leaders are aware of both their strengths and weaknesses.

They are not afraid to admit to the latter. They know how to find support and are humble enough to ask for it. There is no perfect leader who has all the gifts necessary for good leadership.

Community structures

At l'Arche we have a community council of seventeen people, elected by assistants who have been with us for more than two years. This council meets for a morning each week to share about fundamental questions and options for the community and take major decisions. I have learned a lot from these meetings. I have learned about the difficulties of sharing and searching together not for our own will, but for the will of the community and of God. We so quickly become possessive and emotionally involved. I have been helped to discover how I myself have to grow, to become more open to the Spirit and more objective. It seems to me now that all community leaders should have a council like this, where they can discern together, where authority is shared, supported, and directed, and where they can grow to be better able to carry responsibility together.

But it is not easy for a group to discuss peacefully and come to the right decision. They must learn the ways of discernment. I speak about this in the chapter on meetings (ch. 9).

Many leaders are fearful of and too dependent on their community council. They do not seem to be able to give true leadership. I am not sure that a community council can be prophetic, and frequently leadership needs to be prophetic. A council made up of elders is important; it permits the leaders to see all sides of a question. But a council will tend to be conservative: 'We have always done things this way.' Elders can block the growth and evolution of a community. They are often happy with the status quo and fearful of change. A leader needs to know how to use the council wisely, how to help it and how to be helped by it to come to the right decisions.

But how can a leader find the balance and inner freedom between a certain form of dictatorship – telling the council what to do – and just letting the council decide without giving it leadership?

As I write this, Gorbachev is having difficulty developing his policies of reform in the Soviet Union. The old guard is fearful of losing their privileges and want to block *perestroika*. Gorbachev needs support from somewhere, so he is seeking it among the people. Each leader must find his or her charisma to find ways of influencing the elders and advancing in truth and in justice.

It is important for each community to have a constitution defining its structure and mode of government: who makes what decisions and so on. When structures are unclear, and nobody knows who decides what or who is responsible for what, then people will be hurt. Leaders then tend to make decisions secretly, with those they choose, often out of fear of conflict or out of a need always to have their own way. Bad leaders tend to surround themselves with 'yes' people. Such lack of clarity in decision-making will gradually create serious tensions, until eventually an explosion occurs. Then either structures will be defined and a constitution accepted by all, or else some will leave the community in anger, and the leader will continue to lead badly.

Charismatic leaders tend to be frightened of structures, and hesitate in creating them. And yet, structures are essential if a community and its members are to grow.

Structures call for mandates and accountability; they define how leaders are voted or nominated and for how long. They set out how major decisions are to be made and by whom. They define the limits of power and areas of responsibility. They define also the relationship between the leader and the community council. Such structures can sometimes appear heavy, but they are necessary for a healthy community life. If each and every person is called to be responsible for the community, then all must know how decisions are made, even if not all can participate in the process of decision-making.

But, of course, structures must evolve and be redefined as a community grows and matures. I find it unhealthy when a constitution is set from the start and no provisions are made for modifications when they become necessary. People must remain faithful to their community's structures. It is a big mistake when leaders take decisions which should be referred to the council. That process of decision-making takes longer, and it is sometimes hard for leaders to restrain their own 'inspirations'. But this is the way a community comes to mature decisions together.

When leaders of communities are not reappointed as leaders – when their mandate has come to an end – they may suffer very deeply, particularly if they were founding leaders or were expecting to be reappointed. They may go through a form of depression or grief which is hard to bear. And this grief may also make life unbearable for others in the community. Sometimes they even have to leave the community, especially if the new leader is young and inexperienced and is afraid of their presence. Such people need a lot of compassion and help from wise people who accompany them; it can be a time when the cross becomes a reality. They must wait prayerfully for the time of resurrection, when they will again find a place where they can give life.

In l'Arche we give considerable responsibility to the Board of Directors of each of our communities. Like many associations in civil life, there must be legal statutes or a charter according to the laws of each country. The Board of Directors with its chairperson, is legally responsible for property, finances and other matters. It is also legally responsible for what goes on in the community, particularly in respect to people with a handicap who have been entrusted to the community by local authorities.

Our experience has shown that these men and women on the Board are not only competent in legal and financial matters, but that they also play an important role in helping the community to work through crises, to keep its feet well on the ground, to define and develop structures and, in a general way, to help the community to be clear about its established goals.

This means, of course, that Board members must really under-

stand the vocation and the reality of l'Arche, that they must discover how people with a handicap can nourish them too and bring
them closer to God, and also realise that these people have a specific
role in the church and in society. That means that Board members
must come together not just for business matters but also to enjoy
each others' company, to share together on a deeper level, and
particularly to enjoy being with the community members.

In some communities of l'Arche serious conflicts have erupted
between the Board and the leader. This is natural, of course, when
one acts without referring to the other, or makes decisions about
matters in which they were not *solely* competent. In such cases
there must be some external authority (see chapter 4) to whom
both parties can refer. This external authority becomes a reconciler
who helps to restore dialogue so that a real partnership is born,
but where responsibilities are also clearly defined.

Learning to listen and to exercise authority

People who are given responsibility must be allowed to carry it
out. Over-protection is ultimately a refusal to share responsibility.
People have a right to make their own mistakes, and fall on their
faces. Doing everything for them may protect them from setbacks, but it also prevents them from succeeding – however irrelevant the concepts of 'success' and 'failure' are in community.

However, people should not be left to carry responsibility alone.
They need someone who will counsel, support, and encourage
them. They should not be left to muddle through situations and
tensions which are too difficult for them to handle. They need
someone to whom they can talk freely, who understands and
confirms them in their responsibility. This person should be a
discreet presence who does not judge, who has experience in
human affairs and who instils confidence. Without such support,
leaders will be in danger of closing in on themselves or of cracking
up, and this is particularly true for leaders of communities. All
leaders in communities, like others in the Church and in society,

need help, formation, support, accountability and evaluation in order to exercise their responsibility with greater wisdom and love.

Jesus promised the Paraclete to his disciples, and we all have to be paracletes (counsellors who give support and love) for each other, responsive to their call. The cross of responsibility is sometimes heavy and we need a friend who understands, an older brother or sister, to make our task less onerous.

In order to be able to assume the responsibility for other people's growth, leaders must themselves have grown to true maturity and inner freedom. They must not be locked up in a prison of illusion or selfishness, and they must have allowed others to guide them.

We can only command if we know how to obey. We can only be a leader if we know how to be a servant. We can only be a mother- or father-figure if we are conscious of ourself as a daughter or a son. Jesus is the Lamb before he is the Shepherd. His authority comes from the Father; he is the beloved son of the Father.

I am discovering more and more how hard it is to carry authority. I very quickly come up against a hard and defensive aspect of myself. I sometimes find it difficult to link listening to people and compassion with firmness, objectivity, and the hope that they will grow. I am too often either timid and indecisive, letting people go their own way, frightened of speaking out clearly to them, or else rigid and legalistic. Each day I have to gain wisdom in responsibility, as well as strength and patience. My brothers and sisters on the council of l'Arche have helped me a lot. But I have a long way to go yet!

One of the essential qualities of people with responsibility is an ability to listen to everyone and not just to their friends and admirers. They have to know how people are feeling about the community and how they are growing. They have to create bonds with them which are true and, if possible, warm. People who carry responsibility badly hide behind prestige, power, the rule-book and their own commands; they listen only to their friends. They talk a lot but don't stop to listen to how others are receiving what they say. Above all, they do not try to understand other people's deep needs, aspirations, difficulties and sufferings or the way God has called them. People with authority who do not know how to listen to those who disagree with them, or to grasp the grain of truth hidden among the weeds of discontent, are living in insecurity. They would do well to allow the members of the community to discuss with the 'external authority' their view of how authority should be exercised (see chapter 4).

One reason that people with responsibility fail to listen is that they are unable to see the community as it really is. They become lazy optimists: 'Everything will sort itself out,' becomes their slogan. Basically, they are frightened of acting, or feel incompetent in the face of reality. It is hard to be constantly conscious of reality, because it can be disturbing. But it sharpens our awareness too. An aware authority is one which seeks to understand, prays, and cries out to God. Its thirst for truth will grow and God will answer its cry. But at the same time, it has to be very patient, a true friend to time.

Bad leaders are concerned only with rules and regulations. They do not try to understand how these affect people. It is easy to use the law to cover an inability to understand and listen. We tend to impose rules when we are frightened of people.

Founders of communities can be burdensome if communities always keep referring to them long after their death on matters other than the spirit of the community. New leaders need in some ways to be like founders. They have to adapt the community to new situations; they have to feel free to steer it with vision, accord-ing to the ways of the Spirit. But in order to do this, and to call the community to new growth, leaders need a lot of inner strength, particularly as elders of the community are frequently fearful of

change. Leaders who refer only to the past stifle life and tend to
be legalistic.

It is important for people in authority to listen to the young people
who enter the community. Their call, inspiration and wishes can
reveal a lot. The people in authority have to know how to listen
to them with interest and marvel at God's work in them. Their
call can show what the community should be and its failings as
well. In his rule, St Benedict says that each time there is something
important to discuss, the Abbot should call the whole community
together to get the advice of his brothers. And 'God often inspires
the youngest to make the best suggestions'.[3]

Don't hide!

People with responsibility are in danger of throwing up barriers
between themselves and those for whom they are responsible.
They give the impression of always being busy. They impress
others with the size of their car or their office. They give the
impression that they are superior, or at least the most important
person around. These leaders are afraid and create fear in others.
They keep their distance because they are insecure. Truly responsible people are open to others. They don't always use a car, even
for short distances, because walking gives others the chance to
meet them and talk to them like friends. They do not hide in their
offices, and so stay vulnerable to criticism. People in authority
should always stay close to those for whom they are responsible,
and encourage true and simple meetings. If they stay aloof, they
cannot know their people or their people's needs.

It is important for people in authority to reveal themselves as
they are and to share their difficulties and weaknesses. If they try
to hide these, one day people will see their faults and become
angry. After having put their leaders on a pedestal, they may

3 *Rule of St Benedict*, vol 15 (Regency Publishers, USA, 1968).

throw them into the pit. Leaders have to be seen as fallible and human, but at the same time as trusting and trying to grow. If leaders are to be true servants of communion, they must themselves be in communion with other people as a person, not as a leader. They must set the example of sharing.

A community is a body. The way a leader exercises authority is not from 'on top'. The diagram for community is not a pyramid but a circle. A community leader leads with others, and amongst others. The pyramid is the diagram for an army or for industry.

> We do not think so much of Brother Roger as being at the head of the community, as being at the centre of it. We are inspired by his vision and he is very good at expressing what the community is trying to live. He is a man who listens and he has an extremely practical side to him, but if he has gifts that others have not, the reverse is also true. Brother Roger is searching with his brothers. Together they are seeking to mature in the common life and in their 'adventure with God', and so no brother is looked upon as more advanced than any other.[4]

It is good if people with a responsibility do a bit of manual work, whether this is washing up or cooking the occasional meal. This keeps their feet on the ground and ensures that they get their hands dirty. It creates new relationships; those who work with them see them as people and not just as functionaries.

Some people in authority will always need to have someone close to them who knows how to knock them off their pedestal, tease them, and sometimes give them a kick in the pants. They so often meet either adulation or aggression. They can very quickly shut themselves up in their role because they are afraid or believe themselves to be a little god; then they will lose touch with reality. They need people who refuse to take them too seriously, who see

4 This is a quote from one of the brothers of Taizé in Kathryn Spink, *A Universal Heart* (SPCK, London, 1986), p. 55.

them as they really are and bring them back to earth. Of course, they must have confidence in these people and know that they are loved by them.

Personalised authority

Some communities refuse to have anyone in charge of them at all. They want to be governed democratically, through consensus with no co-ordinator or leader. It would be silly to say that this is impossible. But, from my experience of l'Arche, it seems to me that the members of a community need someone to whom they can refer and with whom they can have a personal relationship. People can reject all personal authority because they feel that it is always subjective and to do with personal prestige: for them, only consensus allows for objectivity.

It is true that consensus or collegiate government does allow for greater objectivity (though as we have already said, the elders of a community can get closed in on themselves). It is also true that none of us is more intelligent than all of us together. A group will tend to make juster rules than an individual. But, on the other hand, a group will always have difficulty in allowing for exceptions to its rules and will lack a prophetic vision to move wisely into the future, adapting the community to changing needs. In a community which has to do with the growth of people, it is good for there to be an authority which speaks to individuals and establishes trusting relationships with them. Communities which refuse the idea of a leader are often made up of people who are oriented towards effective and absorbing work, or else to causes and other forms of action. An older community, which knows the weaknesses of its members and which welcomes vulnerable people of all sorts, realises its need for an authority which is personal, loving, trusting and confirming.

The quality of life of a community can decline very quickly; weakness, fragility, egoism and apathy are quick to appear. The role of the 'father' or 'elder brother' is to nourish, encourage, support, forgive and sometimes to direct and restore order, so that the quality of life remains high. We enter community not because we are perfect, objective and intelligent, but because we want to grow towards a truer wisdom and love. And if this human growth is to be possible there must be someone who listens very personally, affirms, supports, brings security and helps people regain confidence in themselves, so that they can walk with greater courage and trust. Community questions have also, of course, to be settled through communal discernment, and people with responsibility help with this. But there are always those whose human, spiritual or psychological weaknesses makes them exceptional. They need to find another, compassionate human heart, to which they can open in confidence. We don't open our heart to a group; we open it to an individual.

Aristotle speaks of *epiki* as one of the virtues of the leader. It is this which enables him to interpret the law. The people who make that law cannot foresee every case. The leader, faced with the exceptional case, has a sense of justice and of the needs of individuals which enables him to act as the lawgivers themselves would have acted in the circumstances.

A group tends to act according to the precepts of justice and the law. It is impossible in a community to take each decision on its individual merits – that would lead to all sorts of comparisons, jealousies, claims, and counter-claims. There must be a rule. But at the same time, there must be the possibility of allowing for exceptions to that rule. A personalised authority will always put the good of the individual before that of the group and before the law; such an authority will show compassion and goodness towards the weak and be able to deal with the exceptional cases.

All this, of course, presupposes a loving authority which is at the service of individuals!

There is a crisis of authority these days, partly perhaps because some psychoanalytic doctrines tend to undermine the role of the father and of all authority. But we cannot accept a law unless we first have confidence in the person in whom it is embodied. Delinquents rebel against the law because they have not made the transition from reliance on the tenderness of their mother to trust in their father; that is why they find authority unbearable. We can only accept a law if it is embodied in a person who is able to forgive, take account of exceptions to the rule and, above all, to understand and have mercy.

Father Léon, founder of a community in Brussels, La Poudrière, has said that when no one carries responsibility in a community, its aggression is directed against its weaker members. Something is always going badly in a community and it is important that the people with responsibility recognise that one of their roles is to receive and channel the aggression, arising from this.

Attitudes to authority

Some people in community say that they cannot obey authority unless they have trust – and they mean complete trust – in those in whom authority is vested. There is something infantile in that; it is like the attitude of children who obey their parents until the day they discover that their parents have human failings.

Authority in a community is not all-powerful. There are always limits to it. The responsibility of the leader should be well defined in the community's constitution, and that constitution must also guarantee the right of all members to express their concerns about the way authority is exercised. If it does not do this, the door is open to division and dissent.

When people say that they can only obey an authority in which they have total confidence, they are looking for an ideal father. Their demand excludes any authority elected for a limited period; it excludes any real sharing of responsibility. We have to learn how to obey people who have been appointed or elected to responsibility according to the constitution, even if we do not feel any great friendship or affection for them. If we can feel this, so much the better; but it is unrealistic to expect it. If the condition of obedience is emotional trust, the way is open to anarchy and the possible death of the community.

It is not necessary to have total trust in the individuals with authority. But we should trust the people who have elected them and the constitution, the community's structures, dialogue, and God, who is watching over the community. He knows how to use even those who appear incompetent; he knows how to give them the grace to achieve their tasks without too many mistakes. We have to believe that the people with responsibility will find the grace necessary for the task.

In one community I visited, a person holding an important role told me: 'I have no trust in the director.' I was surprised and rather shocked. I said to the person: 'My goodness, do you think he might leave with all the money in the bank?' She answered rather sheepishly, 'No.' Then I said: 'Do you think he might sexually abuse a person with a handicap?' The person replied even more sheepishly 'No.' 'Tell me then in what precise ways you do not trust him.' People say too quickly: 'I do not trust someone.' It is not fair to continue saying that; trust is always relative.

If there is no obedience the community will fall apart, because obedience is trust. But this obedience is not something external and servile. It is an internalised support of legitimate authority, of the structures of decision-making and of the communal conscience of the community; it is a search for a communal vision; it is a belief in the principles on which the community's life and action are based.

If this communal conscience is rejected, there will be division. We create division when we believe that we are the only ones to see the truth, when we set ourselves as saviours against authority, when we reject the legal structures and when we want to prove we are right.

Of course people in authority can make mistakes. They may refuse to make decisions and to act at times when there is real danger for people and for the community and a decision is necessary. They may seek to defend their privileges or their way of doing things and no longer behave like servants of the common good. Individual members should then confront leaders but in a friendly dialogue. Those with responsibility are often criticised behind their backs; people are sometimes frightened to speak to them directly, in truth and in love.

It can be very difficult when leaders of communities lack vision and wisdom, or when, because of their limitations, prejudices or insecurity, they make serious mistakes and hurt people and the community. Mistakes in governing or shepherding can have terrible consequences, and particularly they may sap energies, destroy the spirit of a community and bring about a sort of inner depression in the group.

In face of recognised incompetence and serious limitations on the part of leaders, the danger for community members – or at least for the most perspicacious of them – is to become frustrated, angry and to create pockets of criticism and resistance; or else just to submit passively, watching the community slide down a path of disintegration.

Of course, some members can assume unjustly that leaders are incompetent, prejudiced, or are making the wrong decisions. Leaders are not necessarily bad leaders simply because they are not doing what these members think they should do. But when there is objective evidence of incompetence, lack of openness and vision, and this has been confirmed by a few wise and experienced members, then there can be a great deal of pain and anguish. What is to be done?

The first and most fundamental need is for patience and prayer. Members will be called to carry and offer the pain of such a situation, in silence and love, without harsh judgement and without creating divisions. They will also be called to be wise and vigilant in order to help the leaders come to right decisions, either through personal contacts with the leaders or through the appropriate structures. Members learn thus to wait and to put their trust in God. Of course, when necessary, an external authority and those who accompany the community should be advised of the situation; they will be called upon to influence such leaders and to rectify situations, but they cannot always turn a person who does not have the qualities of leadership, into a loving, good and wise leader. Once everything has been done to help the leader, there is always the possiblity that the Board of Directors, or another exterior authority, can ask him or her to resign. But this is exceptional. It is better to help the leader to finish the mandate, possibly with special help.

I have found so many communities living in such pain, not because the leaders were bad, but because there was nobody capable of wise leadership. Because of this, young people leave, others are hurt, and the spirit of love is wounded or, at least, not enhanced.

It is so painful to see a community disintegrating and yet, even then, this disintegration can become a source of life, if it is accepted and held in prayer and offered to the Father in sacrifice. And God in his time can bring about the rebirth of the community, by calling new people to it.

We must always remember; a community is not an end in itself; it is each individual person that is important. And people can grow in holiness and in communion with God in the midst of a broken, dying community, and through persecutions of all kinds.

We all look for perfect leaders who are compassionate and wise; we can all be disappointed when we see their failings and limitations. We risk then closing up against them. One of the greatest pains of a child is when it discovers that its parents are not perfect; that they have many failings, and even hardness, in them; and yet, it is called to obey its parents. It is then that the child risks closing up to authority, and this causes something to break deep inside the child, so that it says 'yes' outwardly, but remains angry and in revolt inwardly.

Members of communities who see the failings of their leaders may close up as well. They may relive certain pains and anger of their childhood. Yet they are called to learn how to remain in communion with their leaders, even if the latter do have failings. They are called to give their leaders support, to pray for them and to help them to grow. Leaders have their inner wounds and limitations like everyone else; we are called to love them as brothers and sisters. Members who have difficulty with authority and with the limitations of their leaders need good accompaniment in order to avoid falling into the trap of closing up.

We beseech you, brethren, to respect those who labour among you and are over you in the Lord and admonish you, and to esteem them very highly in love because of their work. Be at peace among yourselves. And we exhort you, brethren, admonish the idle, encourage the faint-hearted, help the weak, be patient with them all. See that none of you repays evil for evil, but always seek to do good to one another and to all. Rejoice always, pray constantly, give thanks in all circumstances; for this is the will of God in Jesus Christ for you. Do not quench the Spirit, do not despise prophesying, but test everything; hold fast what is good, abstain from every form of evil. (1 Thess. 5:12–22)

People in authority often become the focus for all sorts of personal and community discontents. Someone has to be the target for blame! We often expect too much of them; we seek an ideal father who knows everything, has all the gifts of a leader and can resolve all problems. We want ideal leaders who bring us security; then we feel insecure when we realise that they do not have all the gifts we are looking for. And so we reject those who fail to live up to our ideal.

We are often too dependent on the people with responsibility. We look constantly for their approval. We become servile. And then, discontented with our own servility, we criticise them behind their back. The leader often attracts either servility or aggression.

The relationship that people have with authority is often linked to the relationship they had as children with their parents. When this was difficult, when the parents lacked respect for their children's freedom and imposed their own wishes, the children may be left with a lasting anger and suspicion of all authority. Their relationships with it will be coloured by these emotions and psychological blocks. As soon as the leader intervenes, they will rebel against him and reject his command. They want him to approve of everything they do. As soon as he seems to question them, they clam up. They often have problems in seeing the person behind the position, who is not all-powerful and all-knowing, but equally does have his or her own gift to offer and has to grow in order to use that gift better each day. They often cannot admit that authority too has its failings. The relationship is a complicated one, and it is hard to talk together in simplicity and truth, because everything is coloured by childish fears and attitudes.

The leader is very often put on a pedestal and idealised. But that can simply mean that he is an easier target for criticism. People are careful not to aim for the heart, though; it is enough to wound him in the leg. His death, after all, would be a catastrophe, because then someone else would have to take on the job and that is not what his critics want.

The hardest step of all human growth may well be that from the child's dependence on and aggression towards its parents, to a friendship and dialogue with them, which recognises their grace and gifts. We become adult when we have acquired an inner freedom and a real capacity for judgement, and when we have fully accepted the gift of others and allow ourselves to be touched by the light that is in them. That is the passage from dependence to interdependence, and the people in authority should play their part in helping all to achieve it. But the passage to a new inner freedom cannot be made without pain and anguish.

To know how to talk with and obey authority is an important quality in community life and is a sign of maturity.

The sign of forgiveness

Forgiveness is at the heart of Christian community and the leaders must be the sign and model of this forgiveness. They must know how to forgive seventy times seven all the aggression and apathy that are focused on them, and this is not always easy. Each day, they have to relearn how to meet people as people and let people meet them in the same way, knowing that the road by which anyone finds a true relationship with authority is a long one. Through forgiveness, the leaders accept their own fears and defences, which had led them to be aggressive towards, or flee from, others. To forgive is to be open, understanding and patient with those who are aggressive.

Stephen Verney sums it up well: faced with aggression or servility,

> The leader can react in a number of ways. He can focus the attention of the group upon its purpose, and thus relieve the pressure on himself. He can make warm personal relationships with each individual member of the group, while retaining his command over the group as a whole. Both these tactics may be beneficial and promote the health of the group. But if he aspires to enable the group to live the life of the new age, then alongside and in conjunction with these two styles of leadership he must adopt a third, which is to be one step ahead of the group in this very process of forgiveness which is its essence. That is to say, he must become more aware of the good and evil that interlock both in himself and in the group, and he must pass through the experience of death and resurrection by which they may be unlocked and transformed. This he will have to do not once, but continuously. As Jesus puts it, hyperbolically but realistically, he must 'take up his cross daily'.[5]

Such forgiveness is particularly necessary when one or more members are always in opposition to and contest the leader's authority and competence. This can be terribly painful for a leader who feels threatened by them. The leader must learn not to avoid these people but to try to remain in dialogue with them and always to accept and forgive them. The leader should try also to see where his or her attitude might have hurt them, in order to change and be more open. For that, he or she needs a special grace from God.

In the same way, the leader must be very patient with the slowness and mediocrity of his community. By the grace of his

5 Stephen Verney, *Into the New Age* (Fontana/Collins, London, 1976).

position, he may have a more comprehensive vision; he may understand its needs better and more rapidly than his brothers and sisters; he may have a better sense of its evolution and of God's purpose for it, and of the urgency of being more true and faithful. But others can be expected to go more slowly. The leader should not hustle them or impose his own vision; still less should he make them feel guilty. Through his tenderness, gentleness, patience, acceptance and, above all, humility, he should engender a spirit of confidence. Then the others, in their turn and in their own time, will evolve, not according to his vision, but according to the vision of God for the community, and will be able to listen, forgive and respect each other's rhythm. I very much like Jacob's response to Esau when Esau invites him to journey with him:

> My lord knows that the children are frail, and that the flocks and herds giving suck are a care to me; and if they are overdriven for one day, all the flocks will die. Let my lord pass on before his servant, and I will lead on slowly, according to the pace of the cattle which are before me and according to the pace of the children. (Gen. 33:13–14)

Letting the community evolve

One of the roles of the person with responsibility in a community is to understand and hold together the group as a whole. This, of course is not done by the leader alone, but with others who carry responsibilities. 'By "holding" the group in this way', says Stephen Verney,

> he provides a secure container (room to move, time to face things, space to change), within which it is safe to test out new ways of dealing with the world, corresponding to the safe containment and control provided by the mother to the foetus and later to the infant, and by the mother to the mother/child complex and later to the family.[6]

6   Verney, *Into the New Age.*

Leaders who are themselves insecure, afraid, and anxious about their own authority will not allow the community to evolve. The leader has to be free enough, and have enough confidence in the group and himself, to allow the group's life to evolve and to allow individuals to take initiatives. To achieve this, he must not let himself be overwhelmed by everyday concerns; he must keep the distance he needs in order to grow and act on new inspiration. The leader is not simply the guardian of the law, although that is one aspect of his role. He is there to guarantee the freedom and growth of individuals according to the inspiration of God. Authentic inspiration is that which helps build the community according to its fundamental goals, even if they are not always recognised straight away. In fact, such inspiration can often disturb the community, and even the leader, because of the prophetic challenges it brings. But these challenges are necessary to remind the community of its goal. The leader must recognise their authenticity and help the community to recognise them.

Solomon's prayer should be the prayer of everyone with responsibility: 'Give thy servant therefore an understanding mind to govern thy people, that I may discern between good and evil' (1 Kings 3:9).

7

Other Gifts in Community

The spiritual guide

At the start of human life, the child receives everything from his parents – nourishment, bodily care and, above all, security. Their love and gift of themselves nourish and awaken its heart. Then the child grows and they give it language and are present at the awakening of its intelligence. They transmit a religious and moral tradition; they answer their child's first questions.

But gradually the child discovers that its parents are not enough. The teacher feeds its intelligence; the priest, or man or woman of God, helps it grow in prayer and the knowledge of God. As different aspects of the child are stimulated, it discovers different sources of inspiration and different forms of authority. The parents' role becomes more specific: they teach it to live in the community of the family, with brothers and sisters, and they pass on a tradition and a sense of what is and isn't done. The priest develops the conscience and secret part of the person, where the seeds of the eternal are sown. This part may be closed to the parents, who have no right to enter it. If the child wishes to divulge its secret, they must receive this with great respect. Teachers at school are different again. They help the child discover the meaning of the universe and of human history, and to be equipped in every way to take its place in society.

In the same way, at the start of a community there is a father- or mother-figure who assumes more or less all the functions. They can be at the same time the leader of the community and its authority, the spiritual father/mother or shepherd, and the educator. But gradually, these functions are diversified. Leaders have to help people find spiritual guides who will guide them in the secret of their hearts, in their union with God. Leaders must also give place to a teacher, someone who can develop the intelligence.

As people grow spiritually, their relationship to a spiritual guide evolves. At first this spiritual guide is like a spiritual father or mother who in some ways brings the person to birth in their inner life and communion with God. Young people who have had an experience of God and heard an inner call to grow in love, need a directive kind of guide, because they are still inexperienced and find it impossible to distinguish between dream and reality. If they are to take a first step in inner growth, they need someone who is firm and loving to whom they can be obedient. If they are not obedient and do not accept a guide they will become dispersed, fluttering around and touching upon many things; they will not grow in the knowledge and love of God and in prayer. As the person grows and becomes more centred spiritually and more mature, the spiritual guide becomes more of a counsellor, a witness to their growth and a spiritual companion.

In all ages holy people have been seen as teachers in the ways of God. People would go to hermits, the desert fathers or monks, to ask for healing and for prayers and to seek guidance. These holy people were seen as messengers of God. In the early Middle Ages spiritual direction was linked to confession. The penitent shared with the priest or monk, who encouraged, gave counsel and words of wisdom, and then – in the name of the Father, the Son and the Holy Spirit – forgave sins, even very minor ones. Today there is a tendency to separate the role of the spiritual director from the confessor. We are beginning to recognise that many women and lay people have the gift of spiritual guide or companion. Nevertheless, for me having a spiritual guide who is also a priest-confessor was and is very helpful. All the sharing is in some ways made sacred through the sacrament where the priest is just an instrument of Jesus' forgiving power.

Jesus was attacked because he dared to tell people that their sins

would be forgiven. The scribes and pharisees said that he was
blaspheming. That is why he was crucified.

After his resurrection, he said to the apostles: 'Receive the Holy
Spirit. If you forgive the sins of any, they are forgiven; if you
retain the sins of any, they are retained' (John 20:22–3). The priest
can help people to discover this forgiveness and so to go forward
in renewed hope. This spiritual power of the priest is a good reason
for him not to hold temporal power in a community.

Teresa of Avila insisted on spiritual guides being truly wise theo-
logians. This is particularly necessary for some people whose spiritual path is difficult and complex.

Spiritual guides must not only be holy – that is to say, wanting
truly to put their lives totally under the light of the Holy Spirit
and growing in the Spirit – but also wise in a knowledge of
spiritual things, of the Word of God, the teaching of the saints
and spiritual masters, as well as wise about people, their needs and
their growth.

As people are called inwardly to a change in life, to follow Jesus
along a particular spiritual road or in a particular community, it is
important for them to talk to a spiritual guide. Such a guide, once
they have come to know the person, and trust has been established,
will be able to counsel the person on how to respond to the call.
They will confirm the call, assure the person that it is not an
illusion, and encourage him or her to go forward.

In l'Arche we are seeing how important it is for assistants to
have a spiritual guide to help them in their struggles to love and
to be true, to help them to be rooted in the gospel values and in
the community, to give them support in times of anguish and
doubt or when they have particularly hard decisions or choices to
make at turning points in their lives.

These spiritual guides help them to know themselves and to see
how Jesus is working in and through them. They become a safe
person to turn to; they hold them in prayer; they carry them
through the days and nights, the winters and the summers, the

times of darkness and the times of clarity. It is so important for assistants to find someone who knows the secret of their hearts, calls them to growth and fidelity, reminds them of their initial call and remains close to them over the years.

Some communities fall into the trap of seeing the leader as the prophet and the spiritual guide of individuals all in one. Then this person becomes an all-powerful shepherd. This can be very dangerous, just as it is dangerous if the leader of the community is a psychoanalyst with all the staff under analysis.

If the leader does have these two roles, there is a danger of his using spiritual power to manipulate people for the smooth running of the community. The leader no longer seeks then to help people to be faithful to God in order to grow to greater inner freedom, but acts from the premise that they have to work for the community. That is a situation which can lead to all sorts of abuse.

In the same way, a community's members can trap the leader. Their confidences bind them to the leader which makes the proper exercise of authority difficult. They can even convince the leader that no one else can understand or help them. Then the leader is trapped by a sort of emotional blackmail. People in authority must not be afraid to tell members of the community that they cannot help with their emotional or spiritual life. Their role is to help them find their place in the community and to do their work well, and find the right spiritual guide for them.

I am concerned when I see leaders who are also priests or psychotherapists. These three areas of responsibility should not be confused. There is the role of the father/mother figure called to help each one find their place in community. There is the role of the priest called to evoke the presence of Jesus in the sacraments and the Word; and there is the role of the therapist or doctor called to help members on their road to healing. If these three roles are separated and work well in harmony together, each one according to their gift, then the members will grow to greater inner freedom.

There can be a danger too when a spiritual guide begins to see the flaws in a community and in the leader, and then starts to criticise them in front of the person they are guiding. It is good for a spiritual guide to be independent of the community, but they are called to help the person accept the community that has been given to him or her, and to grow in difficult situations. Spiritual guides need to be wise in the way they work with communities and community leaders.

On the other hand, leaders in society and in communities can feel threatened by priests and spiritual guides; they can seek to lock them up in the sacristy or in the church and to silence them when they speak up against injustices.

The place of priests, outside of the Eucharist and spiritual direction, can only be discovered when there is a community which is truly a body; when there is communion.

My experience with our l'Arche communities is that when the leader and the priest work truly together, in communion one with the other, recognising humbly that each has a gift to offer to the other and to the community as a whole, each one helping the other find their place; then the community will grow in light and in love. But I am not sure that one can define clearly the specific places in the community where each one exercises their responsibility. It will depend so much on the gifts and the temperaments of each one. But priests will obviously have a share in questions touching upon the formation and growth of individuals to greater love and wisdom. They will be called to defend individuals against community abuses. And they will be called to be in communion in and through their priesthood with others outside the community, with the greater church of the diocese and, through the diocese, with the universal Church. A priest is never ordained just for the people of one community, but for the universal Church.

I am sometimes a bit worried about new communities which are carried by a single strong shepherd or a solidly united team of shepherds. As these communities have no traditions, no history and no constitutional control by a recognised ecclesiastic or legal authority, such as a board of directors, there is hardly any check on their activities. The leaders may develop a taste for their role, seeing themselves as indispensable, and so unconsciously dominating others. There is also the risk of mixing community and spiritual power. It is good and useful if these leaders quickly hand over the spiritual direction of individuals to other guides.

A shepherd should never become all-powerful. He or she should never be put on a pedestal as a saint, prophet, or holder of power. The greatest danger for any shepherd or leader is to believe that they are always right, and that God is with them in all their decisions. Every person is fallible. Weak people can tend to seek security by deifying their shepherd. This is unhealthy and wrong. It is their insecurity which makes them want to turn their shepherd into a saint who will instruct them in everything.

Every person is a mixture of good and evil, light and darkness. Spiritual guides must be humble, know their limitations, not interfere where they shouldn't, and respect the gifts and charism of others. They should also know how to disappear. They carry the secret of individuals, their bonds with God, but they leave others to help them find their places in the community.

We should be wary of people who call themselves shepherds or spiritual counsellors without having received the mission or authority for this. They may be wanting spiritual power unsubjected by any controls.

I am struck by how difficult it is for many people to discern well. In the past, judgements were made according to the law and objective criteria; people obeyed and that was it. Now, discernment is increasingly made by subjective criteria. People gauge their own emotions, and if they feel troubled, they think this is because they are not acting according to God's will. We are passing from objectivity and the rule of law to subjectivity. People seem to forget that there is a huge difference between the peace which is a gift of God and passes all understanding, and peace in the psychological sense. If we are living in a dream or illusion, or have certain psychological blocks, we should not be surprised that we become troubled when someone brings us face to face with reality. Sometimes we have to lose psychological peace before we can live in true peace. Divine peace often grows from humiliation and acceptance of a psychological problem. It is a gift of God which springs from our inner selves and a desire to serve our brothers and sisters. It helps us to carry our cross.

In the same way, people who are searching for their vocation are sometimes so taken up by their own small concerns that they no longer hear the cry of those who suffer or the call of the poor. We often discover our own call only when we listen to the call of others.

The present time is also characterised by a struggle in many people between a desire for independence and acceptance of interdependence. Some modern psychology seems to tell us that we have to become free of the father, as if we would then be totally independent in our thought, judgement and emotional life. But often, when we believe ourselves to be free of the father-figure, we are in fact influenced by, and so dependent on, the currents of thought around us. It is not easy to know when and how to be free. The important thing is not freedom for its own sake, but freedom to love and serve better.

There is then an increasing need for spiritual guides who can help people go beyond their search for psychological peace and their own identity, so that they can listen to the call of God and of those in distress, and enter into covenant with them.

Spiritual guides must understand the workings of the human heart. But they must also, and above all, understand the ways of God, and how the Holy Spirit, the master of love, is leading people. Psychology is helpful as far as it goes, in its aim to bring a certain psychological freedom. But men and women of God help others to live with their psychological blocks and to grow in the will of God and in love for Jesus and their brothers and sisters. They help them to do this in fidelity and in humility, in the certainty that this is one of the best ways to make the blocks disappear. They help people to stay in the light of God.

It is the men and women of God who help us discover the meaning of our setbacks and how to use them constructively. When we are going through difficult times in community life and feel rejected, these people remind us, 'Don't worry; it's just a difficult moment. It's a time of death – but don't you know that you have to die with Christ in order to rise again with him? Wait for the dawn. Be patient. Remember your covenant.' We have to learn to draw on our suffering, distress and setbacks so that we can grow spiritually. It is so easy for us to get locked into frustration, anger and depression.

A spiritual guide does not always need to give advice. We all have the light of truth in our hearts, and if we are peaceful and mature enough, we will discover the answer within ourselves. But we always need someone who will ask the right questions.

The specific role of the priest or ordained minister

I have already mentioned the role of the priest as spiritual guide, but a spiritual guide can be a lay person. The priest's essential responsibility is for the sacramental life of the members of the community, in particular, the transforming of bread and wine into the body and blood of Christ. The priest is ultimately linked to the Eucharist.

Our l'Arche communities are always in need of these priest-shepherds who bring the nourishment of the Eucharist and the gift of forgiveness. As a community and as individuals we need them; we need to put the secret of our hearts in the heart of God through the priest. But they must be men of prayer, transparent, gentle and yet firm and sometimes even bold in the struggle against the powers of darkness and evil. And, by the word they preach, they must remind us constantly how the Body of Christ in the Eucharist calls us to see the Body of Christ in the broken bodies of the poor.

If a community finds its centre in the Eucharist which is sacrifice and union, then the priest will necessarily have an important role in the community – not in its government or structures, but by offering himself up in prayer and sacrifice for the community and by nourishing the community members with the Body of Christ. It is the Body of Jesus welcomed with love, that sanctifies each member and makes them holy and whole, and that unites all in one body of the community and of the Church. The priest is not holier than others; he is the chosen minister and servant of the Lord Jesus. The holiest person, the most loving one is the one who welcomes the body of Christ with the greatest desire and love. And this may be a very weak and broken person.

Priests have a further role when they are members of the community or have a mandate to help the community in its growth.

Here we touch upon the very delicate question of links between spiritual and temporal power. Human beings are always craving for power, and priests are no exception to this. Very quickly they can feel uneasy in a spiritual role and then use spiritual power for temporal power and privileges.

When the priest or minister has no power, other than that which comes from his ordination, he has enormous freedom to be truly present throughout the community, and in all aspects of community life, on equal terms with everyone. He is stranger to nobody and there is no situation beyond his touch – which must always be that of Jesus. He is free to meet everyone, to be anywhere, and by his presence to be a living reminder of the place of Jesus and the gospels in the community. It is by simply being present among his people that the priest will come to know their joys and anxieties and there he will find a thousand opportunities for shining the light of God on all that touches the lives of the members of the community.

We are discovering in l'Arche the special place a priest or ordained minister has in accompanying someone who is in their final passage of death. They seem to be able to bring something to the person, and to the community that bears the pain of loss, that others cannot.

Community and work accompaniment

In l'Arche we use the word 'accompaniment' in a way that is very unusual in English. It is the noun coming from the verb 'accompany', and we have not found a better way to express the reality of being alongside people as a companion and friend in order to help them grow in freedom and in the spirit of the community. 'Accompaniment' has its roots in the Latin *cum pane*, eating bread together, which signifies a bond of friendship, a covenant.

We distinguish three forms of accompaniment. *Spiritual accompaniment* touches the deepest part of our being, our life in the Spirit and our union with God. It is carried out by the spiritual guide. *Work accompaniment* is a kind of walking with a person, by someone 'higher' in authority to whom the person is accountable for the work they do; he or she shows them what has to be done and how. The leader of a community, for example, accompanies the heads of houses and heads of work projects; the head of house accompanies the assistants in the house and so on. This kind of 'walking with' is not just helping someone to work with greater competence, but also with greater love and in a certain spirit.

Community accompaniment is carried out by somebody who is outside the assistant's immediate work hierarchy and who is appointed by the community to accompany him or her. This person is called to enter into a more personal relationship, to share together about the spirit and traditions of the community, the needs and difficulties and the growth of the assistant in the community and in the place of work. It is a relationship in which assistants can share on a more personal level about their day-to-day life; and they can be helped to look at problems that come up, to see where their own wounds and blockages are causing conflicts and difficulties. In this way they can be helped to deepen, and to grow in truth and love and wisdom in community life. Many people need desperately to be able to communicate some of their inner pains and joys to someone who can hold them without making judgements, but with understanding, compassion and a certain wisdom.

Because in l'Arche there is no one rule of life for all assistants, no fixed spiritual formation for all, these three forms of accompaniment are vital in order to make the transition from the values of the world to the values of the community, and particularly the values of the Gospel. Only if there is a wise and clear accompaniment will people be able to root themselves in a community of faith and in a covenant with the poor.

The essential aspects of these three forms of accompaniment are: listening, caring, clarifying, affirming and challenging. Assistants need to feel that they are listened to, that someone cares for them and clarifies with them work expectations, community expectations and expectations in their spiritual life; and finally, they need to be challenged and affirmed in their growth and struggle to make choices and efforts. All this rests on a basis of trust.

Psychological accompaniment

Some people need yet another kind of accompaniment. Because of severe conflicts with their parents or the indifference or absence of their parents during early childhood, they were obliged to create strong barriers around their hearts. In this way they protected themselves from the pain, anguish, loneliness, guilt, confusion and anger which could have overwhelmed and killed them if these had remained on the surface of their consciousness. In order to live and get on with life, human nature is such that children can hide all this pain away in the secret recesses of their being and forget it. But this inner pain or darkness, stored up in the shadow side of their being in a sort of inner tomb, continues to govern unconsciously many of their attitudes and actions.

Sometimes, hidden in this secret place, there is too much unresolved anger, too deep a yearning to be seen and loved as unique; too much loneliness transformed into guilt and lack of self-confidence; too much ambivalence in respect to authority for them to be able to live harmoniously in community.

Some people with a lot of pain in them are able to enter community; their generosity and deep need for belonging seem to cover it up. They are able to function quite well, obey all the rules and find quite a lot of personal satisfaction and peace. Their hidden anguish can even become a drive toward greater competence and achievement. But when they are finally accepted as permanent members, and frequently at a moment of a personal set-back, there can be a terrible explosion. All the mess hidden in the tomb seems to rise up into the consciousness. Living in community becomes unbearable for them.

It is then that they will need far more professional, psychological help, or some more specialised spiritual support. They will need someone to whom they can reveal all the pain, even all that their mind had forgotten but which their being had not. Then they can gradually be liberated from these deep powers that have been governing them, or at least come to a better understanding and acceptance of them. They start then on a journey towards inner healing and wholeness.

It is not the scope of this book to elaborate on the values and dangers of these more specialised forms of accompaniment. There are so many therapies and therapists today, so many healers. Suffice it to say that great wisdom must be exercised in the choice of therapy and of therapist, and the person him or herself must want and request the therapy. There is always a danger of a community wanting a person to be healed and to get therapy because the person is a thorn in their flesh.

Each person has a gift to share

A community is like an orchestra: each instrument is beautiful when it plays alone, but when they all play together, each given its own weight in turn, the result is even more beautiful. A community is like a garden full of flowers, shrubs and trees. Each helps to give life to the other. Together, they bear witness to the beauty of God, creator and gardener-extraordinary.

Community brings together people of very different temperaments. Some are organised, quick, precise and efficient; they tend to be defensive and legalistic. Others are open, flexible and love personal contact; they are less efficient – to say the least! Others are shy and tend to become depressed and pessimistic. Others again are extrovert, optimistic, and even a bit exalted. God calls all these opposites together to create the wealth of the community. It may not be very easy at first. But gradually we discover what a richness it is to live with such a diversity of people, and such diversity of gifts. We discover that difference is not a threat but a treasure, or that 'variety is evidence of life: cold conformity presages death'.[1]

When people are using their gifts, it is important that the community prays for them to be more open to inspiration and more an instrument of God, so that they can use those gifts better. It is important, too, that the community welcomes those gifts in love and gratitude. It should also pray for the people who carry authority and those who inspire through their words. So we participate in each other's gifts, and help each other build community.

At l'Arche, we need people who are competent teachers and trained workers. We also need people to live in our houses who are open to whatever comes, love community life, and above all want to live with and discover the gifts of people with a handicap. We need people who are well rooted in their spiritual and religious life, who spend time with God in prayer. They all bring their own gift, and all these gifts are needed for the building, well-being, radiance and unity of the community. Each person is indispensable in his or her own way.

Of course we all have to grow in wholeness, becoming more competent, more open to the demands of community life, closer to the handicapped people, and more prayerful. Some people are called to exercise in a special way their own particular gift.

1 Parker J. Palmer, *A Place Called Community* (Pendle Hill, Philadelphia, 1977).

To love people is to recognise their gift and to help them use and deepen it. A community is beautiful when all its members are using their gifts fully.

'Bear one another's burdens, and so fulfil the law of Christ' (Gal. 6:2). The burden for a Christian is above all the freedom of another.

> The freedom of the other person includes all that we mean by a person's nature, individuality, endowment. It also includes his weaknesses and oddities, which are such a trial to our patience, everything that produces friction, conflicts and collisions among us. To bear the burdens of the other person means involvement with the created reality of the other, to accept and affirm it, and, in bearing with it, to break through to the point where we take joy in it. . . . The service of forgiveness is rendered by one to the others daily. It occurs, without words, in the intercessions for one another. And every member of the fellowship, who does not grow weary in this ministry, can depend upon it, that this service is also being rendered him by the brethren. He who is bearing others knows that he himself is being borne and only in this strength can he go on bearing.[2]

The gift of listening

This is an important gift in community. But if we are to be able to listen, we must offer security. None of us would speak to people unless we knew that they were safe and would respect our secret. An assurance of confidentiality is an essential part of being a listener. This means knowing how to respect the wounds and the sufferings of others and not divulging these.

2   Dietrich Bonhoeffer, *Life Together* (Harper & Row, New York, 1976).

The gift of discernment

Some people have a true gift of discernment. They can seize what is essential in a complicated discussion or a confused story. They are quick to understand what is really needed and at the same time, if they are practical, they can suggest the first steps towards putting people on the road to healing. Some people in a community who do not have an important position may have this gift of light for us. We have to learn to listen to them.

Fidelity over time

A Benedictine abbot once told me how he marvelled at the fidelity of his monks. But, he added, they also needed refreshment and rejuvenation.

At a time when so many new communities are being born, which are sometimes clamorous in their songs, youth and excitement, we should not forget the old communities, which have worked the earth and lived peacefully, in prayer, silence, worship and forgiveness, and whose tradition goes back for centuries. People who are coming into community have a lot to learn from the wisdom of these foundations which are living fidelity without making too much noise about it. Many young communities, with all their enthusiasm and emotionalism, will die, while those which are more silent and serene will continue their journey through the generations.

We who are young in community should beware of believing that we have the only answer and can teach these wise men and women who have so much experience of the human and the divine, and have been walking with Jesus for so many years. They have the gift of fidelity.

The gift of wonderment

People who have spent a long time in community tend to forget what is beautiful in it. They may be too taken up with immediate needs; they may have got stuck in a rut. They have lost the grace of wonderment. They need to be renewed by listening to the sense of wonder in the younger people who feel called to commit themselves to the community.

The greatest sin of people who have spent a long time in community is to accuse the newcomers of naivity and condemn their enthusiasm and generosity. The sense of wonderment in the young can blend with the fidelity, wisdom, and ability to listen of the older members to make a community which is really beautiful.

A grandmother is always given new life by her grandchildren. Communities need 'grandmothers', who may have more time to marvel than other people, because they carry few responsibilities. It is always good when a community has a wide spread of ages, from the very young to the very old. The complementarity, as in a family, brings peace. When everyone is the same age, it can be exciting for a time, but weariness soon sets in. We need to refind the gift of youth and the peaceful wisdom of age.

The gift of the 'grandmother'

A community needs this gift too, especially if their 'grandmother' also has a fund of commonsense. We too often tend to dramatise our weariness and anguish. We weep and forget why we are weeping. We identify with the agony of Christ or with the most disadvantaged of the world. An older woman who has experience, who is comfortable with herself, knows that what we really need is a week at the seaside. St Teresa of Avila advised her sisters who were going through a bad patch to eat a good steak rather than force themselves to pray. We have to remember that we have a body which has its own laws, and that the physical has its effect on the spiritual. We have to respect our body and its needs, and care for it even more than a craftsman cares for his tools. Our body is more than a tool. It will be resurrected. It is an integral part of our being, of our self.

'Grandmothers' sense certain things. And there are things which can be confided only to them. They are important to a community. And of course the same could be said about wise 'grandfathers'.

The gift of men and women

L'Arche communities are a great mixture – men and women, single people and married couples. This is precious and indeed vital. The men and women we welcome sometimes have deep emotional wounds. They need people they can turn to as mother- or father-figures, older people who are a source of healing and growth. They also need models of femininity and masculinity lived in beauty and truth. People of different sexes who live together in communities can discover a richness and call to growth and fulfil- ment that is truly God-given. This is so, particularly, when people have not come to a mature knowledge of their identity and call. There is the difficulty of people in community who fall in love and cannot take the distance they need from each other to see if this is real love, which will lead to marriage, or a love which has grown in each of them out of their loneliness. There are many people who have emotional difficulties because of a lack of love in their own childhood; they can confuse their search for the security of a parent with their search for a husband or wife. The community can help them to integrate their sexuality and find emotional stability, especially if it has very clear and challenging goals, if there is a lot of laughter, and if there is acceptance of clear ethical values concerning relationships between men and women.

It is important in such communities that there be a continual and deepening reflection on the meaning and needs of the human heart - this heart so vulnerable and yet so yearning for a total and a healing love. In these days there is much confusion around the whole area of sexuality and of the place of man and woman in society. People need to see sexuality in a holistic view of the person: not cut off from faithful and covenant relationships, but rather flowing from and to them; not cut off from fecundity and responsibility but always in view of a true fecundity and of giving life; not seen in a vision of competition and aggression but rather of complementarity and of unity in the same body of community. In such a vision people will discover the great gift it is for men and women to be united together in the service of God, in communities oriented towards the giving of life to the poor and the broken.

There is a trend today to suppress the differences between men and women. We seek equality in everything. Of course we are all equally human, and of course for equal work there should be equal pay. But in our bodies and in our psychology there is a difference. It is this difference we must love and respect, and then men and women can discover how much they need each other. In community we are called to discover that that difference is not a threat but a treasure and that each one of us can develop our own gifts.

It is certainly still true that men sometimes see themselves as superior – more powerful, strong, and intelligent – and tend to relegate women to a subordinate place, as if only they have gifts. There is something shocking about men who spend their time and money in bars while women raise their children. We can understand that, when men behave like this, they are trying to prove their virility and putting all their energies into external things – like physical strength and the ability to use this to dominate. Women are often more internalised and, by their physical capacity for having children, much closer to the reality of love and the world of emotions. They have their gift, which is called to grow and to flourish.

Men are in danger of fleeing from their own vulnerability and capacity for tenderness. They seek a wife-mother and then, very quickly and like small boys, they reject her because they want their freedom. They will throw themselves into the world of efficiency and organisation and reject tenderness and true mutuality. But in doing that, they will cut themselves off from an essential part of their nature. Then they will either idealise women as pure virgins or condemn them as sirens, instruments of the devil and prostitutes, or else use them as servants. This is a rejection of sexuality, whether it is condemned as wicked or is denied. Either way, the man will reject any true relationship with a woman because he can see her only as a symbol of either purity or sin or as somebody inferior.

A man has to grow into mature relationships with women, to get beyond the stage of mother-child or seduction-revulsion. This means he has to discover his own true identity as a man and to be able to integrate his sexuality into clear community relationships. He will often need a woman who is comfortable with herself to help him discover his own capacity for tenderness and his own vulnerability, without any threat to his own disturbed and disturbing sexuality. Then he will find a balance between the virility of effective action and power, and his own heart. He will be on the journey to healing and to wholeness.

Women have to find their balance too. They must neither reject their femininity to seek masculine power, nor envy the masculine capacity for organisation. They have to discover the wealth of their own femininity, the power they have in their weakness, the light and the wisdom of their intelligence, and the capacities to heal and to be compassionate. And in the weakness which comes from their separation from power, women sometimes have clearer and truer intuition, less adulterated with the passions of pride and power which often colour masculine intelligence.

Men who hold responsibility in their communities can be jealous of their own vision. There may be women in the community who are more intelligent than they are, more sensitive in their discernment, and more sure of their own purpose. The man in charge can reject these women because he feels it would be a sign of weakness to admit that they have a truer vision and greater discernment than he does. The same thing can happen in a marriage. In our civilisation, where the man has to be virile and powerful, there can be a curious struggle between the sexes; a man can be afraid of losing something if he admits that a woman is right. Yet each should be able to recognise the gift of the other. God sometimes gives a man power without the ability to discern and a woman discernment but no power. When men and women refuse to work together, it can become a subtle form of warfare which can lead to chaos. When they do work together, it is community.

Clearly we should not generalise too much. There is a quality of receptivity in men just as there are qualities of thrust in women. True creativity depends on the development of both. But it remains true that their different physiological make-up give men and women particular tendencies; men are more turned towards the external world and women, by their physical capacity to bear children, towards relationships. Neither is superior in the heart of God. But women are more sensitive to the realities of community life and men are more sensitive to reason, efficiency and structures. This does not mean that either is necessarily incompetent in the other area, but it is why there has to be co-operation and recognition of the gifts of both sexes.

It is clear that the very first community is that between man and woman. They are one family, one body. If their differences cannot be loved and respected by each other, then unity breaks down; they become rivals and are no longer members of the same body. So it is in community; men and women bring so much to each other and to the community. Much should be said about this question in a book on community. But I have already written a great deal about it in *Man and Woman He Made Them* and in *The Broken Body*.

To exercise authority one has to grow to wholeness, seeking continually to harmonise the masculine and the feminine. For many years I have exercised authority together with women. I have seen how we help each other. I had certain gifts that were less developed in them, as they had gifts that were less developed in me. It is good for men and women to exercise authority together.

The anti-gift

A community is founded on the trust its members have for each other. This trust is very fragile and very weak. There is a place in all our hearts where doubt lives. People who sow discord have a flair for finding that place and feeding the doubt, which is how they can destroy community. And that is an anti-gift.

I am struck by the people who come into our communities to stay for a time and very quickly put their finger on failings – of which, God knows, there are enough! – without being able to see anything good. They come to see me, to criticise others, and suggest solutions. They present their own projects – usually involving a particular therapy – and explain how this will resolve the difficulty and put the community or the people with a handicap onto the right track. They believe that their gift is to be a saviour.

These 'saviours' certainly have the intelligence to understand and sometimes to exploit the failings of a community. They are attractive; they talk well. And they are dangerous because they want to do their own thing. They lack self-confidence and they are deeply unhappy. They need to prove that they exist through their projects and so they tend to be aggressive.

If people come into community in this state of mind, it will be a disaster for them and for the community. The right way to come into a community is to feel at ease there, ready to serve and be respectful of structure and traditions. A project has to grow in collaboration with others and not as a way of proving anyone's capability.

The gift of animation

It is always important in a community to have people who have the gift of animating, of giving life to a meeting or celebration. Guy once said that the best way for him to prepare for an event was to spend some time beforehand just listening to the inner

music and the needs of the people who would be there. Coming
with a prepared text doesn't work. We have to be aware all the
time of what people are really waiting for and we have to respond
to this secret, silent wish. A talk, like a celebration, must always
be a dialogue between the person who is talking or animating and
the people who are waiting as the earth waits for water. This
doesn't mean leaving everything to intuition. The person who is
called to speak should know in advance what people really need
and what to say, but at the same time there must be sensitive
response to what people really want as this becomes apparent
during the meeting.

The gift of availability

Availability for service is one of the most marvellous gifts that we
can find in community. People who have this gift trust those in
authority and the community itself, and take on whatever is asked
of them. And if they do not know how to cope, they ask help of
the Holy Spirit and of their brothers and sisters.

There is a tendency nowadays to decry obedience, perhaps
because authority has been badly used in the past; people were
more ready to take on power than to help others grow spiritually
and personally. And it has to be admitted, too, that obedience can
be servile and morose.

But it is marvellous for a community to have among its members people with this child-like spirit, who are ready to take on
whatever is asked of them. They have confidence that it would
not be asked if they were not capable of doing it, by the grace of
the spirit.

The gift of availability can be transmitted from one person to
another, like a fire of love. It brings a community to life.

The gift of the poor

The people with the best sense of what is essential to a community, of what gives and maintains its spirit, are often doing very humble manual tasks. They are not taken up with major responsibilities or 'important' things, so they have a greater freedom to understand the essentials. It is often the poorest person – the one who has a handicap or who is ill or old – who is the most prophetic. These people should not be sucked into the structure of the community; that would deflect them from their gift, which is to love and serve or, even more, to call out for love and awaken compassion and service in the hearts of others. People who carry responsibility must be close to them and know what they think, because it is often they who are free enough to see with the greatest clarity the needs, beauty and pain of the community.

In a mental hospital, it is often the patients who are the most prophetic people. They, more than anyone, can say what is going badly and who are the good doctors.

Not long ago, in an African country, a religious order sounded out local people to see what they wanted of the missionaries. Should they, for instance, dress like local people and eat local food? The response was immediate. They knew, the local people said which of the missionaries loved and respected their culture and way of life and which did not. The way they dressed and their eating habits were irrelevant.

To know whether a community is faithful to its original vision ask the insignificant people, those who surround it, and are in need. These people know very well if authority is being well used and if the community is being faithful. This is why we have to pay heed to them. They nearly always have the best answer to the questions the community is asking.

One of the most precious gifts in a community is to be found among the people who cannot take on important responsibilities. They have no ability to organise, inspire, look ahead or command, but they do have very sensitive and loving hearts. They can recognise people in difficulty straight away and, with a smile, a look, a flower or a word, make these people feel that they are close to them, carrying their cross with them. These insignificant people are at the heart of the community and carry in their hearts those people who are blocked towards each other and who have different ideas concerning the community. It is the love of the hidden people which keeps the community united. The leader brings unity through justice, but these loving people are creators of unity just by being who they are. In their tenderness they are artisans of peace.

The most precious gift in community is rooted in weakness. It is when we are frail and poor that we need others, that we call them to love and use all their gifts. At the heart of community are always the people who are insignificant, weak and poor. Those who are 'useless', either physically or mentally, those who are ill or dying, enter into the mystery of sacrifice. Through their humiliation and the offering of their suffering, they become sources of life for others. 'Upon him was the chastisement that made us whole' (Isa. 53:5). This is a mystery of faith.

At the heart of everything beautiful in a community, there is always a sacrificial lamb, united to the Lamb of God.

Many people are good at talking about what they are doing, but in fact do little. Others do a lot but don't talk about it. They are the ones who make and sustain community.

There are few things worse than adulation. It stifles love. It kills people who want a life which is real, made up of gift and loving presence. Adulation is a poison which, if it gets too deep, can make the whole body sick. And to purify it then takes many periods of trial. Flatterers should know this, and stop making others in community suffer! Confirmation of someone's gift is not adulation. Recognition of someone is not flattery. It is good to recognise, encourage, and affirm gifts.

It is the people who love, forgive and listen who build community. It is those who are sensitive, who serve others, and who nourish and pray for them. And each of us, by the grace that has been given to us, exercises our gifts according to our own good and unique expression of love and tenderness. A community is only really a community when all its members realise how deeply they need the gifts of others, and try to make themselves more transparent and more faithful in the exercise of their own gift. So a community is built by every one of its members, all in their own way.

8

Welcome

Giving space

To welcome is one of the signs of true human and Christian maturity. It is not only to open one's door and one's home to someone. It is to give space to someone in one's heart, space for that person to be and to grow; space where the person knows that he or she is accepted just as they are, with their wounds and their gifts. That implies the existence of a quiet and peaceful place in the heart where people can find a resting place. If the heart is not peaceful, it cannot welcome.

To welcome is to be open to reality as it is, with the least possible filtering. I have discovered that I have many filters within my own self where I select and modify the reality I want to welcome: the reality of the world, of people, of God and of the Word of God. I select what pleases me, boosts my ego and gives me a sense of worth. I reject that which causes inner pain or disturbance or a feeling of helplessness; that which may bring up guilt feelings or anger or a broken sexuality. We all have filters created from our early childhood, protecting our vulnerable hearts and minds. To grow is to let go of these filters and to welcome the reality that is given, no longer through preconceived ideas, theories, prejudgements or prejudices or through our wounded emotions, but just as it is. Thus, we are *in truth* and no longer in a world of illusions.

But to be able to welcome means that our inner person and freedom have been strengthened; we are no longer a person living in fear and insecurity, unclear about who we are and what is our mission. It takes time for this inner person to grow. It takes many painful meetings, many times when we have been wrong and have asked for forgiveness, much grace from God and much love from loving friends. To become humble and open, we have to live through many humiliations.

It is not surprising that Jesus comes under the guise of a stranger: 'I was a stranger and you welcomed me.' The stranger is a person who is different, from another culture or another faith; the stranger disturbs because he or she cannot enter into our patterns of thought or our ways of doing things. To welcome is to make the stranger feel at home, at ease, and that means not exercising any judgement or any preconceived ideas, but rather giving space *to be*. Once we have made the effort of welcoming and accepting the disturbance, we discover a friend; we live a moment of communion, a new peace; a presence of God is given. The stranger is frequently prophetic; he or she breaks down our barriers and our fears, or else makes us conscious that they are there and may even strengthen them.

It is always a risk to welcome anyone and particularly the stranger. It is always disturbing. But didn't Jesus come precisely to disturb our routines, comforts, and apathy? We need constant challenge if we are not to become dependent on security and comfort, if we are to continue to progress from the slavery of sin and egoism towards the promised land of liberation.

Welcome is one of the signs that a community is alive. To invite others to live with us is a sign that we aren't afraid, that we have a treasure of truth and of peace to share. If a community is closing its doors, that is a sign that hearts are closing as well.

But before we welcome people, we have to exist as a community. When a community starts, it is frequently more closed, so that its members can get to know each other and a unity be created. The same is true in marriage; if a newly married husband and wife are constantly inviting friends in, they will have no time to forge their own unity.

There is a time for everything – a time to build community and a time to open its doors to others. The second period doesn't necessarily follow the first: they are bound up in each other. A community will always need times of intimacy, just as it will always need times of openness. If it has only one or the other, it will die, or at least suffer periods of setback. A community which is constantly welcoming people will soon become dispersed; it will end up like a railway station where people just run into each other and part. A community which is closed can become stifling and suffer from dissension and envy, and may cease to be alive.

A loving community is attractive, and a community which is attractive is by definition welcoming. Life brings new life. There is an extraordinary *gratuité* in the power of procreation: the way a living being gives birth to other living beings is marvellous, and this is true for the living body which is community.

Love can never be static. A human heart is either progressing or regressing. If it is not becoming more open, it is closing and withering spiritually. A community which refuses to welcome – whether through fear, weariness, insecurity, a desire to cling to comfort, or just because it is fed up with visitors – is dying spiritually.

But there is a time for everything: a time to be and a time to welcome.

Sometimes when people knock at my door, I ask them in and we talk, but I make it clear to them in a thousand small ways that I am busy, that I have other things to do. The door of my office is open, but the door of my heart is closed. I still have a lot to learn and a long way to go. When we welcome people, we open the door of our heart to them and give them space within it. And if we have other things to do which really can't wait, we should say so – but open our heart all the same.

To welcome is not just something that happens as people cross the threshold. It is an attitude; it is the constant openness of the heart; it is saying to people every morning and at every moment, 'come in'; it is giving them space; it is listening to them attentively.

To welcome means listening a great deal to people and then discerning the truth with them. A community cannot accept as a resident every single person that knocks at the door. In order to welcome there must be a peaceful space in the hearts of those welcoming and a peaceful space in the community for the person to find a place of rest and growth. If that peaceful space is lacking, then it is better not to welcome.

At the same time, the people welcomed must try to accept the community as it is, with the space that is offered, be willing to abide by the spirit, traditions and rules of the community, and desire also to grow and to evolve. If the newcomer only wants to change the community and get everything they can out of it, without any modification on their part, there can be no true welcome.

That is why there must be a double discernment when deciding whether to welcome a new member into the community. Can we in the community give that person the peaceful space and the elements they need to be at ease and to grow? And then will they, so far as we can know them after dialogue and prayer, really benefit from the community as it is, and truly adapt to its minimal expectations? Or does the person have expectations that cannot be fulfilled?

A community needs wise people to discern peacefully and prayerfully. Of course, this careful discernment is only for new members and, at most, those who want to stay a while in the community; it is not necessary for casual visitors.

A community must not fall into the trap of thinking it can be the saviour of all. It must not feel guilty if, after discernment, it says 'no' to someone. But there is a way of saying 'no', with compassion; there is a way of taking time, listening, explaining why the person cannot stay and offering suggestions where he or she could go. It is such a wounding experience to be turned away. We must always remember that.

When I started l'Arche, I welcomed Raphael and Philippe, who are both mentally handicapped. Several months later, I welcomed Gabriel, a tramp without work. He stayed a few months, but his presence quickly became incompatible with community life. He terrorised Raphael – perhaps because he was jealous of him. If he hadn't left, Raphael would have been in real danger. When we have welcomed people who are weak and without inner stability and have made a commitment to them, we cannot then welcome people who seriously threaten their growth. We have no right to accept someone who refuses to accept others or community life with all that it implies.

Each community has its own weakness, its limitations which are also its wealth. It is important to recognise these limitations; we have to know what our norms of welcome are, who can be accepted within them and who the community can truly help. We can certainly hope that, with time, the community will deepen and so be able to welcome more and more difficult people. But strangely enough, that doesn't always happen. When l'Arche started, we welcomed some people who were very difficult, unstable, and violent. With time, they have become more peaceful and found a certain inner harmony. So now it would be unwise to welcome others who could reawaken all their anguish and darkness. We have to respect the rhythm of fragile people who are still finding their own peace and inner healing.

Openness and welcome sometimes challenge us to go beyond our fears and prejudices to the depth of compassion and understanding. At the same time we must respond from our own deepest search for truth. I, for example, am deeply moved by the pain and immense suffering of those who are homosexual. I desire to enter into the sense of misery and guilt that some homosexuals experience. I can sympathise with their anger – though at times it frightens me – at the injustice of being denounced or labeled 'abnormal' by society and church. The causes of homosexuality are not clearly known. For some it is more evidently related to early experiences in a kind of suffering that can be healed. For others it seems less readily accessible to healing, and some even suggest that it is genetic and part of the natural order. Whatever the cause or origin, it is rarely, if ever, a matter of choice. I sometimes wonder how I would have coped with the pain of being different because of an attraction to men rather than to women. People who have experienced a profound psychological hurt often have a quality of sensitivity and spirituality that can be a gift and a grace.

At the same time we should be attentive to those attitudes – particularly with regard to genital sexuality, whether with a person of the same or other sex – which can be destructive to truth and community. Community implies open relationships and not possessive ones. It is built on relationships that give life to others rather than on ones that turn in upon themselves. It requires relationships which do not undermine others in their search for wholeness.

Who welcomes?

Leaders who take responsibility alone, for welcoming people without living with them every day, may be imposing their own ideal of welcome on to those who do live with them; that is not always just. It is the whole community - or a few designated members – which should decide who is to be welcomed, because it is the community which has to live with the difficulties as well as the joys this brings.

In l'Arche communities, especially those which have been going for some time, more and more handicapped people are reaching a certain maturity. They have been in the community for a long time, often for longer than the assistants, and sometimes longer than the person in charge. It is important to consult these handicapped people before we welcome someone in distress.

Some people who appear to be very welcoming are, in fact, seeking to calm their own anguish. They need to meet people and to have a certain power over them. They need to have others dependent on them. They lack the necessary objectivity to really understand a person's weakness and discern whether he or she can grow.

One of the marvellous things about community is that it enables us to welcome and help people in a way we couldn't as individuals. When we pool our strength and share the work and responsibility, we can welcome many more people, even those in deep distress, and perhaps help them find self-confidence and inner healing. But that implies that there is not just one person welcoming but a group of people who have a real gift for welcome and who discern together. Each of us is different and each has his/her ups and downs; each one of us welcomes others in a different way, with larger or smaller filters, or none at all. While I can welcome and understand certain people very well, another will welcome other people better than I. And we all have to beware of our likes and dislikes and our preconceived ideas.

Members of a community should pray for this gift of welcome. For it is truly a gift. Our hearts must be opened to welcome. This gift is love, and love for the different and the unexpected. And this love comes from the Father. We must ask for this love and expect it to be given. Genuine welcome is an energy of peace felt and appreciated.

And of course we can only welcome someone as a gift of God if we have come to the awareness that we too are loved by God just as we are; that we too are a gift for the community.

It is easy to welcome when one feels lonely and does not have much to do. But it can be painful to be welcoming when one has had a busy day with meetings, or is surrounded by people, or when one is tired. It is terribly difficult to tell one's story or the story of the community for the hundredth time. It is then that our welcome is truly from the Holy Spirit. One has to be centred in him in order to welcome in this way. We then become truly instruments of God.

Some people are called to announce the good news by travelling far and wide, meeting and telling people about community and love and the gift of God. This is good and necessary.

We are also 'missionaries' – that is, people who are sent – when we welcome someone at our table, when we show them that they are loved and appreciated, when we tell them with love how we have been called by Jesus to live, when we make them feel at home. At that moment we are also truly announcing the good news.

Welcome: true and false

The welcome a community offers visitors is an extension of the welcome its members offer each other. If our heart is open to our brothers and sisters, it will also be open to others. But if we are withdrawn from other members of the community, we are likely to close ourselves off from visitors. We may of course – and this does happen – be delighted to use visitors as an excuse to flee from the community. We can get bored with each other's company and so become aggressive; visitors then become a distraction. That can be valuable and even lead to better welcoming of each other. But it is not true welcome. It is sometimes easier to welcome a visitor than to welcome someone with whom we live all the time. It is rather the same as husbands and wives who are always away from home, caught up in a whole variety of good works. They would do better to spend more time at home, being a bit more welcoming to each other.

Can we truly welcome strangers as they are, if we have not welcomed the community as it is and the members as they are? If we are angry with the community and its members, we risk using strangers to compensate for our anguish. That is not welcome.

A divided community has no business to welcome people. It would only do them harm. We should put some order into our own house before we invite others into it.

I'm sometimes worried about the way l'Arche welcomes people who come as assistants. Do we welcome them because we need them to do a specific job, or do we welcome them for themselves, because Jesus has sent them? 'I was a stranger, and you welcomed me.'

Of course people have to be able to find their place, and that implies finding a role and a function. They have to be able to use their gifts, too. But we are sometimes in danger of no longer seeing them as people, because we need them to fill a particular job. It is hard to find the balance between using people for the community and leaving them too much space, without a useful role.

Welcoming Providence

The longer we live in community, the more we realise how central the role of Providence is to us. A community can only stay alive when new people arrive and commit themselves to it. What explanation is there for the fact that one person is touched by the community and another isn't? We realise very quickly that people are drawn by something greater than the community itself – a call and gift of God.

And each new person who joins the community brings his or her own qualities, gifts, and failings which will, with time, modify the way the community develops and grows. The people we welcome today will commit themselves tomorrow and carry the community the day after that. Welcome is vital for a community. It is a question of life and death and the first welcome is very often the important one. People can flee because it has put them off. Others stay because of a smile or an initial act of kindness. People should not be made to feel that they are upsetting things when they arrive. They should be able to feel that we are happy to share with them. We have to know how to respond sympathetically to a letter or a phone call, how to add a personal note of *gratuité*. If we really welcome each new person as a gift of God, and as his messenger, we would be more loving and more open.

Welcoming the vulnerable

I am discovering more and more how many people are deeply lonely. They bring certain emotional problems with them into community, together with what may look like a 'bad character' which is often the result of suffering and lack of understanding during childhood. It is good that these people can come into a community, which can be a place of support, opening and growth for them. But clearly they are going to suffer there and make others suffer too. Perhaps they need a community whose life is structured, where the sharing is not too threatening, where there are not too many meetings or demanding situations which could make them explode. They need space to be alone and work that brings inner security. It would be sad if communities accepted only perfectly balanced, flexible, open and available people. Those with difficulties also have the right to the possibility of community life. But we need communities with different structures, to welcome people with different needs.

When a community welcomes people who have been on the margins of society, things usually go quite well to begin with. Then, for many reasons, these people start to become marginal to the community as well. They provoke crises which can be very painful for the community and cause it considerable confusion, because it feels so powerless. The community is then caught in a trap from which it may be hard to escape. But if the crises bring it to a sense of its own poverty, they can also be a grace. There is something prophetic in people who seem marginal and difficult; they force the community to become alert, because what they are demanding is authenticity. Too many communities are founded on dreams and fine words; there is so much talk about love, truth, and peace. Marginal people are demanding. Their cries are cries of truth because they sense the emptiness of many of our words; they can see the gap between what we say and how we live. If the community reacts by showing them the door, this can create a terrible uproar, and then it is easy to label them unbearable, sick, lazy, and good for nothing. It has to devalue them as far as it can, because they have shown up its hypocrisy.

Yes, we have to discern wisely when we welcome. It is so much better to refuse someone at the outset because the community is conscious of its limitations, than to welcome him or her naively and then ask them to leave.

Marginal people in community have very particular needs. They are wounded and lack self-confidence; they are often despairing. They can be buffeted by terrible anguish, which drives them to attack others or themselves in ways that even they cannot understand. They often lack inner stability, and so are deeply confused. They can move quickly from a state where they have no desires at all to a state where they are faced with a complete anarchy of competing desires. A terrible struggle is going on in them between darkness and light, life and death. They have nothing to look to for guidance, neither people nor laws. And it is the realisation of their loneliness and their poverty that makes them despair.

If they are to refind hope, marginal people have to feel loved and accepted. It is not simply through being welcomed that they will rediscover their own value and capacities for positive action. They need people who will listen to them, with all their wounds and needs, and sense what they really want. This demands time and patience, because they are afraid of revealing themselves and won't open up to just anyone. They need to sense that they are not being judged, but are really understood. They need someone who can listen to them, a stable reference person who can guide and support them and bring them security, who can encourage and help them to discover their abilities and take on responsibilities. Because of their very deep confusion, marginal people have to learn to trust that reference person, that father- or mother-figure who unites tenderness, goodness, and firmness.

A community which welcomes marginal people has to make clear to them when they arrive exactly what it expects of them. They have to accept its rules, even if these are very flexible and, in a sense, have been made for marginal people! They have to sense that the community will not let them do exactly as they like, but will demand this minimal conformity. If they refuse this, that is their way of saying that they do not want to stay.

Their reference person is an intermediary between them and the law or the rules. This person has to explain the reasons for these rules, and has to know how to be firm as well as how to encourage and forgive.

Above all, these reference persons must not set themselves up against the community. Generous people sometimes want to be saviours and show the community that it is neither open nor evangelical. They exploit marginal people to show up the community's failings. People who act as reference persons must do so in the name of the community and reflect its wishes. Their task is to help the marginal people progress from this single, individual relationship with them to the demands of relationships with others in the community. This will be gradual; marginal people will have crises of jealousy; they will test the community to see how far it really accepts them. But eventually, through these crises, they will begin to feel part of the community and at home.

So if a community is to welcome marginal people, it must be able to offer them reference persons who are solid, welcoming, understanding and firm. If it cannot do this, if it doesn't have the people who can accept the occasional blows and crises, it would do better not to welcome marginal people at all. If it is to welcome them, it has to be very deeply united and solidly structured. If this unity is not there, marginal people may well accentuate the tensions and disharmony.

Marginal people live in darkness, without motivation or hope. They are forced to compensate for their anguish – which may even prevent them from sleeping or eating – in drugs, alcohol, or 'madness'. It takes time for hope to be reborn and for their anguish to be transformed into peace. The rebirth can be very painful for them and for those around them. Sometimes they have to test the community to see if it is really concerned about them. Sometimes they have to unload their personal anguish on to the community, and this anguish can spread like wildfire if it finds inflammable material – just as it can be put out if it runs into people who can accept it. Marginal people are the product of the injustices and violence of their past. Their attitudes are the reflection of these rejections. If they are very sensitive and vulnerable, their wounds will be deep and be revealed in a confusion, lack of self-confidence, and sense of guilt; they may even feel guilty for being alive at all.

Only another person can bring the light which will chase away this darkness. And the struggle with darkness can be a terrible one for marginal people. They are always ambivalent; they vacillate between love of light and a desire to remain in chaos and tragedy. Their ambivalence spills over on to the community, and especially on to the one who has become their reference person - whom they both love and hate. In their insecurity, they want both to become attached to these people and to reject them.

The liberation of marginal people from their darkness may involve a long struggle. The reference person and the community have to know how to accept the violence into themselves, so that they can transform it into tenderness and gradually liberate the marginal people from their anguish. The role of a community of reconciliation is to break the cycle of violence and so lead people to peace.

Many marginal people are in anguish because they have not experienced a true relationship with their own mother. This leaves them wounded: they are seeking a relationship of unconditional acceptance. Deep inside, they are crying out for this privileged love. Because they have never had it, they haven't lived through the normal frustrations of a child whose mother later gives more attention to a new baby. Because they haven't lived through these first jealousies, they haven't integrated them. That is why the thirst of marginal people is insatiable: they want to possess their reference person totally – they refuse to accept that anyone else has any claims. And that is why people who want to help them should never be alone. It is dangerous when a child monopolises its mother's attention, as can happen if she is on her own or emotionally estranged from her husband. The mother and child become emotionally dependent on each other, each possesses the other. Their relationship is no longer liberating. This dangerous sort of relationship can grow in our communities when an assistant concentrates on a particular child with a handicap to the exclusion of all other relationships.

This is why the reference persons are a part of the community. And the children with a handicap or marginal people must clearly understand that they can never possess these people, whose strength comes from their link with the community.

In some of our l'Arche communities a person with a handicap has become quite violent and anti-social, after many years in the community. We have to learn to interpret these different forms of behaviour. Sometimes the person is saying through their action: 'I don't want to stay here! I want to go somewhere else!' We have to listen and understand the message of violence; we have to enter into dialogue with the person.

Sometimes a community feels guilty when it is not able to keep the person. They feel they have failed. But there is no community that can save everybody. Sometimes a professional person can help the community make the right decision and ask the person to leave.

Sometimes, however, violence springs up because of the inadequacies of the assistants who are not attentive enough to the needs of the people. Sometimes it is because assistants are not permanent enough and people are angry because someone has left. Violence must be listened to attentively, the causes understood and, if possible, remedied.

Bruno Bettelheim wrote a book called *Love is Not Enough*.[1] He is right – even if he is a bit too analytical in his approach. Here is an important message for anyone who tries to help people in anguish and distress, people who are marginal, or living in darkness and confusion. We have to know how to accept crises, violence and depression. We have to understand what people are trying to say through all the regression and confusion. We have to be able to decode the messages that are sent through bizarre behaviour and to respond authentically to these cries for help. We have to understand certain laws of human nature and how human beings grow

1　The Free Press, New York, 1950.

through work and relationships. We have to know how to lead people towards inner healing. We have especially to know how to enter into authentic relationships.

This doesn't mean that we have to become psychiatrists, nor go through analysis. But it does mean being sensitive to the deep needs of other people, being experienced, and knowing when we need the professional help of doctors, psychiatrists and different therapists. There is no conflict between faith and psychiatry; there is only conflict between people who deny the value of one or the other. That isn't to say, though, that it is easy to sort out what has to do with the priest and spirituality, and what has to do with the psychiatrist; the two areas often overlap.

At l'Arche, we are beginning to discover our own therapy, which is very different from that offered by hospitals or from other therapies based entirely on drugs or analysis. Our therapy is based on authentic relationships lived in community, work and a true spiritual life. All these bring people hope, self-acceptance, and motivation. Through this, people discover gradually that they are part of a family and a community, and this brings them security and peace. But some people, before they can find that inner harmony necessary for community life, need professional help.

A Christian community which welcomes people who are on the margins of society and in distress needs professional help from psychologists, psychiatrists, and others. But above all, it needs to deepen its own therapy. And professional people have to recognise this therapy and work with it.

A Christian community is based fundamentally on relationships which are authentic, loving and faithful, and on forgiveness, and the signs of that forgiveness. The role of the priest can be essential in leading people towards inner healing. Through confession, and the secret he keeps, he can help people discover the forgiveness of Jesus; this can be central in bringing those in distress to inner healing by lifting the yoke of guilt. The discovery through faith and the love of the community that Jesus loves us all, and especially those in distress, can help people discover their own value as children of God. The way in which a community welcomes the death of a brother can help others overcome their own fear of death. The Eucharist and communal prayer can help us discover that we are all brothers and sisters in Jesus and that, in the end, there is no difference between those who are well and those who are sick or disabled. We are all handicapped before God, prisoners of our own egoism. But Jesus has come to heal us, save us and set us free by the gift of his Spirit. That is the good news he brings to the poor: we are not alone in our sadness, darkness and loneliness, in our fears and emotional and sexual problems. He loves us and is with us: 'Do not be afraid, I am with you.'

When we welcome people who are deeply wounded, we have to be fully aware of the seriousness of what we are doing. This welcome implies that we accept them as they are, imposing no ideal on them; that we understand what they are seeking in relationships, and that we are ready to 'believe all things, hope all things, endure all things' (1 Cor. 13:7). But at the same time they too must understand the limitations of the community.

Sometimes, even when our welcome has been authentic enough, we find that we cannot keep people, because they are damaging themselves and others. We then have to learn how to be true and firm, and at the same time tender and compassionate. If people have to leave, we should try to find them a place which will help them in ways we could not.

Marginal people at the heart of the community

Many communities carry one or two marginal people at their heart - people who, having lived in the community for some time, seem to withdraw into a kind of mental illness. They become bitter, depressed, and sullen. It seems impossible to reach them; they reject even the most sensitive approaches. Often when these people were younger, they had the strength to hide their difficulties. But now, unconscious forces are exploding in them. They are ambivalent: they want to leave the community and at the same time they know that there is nowhere else for them to go. Because they reject all relationships, they feel useless and unloved. They are carrying a terrible cross of loneliness.

Sometimes the community should help these people to find a place which will offer them what they need; sometimes it should find them professional help if they themselves want this. But above all, it should welcome them as a gift of God. These people who become marginal to their community are often harder to help than those who come from the margins of society outside. But although they are disturbing, they also help the community to be constantly alert to ways of becoming more loving, better at listening, and at finding the small things which bring peace. We have to help these marginal people not to feel guilty, and not to withdraw completely into their illness.

The community or its leaders may be partly responsible for this situation. Perhaps they asked too much of these people when they were younger and didn't take enough care of them then; perhaps they didn't confront them when the first signs of their difficulties appeared. If notice had been taken of them earlier, if they hadn't been left alone, there would perhaps have been less suffering later.

Some people hide their difficulties behind a mask of efficiency. Their 'job' in the community becomes their 'thing' and they let no one interfere or give advice; there is no dialogue about their work, no accountability. When we sense this, we have to be careful. Our tendency might be to enable them to go on doing this by emphasising their function. But a time will come when they will no longer be able to hide their difficulties: they will sense too great a gap between their function and their fragility. Then they may become either deeply depressed or violently aggressive. It is sometimes better to listen to their cries earlier, when there is still time to help them.

In such situations it is better to provoke a crisis earlier on, by not letting them close up on their work. This might be very painful but it is sometimes better than pretending that there is no problem and letting things slide. The most important thing is that we are always truthful and always tell people how we feel towards them.

Welcome and service

A community has to be careful that it is not welcoming people because this salves its conscience or gives it a sense of 'saving' others. It should welcome people because it wants to serve them and to help them find their freedom.

Many welcoming communities want to be Christian communities – which means communities of prayer. A Christian community has to know its own aims and who it is going to welcome. Is it going to give priority to people who are disabled or in distress, or without families, offering them a new family in which they can find greater peace and security and so, perhaps, learn to rejoin society in a really integrated way? Or is it going to give priority to creating a community of prayer, welcoming people who are either Christian already or who will, it hopes, become so?

At l'Arche, we have decided to welcome people because they are in need, whether they are Christian or not. Our aim is to do all we can to help them grow in human and spiritual terms, according to their own rhythm and their own gifts, through the security of relationships. This means that not all our members are necessarily Christian; they do not all join in our prayers. And yet, we are all members of the same family.

The important thing is to know exactly what we want and then to be vulnerable enough to show that we really care for people. This can be terribly disturbing, because we have no firm framework or rules. It is always easier and more comfortable to welcome only the people who come to prayer and Mass! But the danger then is that they feel they will only be able to stay if they pretend to share our faith. It seems preferable to let them discover their own way and the person of Jesus Christ gradually, so that they can decide freely. This way is certainly slower, but because it respects individuals in their own deepest choices and growth, the results will be deeper too. Of course there is always the danger of indifference. But we have to pray that the Spirit will keep us alert to that.

The need for community

There are so many people who live alone, crushed by their loneliness. It is obvious that too much solitude can drive people off the rails, to depression or alcoholism. More and more people seem to have lost their balance because their family life has been unhappy. There are so many who are lost, taking drugs, turning to delinquency or just hiding themselves in a world of rock music, films and distractions; there are so many who are looking for a sense of belonging and a meaning to their lives. In years to come, we are going to need many small communities which will welcome lost and lonely people, offering them a new form of family and a sense of belonging.

In the past, Christians who wanted to follow Jesus opened hospitals and schools. Now that there are so many of these, Christians must commit themselves to the new communities of welcome, to live with people who have no other family, and to show them that they are loved and can grow to greater freedom and that they, in turn, can love and give life to others.

People coming into a community for the first time are usually open, available and often have a child's grace. They have left the responsibilities and the landmarks they had in society and have entered a new world. It is like a new birth. This time of childhood, of naivety, openness and availability will last for varying amounts of time. Sooner or later, people begin to become responsible. The risk for people who leave one community to go into another is that they will arrive as adults and not as children. They will come to offer service. They already know what to do. I really wonder whether anyone can commit themselves in a community if they do not first live a period of childhood there.

9

Meetings

Coming together to share

If a community is to forge its unity, its members have to be able to meet as people, as brothers and sisters, and not just as 'job-doers'. When a community is small, it is easy for all its members to get together and share – meetings happen spontaneously throughout the day. But when it grows and work increases and there are more and more visitors, there is a danger that the members meet only to organise things. So it is essential to set aside a definite time – a day, an evening each week – when there are no visitors and the community's members can meet among themselves more personally.

Community life implies a personal commitment which is made real in meetings between people. But we are very quick to flee from these meetings. They frighten us, just because they commit us. We flee into administration, law, rules, the search for 'objective truth'; we flee into work and activity. We flee from meeting people; we would rather do things for them. But if we are to love, we have to meet.

Creating community is something different from just meeting one with another, as individuals. It is creating a body and a sense of belonging, a place of communion, and this means meetings!

There are different types of meetings, but in a community they all have the same goal: *communion*, the building of one body, creating a sense of belonging together. No matter how much business has to be discussed, all must be directed toward this final goal: a coming together of people in love.

There are meetings to give out *information*. It is important that people know what is happening in the community, in the immediate area and in other communities to which they are linked; what is happening too in specific areas of interest for the community and its vision in other parts of the country and of the world. And this information should not just be written down on paper and given out to save going to another meeting. Written information is different from spoken information, the purpose of which is to inspire and nourish hearts and mind, and to create unity.

There are meetings where *business* and community matters are brought up in order to deepen together a vision and, after discernment, to come to decisions.

There are meetings where people *share together* in depth, revealing their thoughts and feelings and what is happening in their lives.

There are meetings where the *vision* is announced, hearts are touched, nourished and strengthened.

There are meetings where people just relax together, not hiding behind a function or role, just *enjoying each others' company*.

There are meetings which are *celebrations*.

There are meetings where members *pray* together, interceding for the community, crying out to God their pain and their needs; crying out to be saved, but also giving thanks to God and worshipping him in silence.

Each meeting must have clear goals. These will vary and that means that different meetings have to be conducted in different ways. Each sort of meeting has its own discipline and ways of participation. Leaders must know how to animate the different types of meetings and the method involved.

Of course in every specific meeting will be found elements of the other types. In a business meeting, there should also be a time for prayer, at least to begin the meeting, and maybe a time of personal sharing, if that can relax tensions and help people liberate themselves from inner stress. It is not good to bring these tensions out during the business meeting; that would only cloud up the issues. And sometimes in the middle of a meeting it is good to have a moment of relaxation and fun. Leaders have to be wise in using all the different ways and methods to deepen communion and at the same time to be efficient, because decisions must be made.

It takes time to discover the gift and needs of each different type of meeting and how each one builds community and nourishes our hearts and intellects; how we must prepare for and live the difficulties of each one.

We have to be able to bear a lot of suffering, to go through some hard discussions and even some battles. All that is to be expected, because it takes time for us to let go of our own ideas and projects and to support those of the community instead. It takes time to have confidence in the judgement of others and in the community.

We shouldn't expect too much nourishment from a meeting which has to do with administration or other business. Community life means service and these meetings are services we render for the good of the whole. But there can still be a joy and peace in them, if we try to listen to each other's ideas and opinions, and to discover the best way of organising something for the good of us all.

It can sometimes be hard to share in those meetings where we are called to share in depth about our life in the community. We are quick to escape into business discussions, for such meetings imply that we reveal something of ourselves, and thus become vulnerable one to another, letting down our barriers and defence systems and letting go of our desire to prove that we are right and others wrong. For some people this can be difficult, even dangerous. That is why we have to try to make these meetings safe, confidential, and a place of trust. But it can take a long time for some people who have been hurt in the past to truly trust in the group.

Of course, this time of community sharing doesn't mean a total openness. We all have a secret which only God, our closest friends or our spiritual guide knows. Married couples have a secret they do not share with their children or other members of the family. So our meetings are there for us to share what we are living in community. The line that separates our personal secret from what should be shared is, however, a very fine one. That is why some people find it impossible to share at all. Either they reveal everything, using the community almost like a confessional, and delighting in their attentive audience. Or they close up, unable to talk about anything except externals, because they are afraid of revealing too much. But it is right and good to share where we are in the community, what is happening in our lives, and how we are reacting to people and events. It is right to become implicated through our words. It is good to offer a little of ourselves so that others know what community means to us and what our difficulties are.

It is by knowing each other in this way, with our problems and weaknesses, our trust in Jesus and in the community, that we are encouraged to be faithful to each other and to Jesus. If we are concerned only to show our strength, qualities and successes, we will be admired rather than loved and others will keep their distance. The sharing of weaknesses and difficulties and the request for help and prayer are like cement to the community; they bind people and create unity; they help us discover that we need each other if we are to remain faithful and use our gifts. When we meet at a personal level, and are honest about our failings, words flow spontaneously into the silence, which becomes a prayer. And from the depths of the silence can spring another prayer, of intercession or of thanksgiving. So we journey towards a community which is one soul, one heart, one spirit, and one body.

Jesus says that when two or three are gathered in his name, he is among them. Meeting implies a union. Jesus cannot be there if people come together physically but refuse to be in communion one with another.

Coming together in the Spirit

In some l'Arche communities they have what they call 'sacred' meetings. These may be held in the chapel – though not necessarily – and start with a prayer and a period of silence. Then people speak, in a sort of discontinued conversation, each in turn saying what they are experiencing and how they perceive community life. It is entirely subjective; there is no discussion or search for objective truth, but simply a statement of what each person is experiencing. The aim of the meeting is to enable each person to know where the others are, and so to meet them at a personal level. The essential element is that people listen sympathetically; there is nothing to attack, defend or reproach each other for. Many blocks among people in community come from the fact that they do not dare express certain feelings – perhaps for fear of being judged. But when they *can* express them, this brings freedom. There may be no solutions, but at least, when we know what people are experiencing, we can try to modify our own conduct towards them. The simple fact of stating our difficulties or joys can bring us closer together, increase our understanding of each other, and strengthen the bonds between us. When we have all had our say, we pray together. And once the meeting is over, we do not return to it. What was said remains hidden in the heart of God.

We must not go to a meeting carrying within us the pain of another meeting or the frustration coming from a disturbing situation or event in the community. The art of good meetings is in the way people prepare inwardly for them. If members come with an inner space of silence, availability and even excitement, then the meeting will be a living and nourishing one. If they arrive disgruntled and angry – 'Oh, another meeting!' – then we can be sure that it is *not* going to be a nourishing one! And bad meetings (like good ones) become contagious. If we expect them to be bad and a waste of time, then they will be just that! If leaders are responsible for the animation of a meeting, we are all responsible for the quality of it by the way we live it.

Some people enjoy meetings. They find them relaxing –

especially if they are then enabled to escape the demands of work! Others don't like meetings at all. They find them a waste of time, a contagious disease. Some people come to meetings as consumers, for a nice chat. Others resent being dragged from what they are doing and feel threatened when they have to listen to other people. Their activity motor is running so fast that they find it hard to sit and relax.

Participation in a meeting means something much deeper than simply knowing how to talk. It implies a certain death to imposing *our* ideas or defending or proving something about ourselves. That sort of approach does not get you far in community. To participate in a community meeting you must have the certitude that Jesus is present, that he is leading us together and that each one has a gift to bring to the meeting. Our participation then comes from a desire to work together to find the truth and the Will of God. And so participation is a way of listening, in a real effort to understand what the other is saying. It is knowing when to talk, neither interrupting nor challenging. It is knowing how to refrain from whispering to your neighbour or reading your mail. It is a way of sitting – a whole message of the body which tells people either that they are boring or that they are worth listening to. The quality of attention we bring to meetings and the courtesy with which we listen to people who may be stammering or even talking nonsense, out of sheer nerves, are the best indicators of the quality of our participation. People who are shy and lack confidence may express themselves awkwardly or aggressively. If we listen to them disdainfully, we will increase their nervousness. If we really welcome what they have to say, we can help them find self-confidence and discover that they really do have something worth saying.

If we cannot come to meetings in this frame of mind, they will quickly become heavy. One person will have a lot of difficulty in leading them, while the others vascillate between sanctimonious attention and aggression that shows itself in boredom or anger.

Leading a meeting

The first important thing is to start and finish the meeting on time
– and that demands its own discipline! It is always good to start
with a time of silence, even of prayer, if that is what people want.
When there are major decisions to make, it is important to put
ourselves before God, so that we can overcome our own ideas,
desires and passions. Maybe reading a passage from Scripture can
bring people together to greater centredness and communion.

The next important thing is to have a clear agenda, which allows
essential questions the time they need and saves us from drowning
in long discussions on unimportant details. The leader needs to be
firm enough to keep the meeting to the agenda and cut short useless
digressions. But it's good to be flexible, too, because sometimes a
digression can open up new ideas and help people feel more
involved. We have to know how to seize on these moments,
without interrupting the flow of the discussion. It's good too to
draw out or create moments of relaxation and laughter. Knowing
how to make a meeting interesting and nourishing is an art in
itself. It comes with experience and a certain creativity, confidence,
and humility.

Those of us who lead meetings have to know how to enable
everyone to have their say. We have to try to avoid pushing our
own ideas. If we do have an opinion, it is better to wait and see
if someone else puts the same point, and to encourage them to
develop it. There is a danger that it is always the same people who
speak – and they are the ones who find it easy. Their interventions
can seem useful because they fill the silences and stimulate others.
But they can make others aggressive or too submissive, and they
are not necessarily the most perceptive nor those who say the most
important or interesting things. It is often people who find it hard
to talk or who lack self-confidence who do that.

So we have to create structures which encourage everyone to
participate, and especially the shy people. Those who have the
most light to shed often dare not show it; they are afraid of
appearing stupid. They do not recognise their own gift – perhaps
because others haven't recognised it either. We have to help those
who talk too much to hold their tongues and listen. One way to

do this is to ask everyone for their opinion in turn. If there are too many people for this, we can divide them into small groups where they can share more easily. The important thing is that everyone has their say.

Leaders should not be surprised if meetings sometimes bring explosions. If people express themselves violently, this is because of an anguish which we should respect. People who shout are not necessarily marginal, revolutionary, cantankerous, or destructive. They should not be made to feel guilty. They may feel wronged, or maybe going through a difficult time; they may be on the verge of healing or commitment, for this too brings anguish. In any event, they are suffering. If we respond too abruptly, we will not help them to become free and move towards a greater peace and harmony with the life of the community, its structure and its authority. The expression of feelings brings freedom. A community has to be able to listen well enough to allow all its members to find this freedom.

We shouldn't get discouraged when meetings go badly and there are tensions. Each of us has to grow, each of us has the right to a bad patch and to weariness, to moments of doubt and confusion. We have to know how to hold on through these difficult times and wait for happier ones. And we have to discover, through difficult meetings, how to defuse the situation, how to meet in a calmer and more joyful way. People with responsibility have to know how to choose the right moment to bring out a good bottle or a delicious cake. These can bring unity too!

If meetings are well led, if everyone recognises them as a necessary part of community life, respects their discipline and really participates in them, they can become life-giving times when we are aware of the community as a place of communion. Then we are really meeting, recognising each other as brothers and sisters and nourishing each other. Then meetings become celebrations, manifestations that we are indeed members of the same body.

Community discernment is essentially a way of enabling people in a group to come to a common decision where each one has internalised the decision and made it their own. This is different from a group seeing no objection to an idea proposed by the leader and accepting it in a passive and submissive way. It is different also from a decision made after argument and heated discussion. Community discernment implies that each person reflects and chooses in a personal way, after different options have been clearly looked at; it implies that all are seeking only the truth and the will of God, rising above passions and the need to impose their ideas and have their way. But discernment is not easy; groups have to learn how to do it.

I am sometimes concerned by the way some groups are directed by a charismatic leader and when decisions are taken in a very spontaneous and sometimes emotional way, charismatically or pro-phetically. The leader acts as if he has a direct line to the Holy Spirit. Some people do have special charisma, but the spirit of prophecy must always be tested by wise people. There are also false prophets. There are also leaders who unconsciously use the emotional and the spiritual to avoid conflict and to maintain his or her role of leadership, and thus a feeling of superiority or of being blessed by God in a special way.

The role of any leader is to help each member to reflect more personally, to discern and make wise decisions and assume responsibility. A leader must call each one to growth and to assume responsibility.

When the International Council of l'Arche met in February 1977, we decided to hold a large meeting for all the communities fifteen months later. The meeting would be in two parts: the first would bring together directors and delegates from the communities, together with members of their Boards of Directors; the second would bring more participants to join them, including handicapped people. But when the Council met the following September, some people questioned these decisions, and some for good reasons.

Instead of saying that the decisions had been made and that was it, we took time to listen to people's disquiet. We started a process of discernment, trying to see as clearly as we could the advantages and disadvantages of the meeting as planned. After several hours, we reaffirmed the original decision.

Seen from the outside and from the standpoint of efficiency, this dialogue and discernment could seem a complete waste of time. But we discovered that it was important. It allowed all of us to clarify our choice, to see the difficulties and even the risks; it created an inner cohesion in the group which had accepted the original decision in a rather superficial way; our confidence in ourselves and each other grew, and this gave the group as a whole greater creativity. Basically, when people have an inner conviction that something is God's will and not just an individual project, they find a new strength, peace, and creativity.

It will always take time for every member of a group – and especially the slowest and least alert – to reach a point where they have made a decision their own.

Paulo Freire speaks of time that is 'wasted' in dialogue as only an apparent waste of time, for in the long run one has gained a lot in certainty, self-confidence, trust in each other – things which we can never attain when there is a lack of dialogue.[1]

I'm told that in the villages of Papua New Guinea, nothing is decided until everyone involved agrees – however many hours that takes! It is certainly important to take time to discover everyone's opinion and the deep reasons for disagreement. We really have to examine the advantages and disadvantages of a particular course of action until we arrive at a consensus.

Some communities take no decision until there is unanimous agreement, and if necessary, they fast until they reach it. The principle could be a good one – but some people could find fasting difficult! We have to accept that disagreements exist and that we won't always reach unanimity, however much we'd like to. Then

1 Paulo Freire, *Education for Critical Consciousness* (Seabury Press, New York, 1973; Sheed and Ward, London, 1974).

we have to vote. For important things, a simple majority isn't enough. If there is not a substantial majority, it can be better to wait until time has clarified the issue.

We must always pay attention to the minority which disagrees with a decision or is upset by it. This minority can sometimes be prophetic; it can have a presentiment that something isn't right. Perhaps it says so awkwardly and aggressively; perhaps also it rejects the decision for reasons which have nothing to do with the particular case but go far deeper and have to do with rejection of structures or authority, or with personal problems. If possible, these deeper reasons for opposition should be brought to the surface. In any case, we should always be attentive to disagreements and give people time to express them in the greatest possible clarity and peace, without feeling guilty or that they are being disloyal to the group or to the leader. It is so important in a community for each person to feel free to speak according to the truth of his or her own conscience. It is sad when the individual conscience is stifled and dulled by the fear of disloyalty or, even worse, of religious disobedience. Community is not the stifling of individual conscience but rather the enhancing of it, in truth. Communities must learn to accept and cherish difference.

There is always a tension in a community between, on the one hand, unity and cohesion which give security and efficiency and, on the other, acceptance of difference and encouragement for each one to grow personally in wisdom and to express the truth as each one sees it, So often, through an exaggerated form of obedience, members are expected to obey like children and not to think at all for themselves! That is why discernment is so important in community. It allows disagreements and differences to come up in an open, non-threatening way; it permits the formation of individual consciences; and it permits the Holy Spirit to act in the members to bring about change. There is always a danger that a leader may stifle any form of division and disagreement and be fearful of any conflict, and thus prevent change, evolution and growth in the community. At the same time people must learn to listen to others and understand their points of view.

It is obvious that a community cannot take time for a lengthy consideration of every question. Otherwise it would spend all its time in meetings! They must take time only with essential questions. A community which cannot distinguish what is important from what is secondary has lost sight of its goals. Those who spend a lot of time wrangling over secondary questions are doing so, perhaps unconsciously, in order to avoid looking at the more serious ones.

The basic, necessary attitudes in community discernment are *openness*, the *seeking of truth*, and *trust* that it will be given to the group. It means that members accept that they do not already have the answer and that they are willing to abide by the spirit and method of discernment.

In order to discern well, the question or the problem has to be clearly stated in its simplest form, if possible in a way that brings forth a 'yes' or 'no' answer. If the question itself is muddled, or if there are a number of questions in one, then necessarily the answers will be muddled and unclear.

Once the question is clearly stated, and after a fitting time for reflection, members one after the other give their reasons 'for'; then, after another time of reflection, their reasons 'against'. After every one has heard all the 'fors' and all the 'againsts', there should be another time of silence, prayer and reflection. Then each one is asked to write on a paper their 'yes' or 'no' and the basic reason that brought them to that decision.

If there is disagreement, as there probably will be; those who are in the minority will be called to develop their reasons. The leader of the discernment will then try to name the fundamental point of division, the ultimate reason for the disagreement. And he or she will try to formulate that in a new question, which again should be stated as clearly as possible. Then, there will be another discernment about this new question, each person giving the 'fors' and the 'againsts', and people will again be asked to write down their 'yes' or 'no', with the basic reason for their choice. So, little by little, questions are clarified and the group comes to a final decision.

I do not believe that there always has to be unanimity, but obviously in important matters there should be a high majority in agreement.

It can happen that the leaders of a community are unhappy with the result of a vote and feel that it goes against their conscience as community leaders. As they have the grace of leadership, they should have the right to suspend the final decision in order to seek advice from an external authority, or reference person, who would then be called in to help the group discern again or to help the leader to accept the decision.

Of course, I cannot here go into all the intricacies of community discernment. We need wise people to help us come to wise decisions.

A community discernment, even if well done and in a spirit of prayer, does not mean that the decision comes straight from God. We are mortals and weak, but we are trying to overcome our passions and emotions and to live in truth and the Will of God. We are trying to do our best with what we are and what we have.

The discernment process is thus a unifying one for the community. The fact that differences and concerns are voiced in a positive and non-threatening way is formative for all. People are listening to each other and understanding better the different points of view. Thus, the group is evolving; people's consciences are being modified. Isn't this what is important?

10

Living with Every Day

One of the signs that a community is alive can be found in material things. Cleanliness, furnishings, the way flowers are arranged and meals prepared, are among the things which reflect the quality of people's hearts. Some people may find material chores irksome; they would prefer to use their time to talk and be with others. They haven't yet realised that the thousand and one small things that have to be done each day, the cycle of dirtying and cleaning, were given by God to enable us to communicate through matter. Cooking and washing floors can become a way of showing our love for others. If we see the humblest task in this light, everything can become communion and so celebration - because it is celebration to be able to give.

It is important too to recognise the humble and material gifts that others bring and to thank them for them. Recognition of the gifts of others is essential in community. All it takes is a smile and two small words – 'Thank you'.

When we put love into what we do, it becomes beautiful, and so do the results. There is a lack of love in a dirty or untidy community. But the greatest beauty is in simplicity and lack of affectation, where everything is oriented towards a meeting of people among themselves and with God. The way we look after the house and garden shows whether we feel really at home, relaxed, and peaceful. The house is the nest; it is like an extension of the body. Sometimes we tend to forget the role of the environment in liberation and inner growth.

Our lives in l'Arche are disarmingly simple. We often say that half the day is taken up with dirtying things and the other half with cleaning up! That is not entirely true because we also have work, celebrations, meals and prayer. But that does say something about the littleness and ordinariness of our lives. This is particularly evident when we are with people who have severe handicaps. They need a lot of presence and caring in all the vital acts of the body: bathing, toilet, clothing, feeding and so on. Many of them cannot be left alone during the day, even for short periods; their anguish is too great. Much of our life is situated around touch: holding them, bathing them, playing with them. Of course there is no place for interesting conversation. Play and laughter is the only communication possible. We experience communion with them around all the very little things-to-do of each day.

We are *all* called to do, not extraordinary things, but very ordinary things, with an extraordinary love that flows from the heart of God. St Paul expresses this very clearly when he says that if we do extraordinary things like speaking with all the tongues of angels and human beings; if we have all knowledge and faith; if we give all our goods to the poor and our bodies to martyrdom, but have no love, then all these things have no value at all. And then he goes on to say what love is: it is to be patient and kind, not jealous nor boastful, not arrogant nor rude. Love does not insist on its own way; it is not irritable; it finds its joy in truth. And it bears all things, believes all things, hopes all things and endures all.

Love is communion, communion with God and with our brothers and sisters. Love is manifested in all the little things of life that build community, not in heroic acts.

Some communities are always doing big projects, noble acts. They go from one big project to another. Things are always exciting and prophetic. There always seem to be marvellous interventions of God. All this can be true and wonderful, but then communities must remember that the essential is to be found in all the little acts of love day by day; it is being patient with people who drive you up the wall.

I find a great resemblance between contemplative monasteries and l'Arche communities. At first sight there is nothing more different than these two ways of living. But if one looks more closely, one discovers that both are centred on the reality of presence and communion, manual work and prayer; neither type of community does big things, and both are regarded by many in our societies as useless.

Communities that are always involved in the big and the heroic are perhaps fleeing from the essential. They should meditate on the words of Micah (6:8): 'He has showed you, O man, what is good; and what does the Lord require of you but to do justice, and to love kindness, and to walk humbly with your God?'

> Put on then, as God's chosen ones, holy and beloved, compassion, kindness, lowliness, meekness and patience, forbearing one another and, if one has a complaint against another, forgiving each other; as the Lord has forgiven you, so you also must forgive. And above all these put on love, which binds everything together in perfect harmony. And let the peace of Christ rule in your hearts, to which indeed you were called in the one body. And, be thankful. Let the word of Christ dwell in you richly, teach and admonish one another in all wisdom and sing psalms and hymns and spiritual songs with thankfulness in your hearts to God. And whatever you do, in word or deed, do everything in the name of the Lord Jesus, giving thanks to God the Father through him. (Col. 3:12–17)

A community which has a sense of work done well, quietly and lovingly, humbly and without fuss, can become a community where the presence of God is profoundly lived. All its members will feel at home, living all that makes up daily life tenderly and competently. They will be happy to serve, considering others before themselves, communicating peacefully with God, others, and nature, and living in God as he does in them. So the community will take on a whole contemplative dimension.

Many people believe that community life is made up of a series of problems to be solved. And consciously or unconsciously, they are waiting for the day when all the tensions, conflicts, and problems brought by marginal people and structures will be resolved and there will be no more problems left! But the more we live community life, the more we discover that it is not so much a question of resolving problems as of learning to live with them patiently. Most problems are not resolved. With time, and a certain insight and fidelity in listening, they clear up when we least expect them to.

But there will always be others to take their place!

Very often, we tend to look for 'great' moments or beautiful and ecstatic celebrations. We forget that the best nourishment of community life, the one which renews us and opens our hearts, is in all the small gestures of fidelity, tenderness, humility, forgiveness, sensitivity, and welcome which make up everyday life. It is these which are at the heart of community and can bring us to a realisation of love. It is these which touch hearts and reveal gifts.

Daily rhythm

When I was with Chris, in our community in Kerala in India, I really enjoyed watching the Indian masons who were working on the house. They worked hard, but with a great sense of freedom and relaxation. They seemed to enjoy building something beautiful together – and remunerative, of course! The women laughed as they carried piles of bricks on their heads. In the evening, they must have been tired. But I'm sure they slept with peaceful hearts.

There is something very beautiful in work which is well and precisely done. It is a participation in the activity of God, who makes all things well and wisely, beautiful to the last detail.

In these days of automation, we tend to forget the value of manual work which is well done. There is something contemplative in the craftsman. The real carpenter, who loves his wood and knows his tools, doesn't push himself and doesn't get irritable. He knows what he is doing; every action has its purpose and his work is beautiful.

There is something particularly unified about a community

where the work is hard and precisely defined and all the members have their place. Where there is too much luxury and leisure, too much wasted time and imprecision, a community quickly becomes tepid and the cancer of egoism spreads.

In the community of Kerala, all the water for cooking, washing, drinking, and watering the garden has to be drawn from the well. That sort of activity keeps us close to nature and to each other.

Here's a text I like:

> For this commandment which I command you this day is not too hard for you, neither is it far off. It is not in heaven, that you should say, 'Who will go up for us to heaven, and bring it to us, that we may hear it and do it?' Neither is it beyond the sea, that you should say, 'Who will go over the sea for us, and bring it to us, that we may hear it and do it?' But the word is very near you; it is in your mouth and in your heart, so that you can do it. (Deut. 30:11–14)

Daily life in community is not beyond us.

Sometimes this littleness is hard to accept. I remember one summer I was responsible for a holiday group from my community. There were fifteen of us. Friends had lent us a house near a Trappist monastery. I loved to get up early to go and pray with the monks. The silence and the peace opened up my heart. Then, around 8 o'clock I would walk back down to the house; my heart was a bit heavy. I knew I would have to get some of the people up; they would have dirtied their beds and I would have to wash and dress them. And then there would be breakfast and so on. All the chores and squabbles of daily life together; all its bodiliness. How far from the peace and quiet of the monastery!

All that inner pain obliged me to go more deeply into the spirituality of l'Arche. It was important for me to find unity in my being, not to have just a deep spirituality early in the morning and then business for the rest of the day. I had to find how to put love and prayerfulness into all my activities and bodily gestures, into all the cleaning and washing up, into all the chores and togetherness of community living.

I find it marvellous that Jesus lived for thirty hidden years in Nazareth with his mother and Joseph. No one yet knew he was the Christ, the son of God. He lived family and community life in humility, according to the Beatitudes. He worked with wood and lived the small happenings of a Jewish community in the love of his Father. It was only after he had lived the good news of love that he went out to preach it. The second period of his life was the time of struggle, when he tried to get his message across and used signs to confirm his authority. It seems to me that some Christians are in danger of talking too much about things they do not live: they have their theories on what makes for the 'good life' but they have not really experienced it. They speak from ideas rather than from the heart. The hidden life of Jesus is the model for all community life.

The third stage of his life was the one when his friends deserted him, and he was persecuted by the religious and civil authorities. People who are committed to a community may also go through this third period.

Spirituality of movement and spirituality of the circle

Some people have a spirituality of movement and hope. They are filled with energy; they are called to travel and carry the good news and do great things for the Kingdom. The spirituality of St Paul and the apostles was of this kind. They were seized by the desire to make Jesus known and to create new Christian communities. The spirituality of others is to stay where they are: it is the 'spirituality of the circle'. They have more need of a regular rhythm than of constant movement. They use their energies to remain in the presence of God and of their brothers and sisters. Their spirituality is sensitive and compassionate, rooted in the everyday, rather than one which shows itself in action and movement.

People whose spirituality is of the active kind can sometimes be so taken up with the future that they find it hard to live with the present; their heads and hearts can become blinded by projects. If life is too regular, they become impatient; they need adventure and the unexpected. The others, by contrast, become frightened by too much of the unexpected; they need regularity. A community needs dynamic people who construct and do dramatic things. But even more it needs people whose roots are in the spirituality of everyday life.

The spirituality of Nazareth, or the spirituality of the circle which implies littleness, love of little things and humility, is not easy in our world. We are schooled from an early age to go up the ladder of human promotion, to be outstanding, to succeed and to win prizes; we are taught to fend for ourselves and to be independent. We are taught how important it is to possess knowledge, success, power and reputation. We are taught to put external values over and above internal ones. However the gospels call us to love and live the Beatitudes; to die to ourselves. This implies a huge change of attitude, a conversion. And it can only come about if we are truly grafted on to Jesus and receive his Holy Spirit. We will never be able to live the littleness of love unless we are truly determined to respond to the call of Jesus to follow him. And that means that we have to be rooted in prayer.

The laws of matter

There are some fundamental laws which communities have to obey. We have to respect the budget and the system of accounting, and find the resources we need to live. A community needs structures, discipline and a rule, even if this is only to do with the times of meals. We have to know who does what and how. All this makes up the skeleton and flesh of the body which is community. If it is not respected, the community will die. But of course, the administration, budgeting and community structure are only there to allow the community's spirit and goals to develop and deepen.

Some people reject the physical body – whether their own or the community's – as if there were something dirty in it and its instincts were bad. These people don't want structures; they are afraid of them. They reject all rules, discipline, and authority. They don't respect the paint on the walls, either. They have no sense of the value of money or of responsibility towards material goods. Their ideal of a community is one which is completely spiritual, made up of love, warm relationships and spontaneity. But they are unrealistic: community is both body and spirit.

If a community can be thrown off course by people who reject the laws of matter, it can also be stifled by those who rely completely on rules, the law, well-run accounts and efficient administration. People who look only to these things kill the community's heart and spirit. As Stephen Verney says: 'We are more earthy and more heavenly than we have cared to admit.' The same is true of a community. The body is important: it is beautiful, and we have to care for it. But we do this for the life, spirit, heart, motivation, hope and growth of those for whom the community exists.

Love and poverty

The question of poverty is a hard one! A community can so quickly become rich, for the best of all possible reasons. We need a refrigerator so that we can buy meat cheaper and keep the leftovers – and then we need a deep freeze. It's true that a large initial outlay can bring eventual savings. A car is absolutely necessary if we are to shop economically in the market; so we stop walking and using bicycles. Machines help us to do things more quickly and efficiently, but they can also destroy some community activities. I would be sad if we ever got a dishwasher for the houses in Trosly: if we did, we would no longer get together, relax and laugh over the dishes. Other communities would say that preparing vegetables offers the same chance to share. Machines can also throw the weakest people out of work and this is sad, because their small contribution to the housework or cooking is their way of giving something to the community. We are in danger of organising community life as if it were a factory, a hospital or some other institution. People who are capable of doing things very quickly with the help of machines become tremendously busy, always active, in charge of everyone – a bit like machines themselves. Less capable people are condemned to inactivity and gravitate to the television.

Are there any norms in this question of poverty? One thing is sure – a community which gets richer, has everything it needs and is completely self-reliant, will become isolated, just because it needs no help. It will close up in itself and its wealth. It loses its radiance. It will be able to do things for its neighbours, but they will be able to offer nothing in return. There will be no exchange or sharing. The community will become the rich cousin. To what will it witness then?

A community which has all it needs and more is in danger of running up expenses; it will be wasteful or abuse what it has; it will lose its respect for material goods. It will lose its creativity with matter and become slipshod. It will become incapable of distinguishing between luxury, what is helpful for its moral and physical well-being, and what is absolutely essential. A rich community very quickly loses the dynamic of love.

I remember Brother Andrew of the Missionaries of Charity talking about Calcutta, where he lived for fourteen years. The scale of human misery there, he said, made it the worst city in the world. But it was also the most beautiful, because it had the most love. When we become rich, we throw up barriers; perhaps we even hire a watchdog to defend our property. Poor people have nothing to defend and often share the little they have.

In a poor community, there is a lot of mutual help and sharing of goods, as well as help from outside. Poverty becomes a cement of unity. This is very striking at l'Arche when we go on pilgrimage together: everyone shares gladly, sometimes contenting themselves with very little. But when we become rich, we become more demanding and difficult: we tend to remain in our own corner, alone, and isolated. In poor African villages, people share in mutual support and celebration. In modern cities, they shut themselves up in their own apartments. Because they have all the material things they need, they seem not to need each other. They are self-sufficient. There is no interdependence. There is no love.

A community which spends a lot of time watching television very quickly loses its sense of creativity, sharing, and celebration. People don't meet any more – they are glued to the screen. When people love each other, they are content with very little. When we have light and joy in our hearts, we don't need material wealth. The most loving communities are often the poorest. If our own life is luxurious and wasteful, we can't approach poor people. If we love people, we want to identify with them and share with them.

The important thing is for communities to know what they want to witness to. Poverty is only a means to a witness of love and a way of life.

I very much liked what Nadine said about the l'Arche community in Honduras, Casa Nazareth. There, they have welcomed Lita and Marcia, both of whom are visibly handicapped. They both come from very poor families and it is important that their new home is always open to the neighbours – like the rest of the homes in the area. This is the way that people live there, and Lita and Marcia mustn't live differently, because then it would be like living in an institution; they need to have friends, and live like everyone else. So the local children are always running in and out of the house, laughing, singing, chattering and playing. I asked Nadine if she'd like a tape recorder and she turned it down, because she'd have to keep it locked up to prevent the children playing with it and breaking it. If she did this, a cupboard would become a secret hiding place, and so a barrier to welcome. And then, she said, l'Arche shouldn't have things that the neighbours don't have themselves. If it did, people would want to play with them or have them themselves. So wealth could very quickly throw up barriers of envy, or create a sense of inferiority, because possession means power. Poverty, on the other hand, should mean love and welcome. The question remains the same: do we want to witness to love and welcome, or do we want to retreat behind a barrier of comfort and security?

But larger and richer communities shouldn't despair! They have to witness to another sort of poverty. They can still avoid luxury and waste; they can, for instance, use their space to welcome more people. Their wealth is a gift of God, but it doesn't belong to them – they are only trustees. They should use this gift to spread the good news of love and sharing.

The conflict between living littleness and political commitment

We have a small community in Bethany on the West Bank. There is a lot of pain in the village and surrounding area. The Palestinian people are struggling for survival. The Israelis are also struggling for survival and have been trying to crush recent uprisings, often with great cruelty. It is difficult and disturbing just to be living there with Rula and Siham, helping them to eat, to dress and do all the little things of daily life when there is so much going on around us. If we get too involved in what is happening, we will not be able to be present in mind and spirit to Rula and Siham and to others who need our presence and attention in order to live. And yet we can feel torn and guilty doing little things, when so many important things are happening which could change the course of history for so many people. It is not always easy to trust in the importance of doing little things when political struggle is raging round us.

Political dimension of the community

Christian communities cannot be outside society. They are not bolt-holes for the emotions, offering spiritual drugs to stave off the sadness of everyday life. They are not places where people can go to salve their consciences and retreat from reality into a world of dreams. They are places of resource, which are there to help people grow towards freedom, so that they can love as Jesus loves them. 'There is no greater love than to give one's life for one's friends.' The message of Jesus is clear. He reprimands the rich and proud and exalts the humble. Christian communities have to be at the heart of society, visible to everyone; they should not hide their light under a bushel. They should be a sign that we don't need artificial stimulants or material goods for our hearts to rejoice at the beauty of those around us and of the universe in which we live, a sign that we can work together to make our neighbourhood, village, or city a place of creativity and human growth.

So there is a whole political dimension to Christian communities.

Some Christians are very taken up by politics. They can be terribly anti-communist, forming rather fascist organisations to fight the 'red devil'. Or they can be fiercely anti-capitalist, fighting for new structures and redistribution of resources. Both these tendencies can lead to a centralisation – whether to protect the free-market economy or to further wholesale nationalisation.

I sometimes wonder whether these fighting Christians wouldn't do better to put their energies into creating communities which live as far as they can by the charter of the Beatitudes. If they did this, they would be able to live by, and measure progress by, values other than those of material success, acquisition of wealth and political struggle. They could become the yeast in the dough of society. They would not change political structures at first. But they would change the hearts and spirits of the people around them, by offering them a glimpse of a new dimension in human life – that of inwardness, love, contemplation, wonderment and sharing. They would introduce people to a place where the weak and poor, far from being pushed aside, are central to their society. My personal hope is that, if this spirit of community really spreads, structures will change. Structures are – tyrannies excepted – the mirrors of hearts. But if change is to come, some people should be working now on the political level towards a society which is more just, true and sharing, in which communities can take root and shine, and where human beings can be truly human.

Something similar could be said about people who throw themselves militantly into *causes*. Some people struggling for peace are terribly aggressive, even with 'rival' peace movements. To struggle for a cause it is best for people to be rooted in a community where they are learning reconciliation, acceptance of difference and of their own darkness, and how to celebrate. Isn't there a danger when groups with noble humanitarian causes develop very aggressive attitudes and divide the world into 'goodies' and 'baddies'? This type of elitism can be dangerous and continues a form of apartheid and oppression towards those who do not share the same ideas.

Communities which live simply and without waste, and which do not use television all the time, help people to discover a whole new way of life, which demands fewer financial resources but more commitment to relationships and to celebration. Is there a better way to bridge the gulf which widens daily between rich and poor countries? It is not simply a question of generous people going to work in developing countries. Rich countries themselves have to be awakened to the fact that happiness is not to be found in a frantic search for material goods, but in simple and loving relationships, lived and celebrated in communities which have renounced that search.

Life in industrialised countries has become artificial, its patterns far from nature. Houses are full of electric gadgets; leisure activities are limited to television and the cinema; cities are noisy, stifling and polluted; people are exhausted by long hours of travel in subway, train and car – when they aren't equally exhausted by crawling through traffic jams. The films they watch and the news they listen to concentrate on violence. They cannot possibly integrate all that is happening over the world – earthquakes in Azerbaijan, famine in the Sahel, fighting in the Middle East, disruption in Northern Ireland, censorship of the press, tyranny, torture, people being condemned to prison without trial, or to a psychiatric hospital when they are not ill. It is overwhelming. And people are

overwhelmed by it all. They are not equipped to assimilate all this
dramatic information. That is why they latch on to new myths
which announce the salvation of the world, or rigid sects which
claim to have a monopoly of the truth. The more anguish people
feel, the more they seek out new saviours – whether these are
political, psychological, religious, or mystical. Or else they throw
everything over in the race for instant stimulation, wealth and
prestige.

Communities are a sign that it is possible to live on a human
scale, even in the present world. They are a sign that we do not
have to be slaves to work, to inhuman economies, or to the
stimulations of artificial leisure. A community is essentially a place
where we learn to live at the pace of humanity and nature. We are
part of the earth and we need the heat of the sun, the water of the
sea, and the air we breath. We are part of nature and its laws are
written in our flesh. That doesn't mean that scientific discoveries
aren't useful too. But they have to be at the service of life, applied
to create an environment in which human beings can truly grow
– whether in town or country, middle-class areas or slums.

A community should be primarily not a grouping of shock-
troops, commandos or heroes, but a gathering of people who want
to be a sign that it is possible for people to live together, love each
other, celebrate and work for a better world and a fellowship of
peace. A community is a sign that love is possible in a materialistic
world where people so often either ignore or fight each other. It
is a sign that we don't need a lot of money to be happy – in fact,
the opposite. Schumacher's *Small is Beautiful* gave us a lot to think
about.[1] In our l'Arche communities, we have to put still more
thought into the quality of life. We have to learn to live each day
and find our own internal and external rhythms.

In rich countries today there is a growing opposition to immigrants
from poorer countries; they are frequently badly treated and
housed in terrible conditions. Apartheid exists not only in South

---

1   E. F. Schumacher, *Small is Beautiful* (Blond & Briggs, London, 1973; Sphere,
    London, 1974).

Africa; it exists in all our hearts. We all tend to be clannish and to hide ourselves in fear, in our clubs and with friends, with those who think like us. Isn't it politically important today to give witness that different kinds of people can live together – that the dividing walls of hostility are not inevitable? Isn't it important to show that people coming from different cultures and religious traditions can respect and love each other; that war and oppression are not inevitable? Isn't it important, in a world where people with a handicap are being eliminated before or shortly after birth, that there be communities that manifest their beauty and value?

Village people in African and other poor countries have a quality of life. They know how to live in families and communities, even though they don't always know how to act efficiently. I sometimes meet missionaries who know how to do all sorts of things: build schools and hospitals, teach, and take care of people. They sometimes even know how to play an effective part in political struggles. But they often do not know how to live together. Their house doesn't feel joyful or alive; it doesn't feel like a community where everyone is relaxed, bound together in deep relationship. That is sad, because Christians should, above all, bear witness by their lives. That is as important today, when African countries are torn between village traditions and a taste for money and progress, as it has ever been. Missionaries often seem to be saying that successful living depends on being able to use machinery and costly techniques, on having a refrigerator and a car. I always marvel at the Little Sisters of Jesus, the sisters of Mother Teresa and others who live among their people and bear witness by their lives.

We sometimes wonder what l'Arche is doing in Calcutta. There are fifteen people at Asha Niketan. Some of them used to live on the streets, destitute because of their mental handicap. The house is in a grossly overcrowded area, stuck on the side of Sealdah – the busiest railway station in the world. Life is happy, through the usual ups and downs. There is enough to eat and there is work from a Philips factory. The community is growing slowly towards financial independence – though it's not certain that it will achieve it. In the street, there is a multitude of poor people who have no work at all. A bit further away, there are some very rich people who seem quite unaware of their responsibilities. So we wonder what l'Arche is doing there – a small drop of water in that vast desert of suffering and misery.

But we have to remind ourselves constantly that we are not saviours. We are simply a tiny sign, among thousands of others, that love is possible, that the world is not condemned to a struggle between oppressors and oppressed, that class and racial warfare is not inevitable. We are a sign that there is hope, because we believe that the Father loves us and sends his Spirit to transform our hearts and lead us from egoism to love, so that we can live everyday life as brothers and sisters.

Sartre is wrong when he says that hell is other people. It is heaven that is other people. They only become hell when we are locked into our own egoism and darkness. If they are to become heaven, we have to make the slow passage from egoism to love. It is our own hearts and eyes that have to change.

I marvel sometimes when I visit families with a son or a daughter who has a severe handicap. The parents are living each day, and sometimes the whole day, with little help or times of rest. They are not admired or honoured for what they are doing; sometimes they are even criticised for not having aborted their child or put him or her into an institution, outside the general run of society. We in l'Arche have days off; we get help and encouragement from professionals and clergy. We even receive salaries. And often people see us as wonderful and generous people. And yet, isn't it those families who are living love and truth and humility and abandonment to God in a special way? Isn't it all those families in the ghettos of large cities struggling to feed their children who are radiating a truth about our humanity? People who have chosen to live in community have much to learn from all those people throughout the world who are living love in a simple hidden way, and who are there welcoming and forgiving.

11

Celebration

At the heart of community: celebration

Forgiveness and celebration are at the heart of community. These
are the two faces of love. Celebration is a communal experience
of joy, a song of thanksgiving. We celebrate the fact of being
together; we give thanks for the gifts we have been given. Celebration nourishes us, restores hope, and brings us the strength to
live with the suffering and difficulties of everyday life. The poorer
people are, the more they love to celebrate. The festivals of the
poorest people in Africa last for several days. They use all their
savings on huge feasts and beautiful clothes. They make garlands
of flowers and they set off fireworks - for light and explosions
are an integral part of celebration. These festivals nearly always
commemorate a divine or religious event – they are sacred
occasions.

In richer countries we have lost the art of celebrating. People
go to movies or watch television or have other leisure activities;
they go to parties, but they do not celebrate.

Rich societies have lost their sense of tradition and so their sense
of celebration as well. Celebration is linked to family and religious
tradition. As soon as it gets away from this, it tends to become
artificial, and people need stimulants like alcohol to get it moving.
Then it is no longer a celebration. It may be a party, where we
come together to eat and drink, but when we dance it is usually
in couples and often alone. We have become spectators. Our

society has its theatres, cinema, and television. But it has lost its sense of celebration.

Celebration is the specific act of a community as people rejoice and give thanks to the Father for he has bonded them together; he is looking after them and loves them. They are no longer individuals locked up in their own loneliness and independence. They are one body and each of them has their place in the body. Celebration is a cry of joy from all of them covenanted together, for they have been led through the passage of loneliness to love, of discouragement to hope.

Celebrations certainly have a role in helping people to accept the sufferings of everyday life by offering them the chance to relax and let go. But to see them as nothing but a form of escapism or drug, is to fail to understand human nature. We all live a daily life which brings its own weariness: we make things dirty, we clean them, we plough, sow, and harvest. We have long hours to travel to work, which is frustrating; and at work there is discipline, efficiency and a programme to be respected, and then there is the stress. In family life there are sometimes barriers and lack of communication between people; we may close ourselves off from others in television, books or other things, feeling guilty and making others feel guilty; inside us there is a lot of inner pain. As we need the day for work, activity, prayer, rejoicing and the night for sleep, and as we need the four seasons with their different climates, so too we need the drudgery of dailiness and the joys of celebration; we need the work day and the sabbath. Our human hearts need something beyond the limitations and frustrations of the daily grind. We thirst for a happiness which seems unattainable on earth. We crave the infinite, the universal, the eternal – something which gives a sense to human life and its irksome daily routines. A festival is a sign of heaven. It symbolises our deepest aspiration – an experience of total communion.

Celebration expresses the true meaning of community in a concrete and tangible way. So it is an essential element in community life. Celebration sweeps away the irritations of daily life; we forget our little quarrels. The aspect of ecstasy in a celebration unites our hearts; a current of life goes through us all. Celebration is a moment of wonder when the joy of the body and the senses are linked to the joy of the spirit. It unites everything that is most human and most divine in community life. The liturgy of the celebration – which brings together music, dance, song, light and the fruit and flowers of the earth – brings us into communion with God and each other, through prayer, thanksgiving and good food. (And the celebratory meal is important!) The harder and more irksome our daily life, the more our hearts need these moments of celebration and wonder. We need times when we all come together to give thanks, sing, dance, and enjoy special meals. Each community, like each people, needs its festival liturgy.

Celebration is nourishment and resource. It makes present the goals of the community in symbolic form, and so brings hope and a new strength to take up again everyday life with more love. Celebration is a sign of the resurrection which gives us strength to carry the cross of each day. There is an intimate bond between celebration and the cross.

The greatest pain of human beings is separation and loneliness, which always produce guilt, anger, vengeance, jealousy and such like; these are the seeds of war. All this is a foretaste of death. The deepest cry in the heart of the human person is a cry for life, and life is unity and peace. Joy flows from unity. And unity is born from daily love, mutual acceptance and forgiveness. Celebration is the song of joy and thanksgiving flowing from a sense of unity but also creating and deepening it.

For married couples, their love and tenderness expressed through their bodies is a celebration of unity. They are one body, one being; they belong to each other. Members of communities are called to celebrate their unity, the fact that they belong to one another, and to God. If they don't, then their emotional lives will be frustrated and hurt and they will have more difficulty integrating their sexuality into their capacity to relate.

It is so important for a family to celebrate all together. It is so important for the children to laugh and play and sing with their parents and to see their parents happy to be together.

By contrast, there is a sadness about commemorations of political liberation. There is no dancing, no feasting; there are military parades and fly-pasts instead. There is a show of power which people may watch with a certain emotion. But there is no celebration. In France, even in non-Christian quarters, there is a great difference between the tenderness and sweetness of Christmas, when people quite naturally wish each other 'Happy Christmas' and the national celebration of the Fourteenth of July, when there is a slightly serious moment at the war memorial, when you salute the Republic – then it's off to the café for a drink. In the old days, people used to dance in the cafes – but they don't even do much of that now.

In the same way when people come to honour success and power or to give out prizes to winners; they do not celebrate. They clap and applaud. They are proud if the winners come from their club or group or family or country. In some ways they identify with the winner and feel they are the best. But there are so many who are losers, who have no success nor power. Celebration is a shout of love, and of openness, not a feeling of power and superiority.

Very often these days we have joy without God, or God without joy. That is the result of a certain tradition of God as all-powerful and severe, a tradition which separated joy from the divine. But celebration is joy with God. Each culture and each tradition expresses this joy in a different way, with more or less restraint. At l'Arche, we can celebrate with a burst of laughter and song, and then immediately go into prayer and silence. Shouldn't every celebration end in the silent prayer which is the celebration of our personal meeting with God?

True belly laughs are important in community life. When a group laughs in this way, many pains are swept away.

Laughter is something very human. I am not sure angels laugh! They adore. When human beings are too serious they become

tense. Laughter is the greatest of relaxations. And there is something funny about humanity. Little as we are, poor as we are, with
all our 'animal' needs, we are called to become more than angels;
brothers and sisters of God, the Word made flesh. It seems so
ludicrous and wonderful, so crazy and yet so ecstatic. And the most
rejected are called to be at the heart of the Kingdom. Everything is
upside down. No wonder some people at sacred moments have
the giggles.

Celebration is a time to thank God for an event in the past when
he showed his loving presence to humanity itself or the community
in particular. It is also a reminder that he is always there, today,
watching over his people and the community, as a loving father
watches over his children. We are celebrating not only something
which happened in the past, but something which is happening
now. For the Jewish people, Passover is a reminder of the time
when the angel of Yahweh passed by and God freed his people;
they give thanks to Yahweh today, who continues in the same
way to be their guide, pastor, protector and loving Father.

When people celebrate Christmas, they are celebrating the same
reality, the same love of the Father who sent his only beloved son
into the world to save it. And Jesus is born in our hearts to heal
us, to make us whole and to save us. The feast day reactualises
the event that happened long ago. It is not just remembering what
happened; it is living it today.

It is sad when people forget what it means to celebrate
Christmas, and when everything is reduced to food and drink, and
to giving expensive toys to already spoilt children.

Christmas is the celebration of the poor and the children. It is
the celebration of the family. It is a time of peace.

In many of our l'Arche homes on Holy Thursday, after the Eucharistic celebration when we celebrate Jesus transforming for the
first time the bread into his body, we eat the paschal meal. During
this meal, we bring to mind all the moments of grace we have
lived together during the past year. Then we wash each other's

feet and ask forgiveness one of another. All this is done with love and simplicity and a real sense of the sacred. After that we go to pray in the chapel, spending time with Jesus who had said in the Garden of Olives: 'Can you not watch one hour with me?'

Each community should celebrate its anniversaries according to its own history and traditions – like the moment God inspired the foundation, or a particular occasion when he protected the community.

It is important to remember and to re-read our own personal histories and the history of the community on certain feast-days, and then to give thanks for the way God has watched over us, protected us and saved us over the years. Remembering too that if he called the community into being and looked after it in the past, then he will continue to do so today with all our questions, difficulties and tensions. Yes, he continues to watch over us.

There is also the celebration at the end of the year when a community gives thanks for and rejoices in what it has received in the past twelve months. And then there are smaller celebrations – birthdays, weddings, christenings – through which we recognise the uniqueness, the particular place and the gift of each individual. There are also the small daily celebrations which spring up around meals and happen spontaneously when we meet. When the prodigal son returned, his father told the servants: 'Bring quickly the best robe, and put it on him; and put a ring on his hand and shoes on his feet; and bring the fatted calf and kill it, and let us eat and make merry; for this my son was dead, and is alive again; he was lost and is found' (Luke 15:22–4).

The Gospels speak continually of feast-days and celebrations. Jesus' first miracle was at the wedding feast at Cana where he turned water into wine so that the celebration could be more beautiful, and not just a few good bottles but over four hundred litres and for people who had already had quite a lot to drink! The generosity of God! It was often at a moment of celebration that Jesus appeared at the Temple and announced a special good news. And he died on the feast of the Passover. We need to learn how to use each feast day, each celebration to bring the appropriate message of love and hope through the Word and through mime: there is a message for each day that can nourish the heart and renew and deepen the vision, giving new life.

At the heart of celebration, there are the poor. If the least significant is excluded, it is no longer a celebration. We have to find dances and games in which the children, the old people, and the weak can join equally. A celebration must always be a festival of the poor, and with the poor, not for the poor.

Some people are reluctant to go to celebrations in a community. They feel tired and a bit closed up in themselves. When they do go, however, they come away refreshed and feel liberated inside. But no one should be obliged to go to a celebration. There is always someone who is in pain and who does not want to celebrate. And then there are those who have difficulty being in a group; so they remain outside, listening to everything that is going on. They are in and out of the group at the same time. And then there are some who feel called by Jesus to remain silently with him in the chapel; they participate also in a secret, mystical way.

Visitors are often astonished at the joy they sense at l'Arche. Their impression surprises me, too, because I know how much suffering some people in our communities are carrying. I wonder then if all joy doesn't somehow spring from suffering and sacrifice. Can those who are rich and live in comfort and security with everything they need, and refuse to be close to those who are suffering, be truly joyful? Isn't there a lot of unconscious guilt in them which closes them up? Joy comes from openness. But I am sure that poor people can be joyful. At times of celebration, they seem to overcome all their suffering and frustration in an explosion of joy.

They shed the burden of daily life and they live a moment of freedom in which their hearts simply bound with joy. It is so too with people in community who have learnt to accept their wounds, limitations and poverty. They are forgiven; they are loved. They have discovered liberation; they are not frightened of being themselves; they do not have to hide away; they are free with the freedom of the Spirit.

A wedding is one of the great celebrations. It is a time when all that is most divine seems to meet all that is most human in joy. 'The Kingdom of God is like a wedding feast.' The celebration is a sign of the eternal celebration. And each small celebration in our communities has to be this sign too.

A celebration is very different from a spectacle, where actors or musicians play to entertain an audience. In a celebration, we are all actors and all audience. It is not a true celebration unless everyone participates.

But there is always an element of sadness in celebration. We cannot celebrate without alluding to it, because there are people on this earth of ours who are not celebrating, who are despairing, anguished, starving and mourning. That is why all celebration, which is like a great 'Alleluia' and song of thanksgiving, should end with a silence in which we remember before God all those who cannot celebrate and who are in pain today.

Each community has its own traditions of celebration. Each has its own liturgy, or special Eucharist, its own way of decorating the chapel; each has its own special meal and way of serving it and decorating the dining room with candles, garlands, and flowers; each has its own songs, party clothes, and dances.

And of course, the way a Trappist monastery celebrates a feast day or a birthday will be different from the way the Church of the Saviour or a l'Arche community celebrates. Each community has its charism and its way of announcing that all together they give thanks for being called by God in one body; all give thanks for a particular meaningful day, a feast day. In communities where there is a great deal of silence and prayer, these gestures will be simpler but maybe all the more expressive.

In communities like the l'Arche ones in Africa, where the members come from different cultures, each person has their own idea of how leisure time should be spent. Canadians like to have a drink; people from Burkina Faso like to visit the neighbours; others want to shut themselves away and read a book. Individuals all have their own preferences. Celebration isn't simply a time for relaxation according to our own culture, a moment 'for ourselves'. It is a well-prepared meeting of joy and wonderment, which goes beyond cultural differences.

It is wonderful to see how the Roman Catholic Church has kept its sense of celebration. Almost every day is a feast day – either a great liturgical festival or a saint's day. And then at the heart of each day we 'celebrate' the Mass. I am always struck by the vocabulary of the Mass: celebration and feast, presence and communion, meal and sacrifice, forgiveness, eucharist and thanksgiving. These words sum up community life well. We have to be truly present, in communion, with each other because we are in communion with Jesus. And that is feast and celebration. This communion, this celebration, is a time of nourishment. We become bread for each other because God became bread for us; it is a meal at the heart of the community. Sacrifice is always at the centre of community life, because it has to do with the sacrifice of our own interests for those of others, as Jesus sacrificed his life so that we could receive the Spirit. We begin the celebration by asking for forgiveness and we complete it in thanksgiving.

The Eucharist is not there just to feed our personal piety. It is celebration and thanksgiving for the whole community, for the whole Church, and for all humanity. The celebration of the Eucharist is one of the moments in community life when we are most united; everything is offered to the Father in Jesus. For

Christians it is the summit and the heart of all celebrations; it is the centre of community.

These days, when there are so many people who are depressed and frightened for the future, it is important to announce and celebrate our hope in God. There may be wars and revolutions; there may be sickness and natural catastrophes, but God is watching over humanity with love. Death is not the end of all. Love has conquered hate and death. Celebrations do not have to be loud nor boisterous; they can be very sober, simply announcing our trust and our love; announcing the unity of the body; announcing the good news: God is present amongst us, he is in our hearts; Jesus is risen and is alive.

Meals

Meals are daily celebrations where we meet each other around the same table to be nourished and share in joy. They are a particular delight for the body and the senses. So we shouldn't bolt our food under the pretext of having more important or more spiritual things to do than sit at table. A meal is an important community event which has to be well prepared and fully lived. It is a time when the joy of eating and drinking well merge with the joy of meeting – a marvellous human moment. Meals and love have been linked for us all since we were infants. When a mother feeds her baby, there is mutual presence, joy and play. An infant who is not fed with love and who takes the nipple mechanically, is going to have indigestion. Human beings don't eat like animals, all in their own corner. Friendship and love make the activity human.

This is why meals must not be times for contentious discussion or serious educational attitudes. Working meals are not to be encouraged either. A meal is a time of relaxation for the body and the spirit. Laughter is excellent for the digestion. Serious discussions cause ulcers and other intestinal problems. Some children really do have terrible problems if they can't eat in an atmosphere of relaxation. I know that tensions at table cut my appetite and go straight to my liver!

During the course of a meal, each person has to have the chance to meet all the others. Even the simple gesture of passing the potatoes is a natural moment of communication which can bring people out of their isolation. They cannot remain behind the barriers of their depression when they have to ask for the salt. The need for food encourages communication.

Self-service is the worst of inventions. There we are, all with our own tray, own little bottle of wine, own little sachets of sugar, salt, and pepper. It's like spending every mealtime on an aeroplane. It's terrible to assume that everyone is going to eat and drink a standard quantity, and do it alone into the bargain. How much more human to have a nice big bottle, from which everyone can pour as much as they want, and one nice big dish, so that everyone can make sure that the others have what they need and be willing to offer the best bits to their neighbour. Then meals are no longer a solitary and egoistical business, but a time when each person shares and loves.

Anyone who runs a house knows that a good meal takes careful preparation – from drawing up the menu, to buying the food, to cooking it, to setting the table, and presenting the meal attractively. Everything has to be thought of: the wine, the flowers, who sits next to whom, the way conversations can be encouraged. It is good if people have time to talk to their neighbours. But it is good too to have times when everyone can share in conversations of general interest and laugh together.

I think it was St Louis of Gonzaguez who each day prepared funny stories to make his brothers laugh during recreation. He wasn't naturally gifted for this and would rather perhaps have stayed out of the limelight. But for love of his brothers, he tried to inject gaiety into those recreation times. Things can't always be left to spontaneity, because this is often a question of sensitivity or the emotion of the moment.

We have a duty to learn more creative ways of celebrating. We need to find more rousing and funnier songs, stories, and snippets of information. If these are well prepared, the meal and other community activities can become moments of sharing, celebration and pooling of knowledge, with all the opening of the spirit that these imply. Too many people come to a meal simply as consumers. They don't realise the role which meals can play in the building of community.

When we've had oranges for dessert at l'Arche, we sometimes start chucking the peel about at the end of the meal. Everyone gets into it. An Englishman once asked me if this was a traditional French custom. I don't know about that! But I do know that it is one way to bring people out of their isolation to express themselves joyfully – especially if they can't communicate with words. People who cannot participate in interesting conversations can participate through play. When a piece of orange peel arrives on their nose, they are delighted – and they throw it back.

I was once explaining this way of celebrating during a retreat I was giving in New Zealand for superiors of religious orders. The last evening, we had a celebratory meal to which the bishop came. And, by chance, there were oranges for dessert. It was quite something to see those serious and until now rather formal mothers provincial joyfully chucking orange peel about under the astonished gaze of the bishop! He, of course, didn't know how it had all started. There was a bit of explaining to do!

The way the table is set is important. So is the placing of people around it. If some are a bit strung up, there are others who shouldn't be put next to them. There is a whole discernment of love to be made here. In the same way, when people are sad, we try to make some food they really enjoy. A meal offers the chance of very many gestures of sensitivity and tenderness.

Eating well doesn't mean eating expensively. There is a lot of good food that is cheap too. It's a question of creativity, of culinary skill, especially with sauces – think of spaghetti without sauce! A sauce is a gesture of *gratuité*. A community which eats nothing but plain pasta because 'it's cheaper to buy in bulk' will never be a very cheerful place.

A silent meal, by candlelight and against a background of good music, can create a very warm community atmosphere. Silent meals are often the rule in monasteries, where people, after all, don't have too much news to share. But silence also encourages reflection and inwardness. And it doesn't exclude sensitive non-verbal communication which can sometimes forge unity more strongly than words.

Preparing the celebration

A celebration or other community activity should be at least as carefully prepared as a meal. Things cannot be left to happen spontaneously. A small group of people have to discern the goal and how it is to be reached, for it is within a well-prepared framework that we can best encourage spontaneity and changes in the programme. And we have to know how to capture and prolong the unexpected – the moment of unity, of grace and recollection, or of wonder, the times when the current of life is flowing joyfully. If a celebration is not well prepared, you can be sure that either someone will seize the chance to turn the occasion into 'their' project and impose their view, put themselves at the heart of the spectacle and collect the applause; or that everything will disperse into boredom, with no sense of unity or celebration at all.

Every community activity should be evaluated afterwards, to see whether we have done what we set out to do. We have to recognise our mistakes and omissions, so that we can do better next time. God gave us an intelligence, a memory, and an imagination – and we should use them. Americans love evaluating and they sometimes concentrate a bit too heavily on the material aspects, which is why they are good at commerce. The French are not too fond of evaluation. We should always try to evaluate our activities – but qualitatively.

Some people refuse to take on the organisation of celebrations 'as a job' because they want others to have a chance and because they don't want to be typed as 'animators'. But if this is their gift, why do they deny it to the community? Perhaps they could teach others how to be animators. The same holds true for all the arts – theatre, dance, mime. Every artistic activity can carry a message which can touch people and make their hearts beat in unison. The arts shouldn't be neglected, and each community should find its own expression. Every human activity can be put at the service of the divine and of love. Everyone should exercise their gift to build community.

Song has a primary importance in community. The members of Bundeena in Australia told me that because some of their people couldn't read, they set some passages of the Bible to music, so that the word of God could penetrate more deeply into people's spirits. St Marie Louise Grignon of Montfort set prayers and hymns to popular music. At l'Arche, it seems to me, we are turning more and more to melancholy songs, perhaps because we want to help people reflect. We need to find some more cheerful ones. There is a whole art in discerning the right song for the right moment: there are some which encourage prayer and reflection, others which encourage us to push ahead. More people in our communities should be thinking about and specialising in this. We too often leave everything to the emotion of the moment. Certainly people shouldn't choose songs just because they like them or they reflect the way they themselves are feeling. We need to find the right song for each occasion.

Wolf Wolfensberger, professor in the special education and rehabilitation division of an American university, told me recently that he felt we should invent universal dances, easy to learn and perform, and set words to them. In our celebrations, we always dance farandols – but only because we have never learned anything else. There must be some other dances in which people with disabilities can join.

Sometimes we feel we lack a particular gift, because we don't want to push ourselves forward. But we can still ask God to give us gifts, especially if these are to be used to create community. Each aspect of community life is important; sometimes we have to work hard to participate in it as fully as possible, and to create the atmosphere of joy and awareness which enables it to flourish.

In celebrations – and in any community discussions and prayers as well – those who speak must always make sure that everyone can hear and understand what is going on. That means speaking loudly and clearly, for a start. Meetings where people mumble shyly into their beards so that only their closest neighbours can hear them, are deadly. When we speak in any sort of community meeting, we have to think of the person at the furthest end of the room and, if necessary, stand up. We have to talk simply, thinking of the composition of the audience. It is better to get across one or two ideas that they can grasp easily than to confuse them with a jumble of thoughts that they only half understand. And we have to remember too that what we say is not as important as the faith and enthusiasm with which we say it and touch hearts. It is important that we know how to get across the message we want to communicate.

Nourishment comes in those moments when the whole community becomes aware of the current of life which flows through it. These are times of grace and gift when the community lives the joy of being together in celebration, feasting, and prayer. I remember an evening in one of our communities which had just started. The meal I shared with them was rather sad; each person spoke only to their neighbour and there was no sense of unity round the table. After the meal, we all met in the living room. Someone picked up a guitar and we began to sing. And then, one after another, everyone began to clap their hands and beat out the rhythm with a glass and spoon, or any improvised instrument they could find. You could feel the current of life! Faces began to light up – it was a moment of grace. We were really together, our hearts, hands and voices beating in unison. But it didn't last. Some of the people with disabilities couldn't bear to feel too relaxed and happy; their families' rejection had left them with too much anger. Sometimes we have to wait for a long time for everyone to be able to join fully in a celebration.

Invited to the wedding feast

I have always loved what the King said to his servants in St Matthew's Gospel: 'Go therefore to the thoroughfares, and invite to the marriage feast as many as you find' (Matt. 22:9). We are not made to be sad and to work all the time, to do nothing but obey the law and struggle. We are all invited to the wedding feast!

Our communities should be signs of joy and celebration. If they are, people will commit themselves with us. Communities which are sad are sterile; they are places of death. Of course our joy on earth is far from complete. But our celebrations are small signs of the eternal celebration, of the wedding feast to which we are all invited.

Conclusion

This book has been about community – community as the place of forgiveness and celebration, growth and liberation. But when all is said and done, each of us, and in the deepest part of our self, has to learn to accept our own essential solitude.

In each of our hearts, there is a wound – the wound of our own loneliness, which hurts at moments of setback and can be even more painful at the time of our death. Death is a passage which cannot be made in community. It has to be made completely alone. And all suffering, sadness and depression is a foretaste of that death, a manifestation of our deep wound which is part of the human condition. Because our hearts thirst for the infinite, they will never be satisfied with the limitations which are always a sign of death. We can touch that infinite in art, music and poetry. We can experience moments of communion and love, of prayer and ecstasy – but they are only moments. We quickly find ourselves back in the incompleteness which is the result of our immortality and limitations and those of others.

We will only find peace when we discover that our setbacks, depression, and even our sins can be an offering and a sacrifice, and so open the door to the eternal. We will only find trust when we have accepted our human condition, with all its limitations and contradictions and frantic search for happiness, and when we have discovered that the eternal wedding feast will be waiting for us, like a gift, after our death.

Even the most beautiful community can never heal the wound of loneliness that we carry. It is only when we discover that this loneliness can become a sacrament that we touch wisdom, for this sacrament is purification and presence of God. If we stop fleeing from our own solitude, and if we accept our wound, we will discover that this is the way to meet Jesus Christ. It is when we stop fleeing into work and activity, noise and illusion, and when we remain conscious of our wound, that we will meet God. He is the Paraclete, the One who responds to our cry, which comes from the darkness of our loneliness.

Those who enter marriage believing that it will slake their thirst for communion and heal their wound will not find happiness. In the same way, those who enter community hoping that it will totally fulfil and heal them, will be disappointed. We will only find the true meaning of marriage or community when we have understood and accepted our wound. It is only when we stand up, with all our failings and sufferings, and try to support others rather than withdraw into ourselves, that we can fully live the life of marriage or community. It is only when we stop seeing others as a refuge that we will become, despite our wound, a source of life and comfort. It is only then that we will discover peace.

Jesus is master of community and it is his teaching which leads to the creation of Christian communities, founded in forgiveness and completed in celebration. But Jesus died abandoned by his friends, crucified on a cross, rejected by society, religious leaders, and his own people. Only one person understood and lived that reality: Mary, his mother, who stood at the foot of the cross. This was no longer community. It was a communion which went beyond all community. The master of community even cried: 'Lord, Lord, why have you forsaken me?' and 'I thirst'.

Community life is there to help us, not to flee from our deep wound, but to remain with the reality of love. It is there to help us believe that our illusions and egoism will be gradually healed if we become nourishment for others. We are in community for each other, so that all of us can grow and uncover our wound before the infinite, so that Jesus can manifest himself through it.

But we can only accept our own deep wound when we have discovered that community is a place where our heart can put down roots, a place where we are at home. The roots are not there to comfort us or turn us in on ourselves. Quite the opposite: they are there so that each of us can grow and bear fruit for humanity and for God. We put down roots when we discover the covenant among people who are called to live together, and the covenant with God and with the poor. Community is there not for itself, but for others – the poor, the Church, and society. It is essentially mission. It has a message of hope to offer and a love to communicate, especially to those who are poor and in distress. So community has a political aspect.

Community can only truly exist if there is this vital and loving communication between it and the poor, if it is a source for them as they are for it.

So community life takes on a wider meaning. It is lived not only among its own members, but in the larger community of its neighbourhood, with the poor, and with all those who want to share its hope. So it becomes a place of reconciliation and forgiveness, where each person feels carried by the others and carries them. It is a place of friendship among those who know that they are weak but know too that they are loved and forgiven. Thus community is the place of celebration.

And celebration is the sign that beyond all the sufferings, purifications and deaths, there is the eternal wedding feast, the great celebration of life with God. It is the sign that there is a personal meeting which will fulfil us, that our thirst for the infinite will be slaked and that the wound of our loneliness will be healed.

Our journey together, our pilgrimage, is worth while. There is hope.